Integrating the City of Medicine

Blacks in Philadelphia Health Care, 1910–1965

Integrating the City of Medicine

Blacks in Philadelphia Health Care, 1910–1965

David McBride

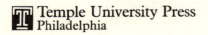

Temple University Press
Philadelphia

Temple University Press, Philadelphia 19122
Copyright © 1989 by Temple University. All rights reserved
Published 1989
Printed in the United States of America

The paper used in this publication meets the minimum
requirements of American National Standard for Information
Sciences—Permanence of Paper for Printed Library Materials,
ANSI Z39.48-1984

LIBRARY OF CONGRESS CATALOGING-IN-PUBLICATION DATA

McBride, David, 1949–
    Integrating the city of medicine : Blacks in Philadelphia health
care, 1910–1965 / David McBride.
        p.   cm.
    Bibliography: p.
    Includes index.
    ISBN 0-87722-546-X
    1. Afro-American physicians—Pennsylvania—Philadelphia—
Biography.   2. Afro-American physicians—Pennsylvania—
Philadelphia—History.   I. Title.
R315.M38 1989
610.69′52′097481—dc19   88-15924
                                                          CIP

To my parents,
Ruth D. Jordan and
the late Andrew D. McBride,
and Hunter L. Jordan

Acknowledgments

In the process of writing this book, I received invaluable encouragement and support from a number of individuals. In the beginning there was Hollis R. Lynch of Columbia University, who supervised my early research there. Others who commented on sections of the manuscript or gave freely of their time to discuss my perspective on specific topics were Cyril E. Griffith, Monroe H. Little, Edna McKenzie, Charles L. Blockson, Sarah Elbert, Carl Oblinger, Shirley T. Parham, and Elizabeth Fox-Genovese. An historical investigator can only go as far as the sources lead. Hence, I must thank those in the medical field who allowed me to interview them for oral history purposes. The staffs of the many libraries and archival repositories cited throughout the notes were helpful in accommodating my questions and locating vital materials. Most especially, I appreciate the assistance that I received from staffs at the Rockefeller Archive Center, Special Collections at Fisk University, Temple University Urban Archives, Pennsylvania State Archives, and Bureau of Municipal Research and Archives–City of Philadelphia. Also, my manuscript benefited greatly from the editorial expertise of Michael Ames, editor-in-chief, and David Bartlett, director, of Temple University Press. A blind referee also devoted much energy to bettering my study, strafing earlier drafts of this book with rounds of critical insights that sent me scurrying back into the research shed and that greatly enhanced its ideas and range. I also appreciate the permission of the Johns Hopkins University Press to republish material in part of Chapter II that appeared in my article "The Henry Phipps Institute, 1903–1937: Pioneering Tuberculosis Work with an Urban Minority," *Bulletin of the History of Medicine* 61, no. 1 (Spring 1987): 78–97.

ACKNOWLEDGMENTS

Finally, I must acknowledge the help of my family. My brothers Andrew Dennis (Jr.) and William and their families endured my late night visits and long distance calls, giving advice on the myriad problems that arise when one is involved in writing a book. My two young sons Patrice and Julian brought me much joy as they tolerated the long stretches of isolation that my research trips and writing required. I recall one sweaty summer afternoon, when I was sitting at my desk trying to type, to get my attention one of the boys climbed on to my shoulders and began to swing my head from side to side while the other ferreted under my chair and tugged at my ankles. But in deference to me, they maintained dead silence throughout this act of affection. Last, my greatest debt is to my parents.

Contents

CONTENTS

List of Tables and Map

MAP

Introduction

A 1983 study of blacks in American medicine points out that there is a severe shortage of black and minority health professionals and that this shortage is a key factor behind the persistent discrepancies in the health status and life expectancy of black and white Americans.[1] As far back as the Flexner Report on Medical Education (1910), medical educators and professionals have had to wrestle with developing medical training and health care policies that would dispose of the "Negro health problem"—that is, the twofold dilemma of blacks' persistently high mortality and disease rates and disproportionately low representation in the medical professions. The Flexner study predicted fatalistically that given American social and educational segregation, as well as the purported biological weaknesses of the black race, America's blacks could always expect an inadequate supply of its own medical professionals.[2]

As race relations, urban growth, government intervention, and health care institutions underwent drastic transformations, the approaches to the black American medical crisis changed from ones that assumed "separate but equal" social, political, and medical institutions to policies built on the premise that racial equality was both a legal and a moral mandate. The *Brown v. Board of Education* movement and court decision opened the doors to the highest level of medical education for all races, and gradually black and minority Americans also gained access to equal patient care and health employment opportunities on either legal or humanitarian grounds.

This study traces the structural development and the social and political experiences of one urban community of black medical professionals as

America passed through "separate but equal" segregation to the post–*Brown* period of legally enforced integration. Philadelphia's black health care providers, like their colleagues nationwide, were shaped by the revolutionary transformation of twentieth-century American medicine from an institution centered around the physician and the office or household to our present massive network of hospitals and health centers serving the national middle class.[3] It is estimated that in 1982 about 10 million Americans earned all or part of their incomes from this health care network, which encompasses more than two hundred professional and non-professional occupations and ranks among the top three or four industries in the country.[4]

Many social histories have documented this growth in the mainstream institutions of American medicine. The modernization of medical education, the rise of the modern physician and specialization movements within the various branches of medical practice, and the emergence of the technically advanced and costly contemporary hospital have all been the subjects of valuable recent historical studies.[5] The subject of racial minority groups, however, both as medical practitioners and as public health workers in the American health care system, is still largely untouched.[6]

In this book I describe the unique historical role of black Americans throughout the development of Philadelphia's modern medical establishment. My interest in this subject was originally stirred by the obvious lack of any previous substantial historical accounts of the experience of black medical professionals and their institutions in a major city. However, I was also stimulated to undertake this investigation after I came across modern occupational statistics that pointed not only to a deep-seated shortage in the number of black medical professionals but also to an "industrial" and racial pyramid that historians have not yet tried to analyze. Nationally in 1966 there were some 1.1 million people employed in hospitals outside of medical professional segments as nurses' aides, orderlies, attendants, and other allied health workers. This was 38.5 percent of America's total health care labor force. By 1970 the figures for non-professional health care labor rose to 1.3 million—over 39 percent of health care employees nationwide. These non-professional health service workers were disproportionately black. In 1970 blacks made up only 2.2 percent of Pennsylvania's 32,573 health professionals—that is, doctors, dentists, optometrists, and the like. In the lower allied health labor segment, however, blacks comprised 26 percent of the state's 51,700 nurses' aides, orderlies, practical nurses, operatives, and so on. Blacks in Philadelphia formed an even greater percentage of such non-professional health employees in 1970, making up 67.4 percent of the city's 11,714 non-professional health care workers.[7]

The historical achievements and limitations of black medical professionals in Philadelphia, America's "city of medicine," are understandable only in terms of the broader social and urban context. Indeed, we will see that a succession of non-medical (non-clinical) factors—especially citywide fears of epidemics, racial customs, technological and occupational changes within the hospital, expanding health care financing, shifting political moods within the black community, and local and federal civil rights measures—played important roles first in sustaining but later in eroding the color divide in Philadelphia medical institutional life. As changes mainly outside medical research and clinical life placed greater pressure on medical institutions within the city to integrate their staffing and institutional programs, Philadelphia's black medical profession also went from a position of wide-scale isolation during the early twentieth century to one of integration. Throughout the course of this transformation, the city's black and white medical communities became increasingly merged or "bridged"— first by small cooperative efforts in the public health sphere but later, after World War II, by more fundamental and citywide movements as Philadelphia's large medical institutions increased both the quantity and the quality of service to the city's fast-growing black population. In this phase, Philadelphia's mainstream, predominantly white hospitals and medical educational institutions absorbed a previously self-enclosed, black medical community.

The first period of this fundamental shift in the role of black medical practitioners spanned the roughly three decades between the immediate pre-World War I years through World War II (Chapters I–IV). During these years, "two worlds" of medicine prevailed in Philadelphia—one black and one white.[8] Blacks were generally excluded from any professional or administrative employment in Philadelphia's large hospitals and also from attending their nursing schools; blacks, in turn, established and sustained their own hospitals and nurse training programs. Moreover, while blacks during these decades were on occasion admitted to some of the city's several medical schools, this and other efforts to aid the training of black doctors and nurses were intended to reinforce rather than dismantle a separate health care network for the black and white communities of Philadelphia. This racial separatism was consistent with larger socio-racial patterns within the city and the nation.[9] Although relatively isolated from the larger hospitals, professional associations, and medical education institutions of the city, black medical practitioners were inspired by the progressivism and "New Negro" ideas pervasive in black America during World War I and the twenties. This cultural and political current stressed self-reliance, as well as strong professional and community ties to improve general black civic welfare. The results were the emergence of a constellation of black medical associations and public health operations in Philadelphia that were sustained by vigorous black and liberal community support.

The second phase in the relationship of blacks to Philadelphia's health care system ran from the post-World War II years through the early 1950s (Chapters V–VI). This period was marked by fundamental shifts in the political and social ordering of racial groups both in Philadelphia and nationally, as well as a simultaneous, dramatic onrush of changes in the city's health care and employment policies. Reflecting the rising political militancy and integrationist advocacy of the NAACP's *Brown* campaign, the Philadelphia black medical community, local lay civil rights groups, citywide political reform movements, and Pennsylvania state political groups, challenged publicly the traditional racial barriers in medical training and professional hospital employment in Philadelphia health institutions. At the same time that this political drive to integrate medical institutions in the city was intensifying, the rapid expansion of patient care and personnel needs within the city's hospitals forced these institutions to begin integrating their staffs and clientele.

The third phase in the collective biography of black medical professionals in Philadelphia occurred during the late 1950s and 1960s (Chapters VII–VIII). In this period, due to the cumulative impact of the civil rights movement and pressure by government agencies charged with ensuring equality in patient care, as well as new educational and employment avenues for black physicians, nurses, and allied health workers, integration of black medical professionals became fully accepted public policy and practice for the city's mainstream hospitals and medical institutions. The result was an enormous "shortage" of black medical practitioners for the newly integrated medical establishment, a shortage that is still debated heatedly today. By 1965 the wall of color in Philadelphia's health institutions had at last come a-tumbling down.

Integrating the
City of Medicine

PART ONE

Two Worlds of Medicine

CHAPTER I

The World of
Black Medical Professionals

O n a winter day in 1916, Nathan F. Mossell, a nationally known black Philadelphia physician, addressed a gathering of black medical professionals and civic leaders at the Allen African Methodist Episcopal Church in Philadelphia. Invited to speak on "Hospital Efficiency" by the Philadelphia Academy of Medicine and Allied Sciences, the local black medical association, Mossell recounted his struggle to establish the Frederick Douglass Memorial Hospital, the first of two black hospitals in the city, which he had founded and directed since its inception in 1895. Mossell had named his hospital for Frederick Douglass, "one of America's most potent . . . advocates of human rights," because to him the hospital embodied Douglass's egalitarian ideal, as well as his belief in furthering human progress through medical science. To Mossell his hospital also stood as a concrete protest against the racial barriers that prevented black doctors and nursing students from training or practicing at any of the white hospitals in Pennsylvania. "The modern hospital is much more to a community than a dwelling place for the sick," he remarked; it embodies the "solemn duty" to advance "a higher and better civilization of the whole people." As such, the hospital or medical school defeated its own purposes if it "recognized any form of segregation, caste, or race discrimination" by refusing to train or treat black citizens. According to Mossell, such racial discrimination "traduced [Douglass's] sacred memory" and the high civic ideals of the modern hospital.[1]

Mossell's speech evokes the dual medical world that existed in Phila-

3

delphia and the rest of the nation through the two world wars and into the Great Society era. It also reflects the first of three key historical currents that would gradually merge during the first half of the twentieth century to transform the separated medical worlds of a racially divided city into one integrated medical system. This first current was the missionary zeal and effectiveness of Philadelphia blacks and sympathetic white reformers in establishing and sustaining medical institutions and practitioners within the city's black community. These institutions met critical black health care and training needs at a time when such concerns were largely ignored by the nation's health and urban political leaders. In the eyes of Mossell and his professional and lay followers, viable health care resources were essential to the survival of black Americans in a largely industrial, working-class, urban environment and had to be sustained even in the face of "the bitterest opposition."[2]

The second historical current that contributed to making an integrated health care establishment in Philadelphia was the changing socio-economic and political character of the city itself. In the early decades of the twentieth century Philadelphia's political and medical leaders could in general evade the issue of the inadequate health care and segregated professional training resources facing its proportionately small black community. However, during epidemics, when threats to the public health of whites posed by ill, impoverished blacks seemed serious, bridges between the two medical communities were encouraged by health authorities. By mid-century, as the black population spiraled upward and the civil rights political impulse gained ground locally as well as nationwide, these leaders had to place the issue of health care for blacks high on their agendas of public concern.

The final factor that would shape an interracial health care community in Philadelphia was the changing nature of hospitals and health financing, which accelerated immensely following World War II. The explosive growth in access to and use of hospitals generated a serious shortage in the professional and allied health workforce of these institutions. Consequently, race relations in health employment and patient care were altered drastically as blacks were absorbed as both staff and patients by the newly expanded hospitals. In short, by the mid-1960s, black health activism, a changing urban environment, and a modernizing health system had so tightly bridged the black and white communities in Philadelphia medicine that traditionally black-operated health institutions became extinct. However, the bridging and ultimate merger of Philadelphia's black and white medical institutions required many decades of gradual change—changes that neither Nathan Mossell nor his black and white medical contemporaries could envision in the opening decade of the twentieth century.

The Roots of Black Medical Life
in Philadelphia

The two black hospitals, Frederick Douglass and Mercy Hospital, along with their nursing schools and the numerous black medical associations found in early twentieth-century Philadelphia, were but one branch of the social welfare institutions that emerged out of the city's complicated mosaic of cultural, economic, and ethnic communities. By the opening of the twentieth century Philadelphia was a major American medical center. Indeed, the city had been central to American medicine since the colonial period. The first hospital in British North America was founded in Philadelphia in 1752 and, in 1765, the colony's first medical school. The life and activities of the most famous American doctor of the Revolutionary era, Benjamin Rush, were also centered in Philadelphia. Many discoveries that influenced international medical science were made at the city's several prominent hospitals and medical schools throughout the late eighteenth and nineteenth centuries.[3]

In addition to its rich medical heritage, Philadelphia had been through the end of the nineteenth century a focal point in American urban life and economic activity. From the colonial period to 1810, it was North America's largest city. For the next eighty years, it ranked as the second largest city (behind New York), and it remained the third largest (behind Chicago) until 1960.[4] As an eastern seaboard city with an extensive industrial base, Philadelphia attracted waves of European immigrants. Native-born whites comprised about 70 percent of the city's population from 1860 to 1910, while southern and eastern European groups were less than 1 percent of Philadelphia's aggregate population in 1860. During the late nineteenth and early twentieth centuries, however, large concentrations of Irish, Russians, Italians, Poles, and Germans arrived. By 1910 more than 11 percent of the city's population had been born in eastern and southern Europe.[5]

During the eighteenth and nineteenth centuries, blacks emerged as a small but integral part of the Philadelphia metropolis. In 1790, the city had 2,489 blacks, comprising about 4.5 percent of the city's population. In 1860, there were 22,185 blacks, who made up slightly less than 4 percent of its residents, and in 1890, there were 39,371 blacks, also a little under 4 percent. As the twentieth century commenced, blacks continued to represent about 4 percent of Philadelphia's overall population and were concentrated primarily in the central wards of the city. Because most of them were restricted to domestic and personal service work, they tended to live as renters in impoverished, largely segregated neighborhoods lining the well-to-do center city section.[6] Since the city's transportation resources, primarily street railways, did not permit much distance between laborer and workplace, blacks needed to live close to the households and businesses of their wealthy employers. Both municipal and private social welfare facilities were segregated. Also health conditions for most black Philadelphians were precarious and mortality rates consistently higher than those of the city's native whites.[7]

Although not a sizable group in relationship to Philadelphia's general population and restricted spatially to clusters of all-black blocks, the black community of the city was internally a multilayered society, rich with entrepreneurs, cultural institutions, and political clubs. Prior to the Civil War, the Philadelphia community was considered the capital of northern black society. Its pivotal institution was the church. The nation's first black church, the First African Church of St. Thomas (1792), and its key black religious denomination, the African Methodist Episcopal (or AME) Church (1796), both emerged within the Philadelphia community.[8] Second to the church in importance were the all-black beneficial societies. In 1815, twelve such self-help organizations existed in Philadelphia, and, by 1847, this number had increased to over one hundred.[9] In addition, by the 1890s, fraternal societies, insurance companies, building and loan associations, libraries, cemeteries, labor unions, and political clubs also sustained Philadelphia black society, and there were approximately three hundred black-owned businesses, the majority of which were caterers, barbershops, and restaurants, as well as a lesser number of grocery stores, cigar and candy shops, mortuaries, and upholstery concerns.[10]

Medical conditions in Philadelphia during the opening decade of the twentieth century reflected the city's racial and ethnic division.[11] Each of the city's approximately fifty hospitals had its own specific ethnic and racial composition. Hospital administration and personnel usually mirrored the ethnic, religious, and racial character of the institution's particular neighborhood and controlling interest group. For example, the Lankenau Hospital tended to serve German-Americans. Mount Sinai Hospital and the Jewish Hospital attended to Philadelphia's native and immigrant Jewish community. The city's Italian-Americans were served by Catholic hospitals. The white upper-class residential neighborhood of Chestnut Hill had the Chestnut Hill Hospital, which served mostly patients who could afford expensive private and semi-private ward care. While several hospitals would admit "colored cases," these blacks were treated under segregated arrangements. Even at Philadelphia General Hospital, the municipal institution traditionally for the city's indigent, the majority of the patients through World War I were white; those blacks admitted were treated in segregated wards.[12]

Like the Catholics and Jews, other religious groups such as the Presbyterians and Episcopalians operated hospitals in Philadelphia during the early twentieth century. Racial separation prevailed in these hospitals as well. Episcopal Hospital, for example, generally cared for white factory working families and, in the main, avoided treating blacks. Moreover, due to the strong denominational and moralistic character of sectarian hospitals at this time, poor black and white women without spouses who were in need of maternity care were frequently barred from treatment.[13]

It was out of this context—a racially and ethnically polarized city and health life—that black hospitals and a black medical professional community emerged in Philadelphia around the turn of the century. Although black medical leaders and their sympathizers frequently questioned the legitimacy of the caste-based health care establishment, most of the city's political and medical leaders accepted racial dualism as unalterable. Because of these racial barriers, black medical professionals were forced to build their own medical "sub-world" or network within the city's larger medical establishment. Their progressivist spirit of self-help produced a reciprocal popular outflow of community support for their institutions. And this civic and racial pride grew and took on a more militant tone as World War I unwound and the "New Negro" impulse swept through urban black America, including Philadelphia. Thus, the two worlds of medicine coexisted tensely, while black health care practitioners enhanced their professional development through their own institutions, becoming elite figures within Philadelphia's black community.

Black Hospitals and
Early Black Medical Leadership

From the colonial period until the end of the Civil War, black physicians practiced in Philadelphia and other cities. Abolitionists had been instrumental in getting a few blacks admitted to medical training in the United States; other blacks had journeyed to Europe to pursue medical study. Owing to the underdeveloped licensing and educational standards of antebellum American medicine, figures on physicians by city and region are at best rough estimates, but it is likely that a few black medical practitioners could be found in business in Philadelphia during the middle years of the nineteenth century.[14] However, throughout the Civil War and Reconstruction decades black presence in the medical profession in Philadelphia was virtually erased by the influx of European immigrants. According to Eugene Foley, during this period "each generation [of immigrants] renewed the barefisted competition with each generation of Negroes" that resulted in violent riots and intimidation constricting black voting, enterprise, and employment in the skilled trades.[15] By the 1880s the handful of black physicians in the city had virtually no private practice clientele and, according to the then young sociologists W. E. B. Du Bois, writing in 1899, "had to sit idly by and see the 40,000 Negroes healed principally by white practitioners."[16]

Even with the intensification of Jim Crow politics in the South and anti-black intimidation throughout the North, a spirit of civic reformism and a deep social belief that a new educated class would provide effective leadership for the race emerged widely throughout Progressive-era black America. While W. E. B. Du Bois and race liberals in the northern cities championed the ideals of scientific social work and political reformism, Booker T. Washington, the nation's most influential black educator, campaigned throughout the South, spreading the ethos of industrial education, business enterprise, and self-help. As James Summerville has stated, "Denied hospital facilities, membership in medical societies, and a forum in their professional journals, Negro physicians and dentists nevertheless [strove] to prove their competence." Black medical leaders of both the North and South rode the black self-help crest and established their own health care facilities and professional associations. Between 1890 and 1910 especially, black hospitals were established in virtually every southern state as well as a number of northern cities. By 1900 there were about forty black hospitals nationally and ten years later nearly one hundred.[17]

In the North, Nathan Mossell led the way in 1895 by founding Frederick Douglass Memorial Hospital and Training School for Nurses. A product of Lincoln University, Mossell was the first black to graduate from the University of Pennsylvania Medical School (class of 1882) as well as the first to be admitted to the Philadelphia Medical Society. Throughout his career he involved himself in local and national political efforts to gain civil rights for black Americans. Around the turn of the century his most notable political activities included his work with the Citizens Republican Club, formed in the 1890s to give Philadelphia's black voters more leverage within the domineering city and state Republican party machines. Mossell was also among the first supporters of the newly formed National Association for the Advancement of Colored People (NAACP), serving on its first national executive committee with Jane Addams, Ida B. Wells, Archibald H. Grimke, Clarence Darrow, and others, as well as on its first board of directors.[18]

Douglass Hospital continued to expand through the first decade of the century and received significant state support. The facility served 3,500 in-patients and 40,000 out-patients by 1912. This level of patient care was small in comparison to the much larger voluntary and public hospitals in the city, but still it was sizable enough to offer a diverse clinical setting for the Philadelphia black medical community. According to Dr. John P. Turner, a leader among the city's black physicians throughout the pre-World War II decades, writing in 1910 in a black professionals' directory, Douglass was "the largest hospital structure in the world operated wholly by Afro-Americans."[19]

In 1907, four young black physicians created an offshoot institution, Mercy Hospital.[20] When Mercy began to come into its own in the 1910s, it, alongside Douglass, provided the only facilities where black doctors could intern anywhere in Pennsylvania until the Depression. In fact, until World War II, these two black hospitals made Philadelphia something of a mecca for the nation's black medical school graduates, almost half of whom could not find internships in any given year due to the small number of fully accredited black hospitals and the bar against black interns at the nation's white hospitals.[21]

As World War I approached, Dr. Mossell and both black hospitals attracted widespread support among Philadelphia's black residents, who were concentrated mostly in the southcentral wards that surrounded these two institutions. Because these largely black sections contained important black Republican voting blocs, they also received substantial support from the state Republican machines in the form of both start-up funds and annual appropriations.[22] Indeed, throughout its first three decades of operation, Douglass Hospital received most of its revenue from the state of Pennsylvania. From its inception to 1912 Douglass received $77,000 in donations and proceeds from numerous fairs and fund-raisers, $50,000 of which was used for construction and the remainder for administrative expenses; during the same period, it received on average $6,000 annually from the state of Pennsylvania, $86,000 of which was used for maintenance and $18,000 for building expenses. Similarly, Mercy Hospital received annual appropriations of around $10,000, increasing steadily through World War II. Annual state allocations amounted to about 50 percent of Douglass's total revenue while earnings from patient services and community donations comprised about 35 and 15 percent respectively of the remaining income. By comparison, state appropriations through the 1920s amounted to only about 10 percent of the financial resources for Philadelphia's other voluntary hospitals that were similar in size to Douglas and Mercy.[23]

While the city's black hospitals served as the institutional center for the black medical professional, it was the black private practice physician who emerged as the foundation of the black medical world in early twentieth century Philadelphia. Health and civic leaders of the black community viewed the independent black private practice physician as the most essential resource for the health care needs of black Philadelphia. In this city and throughout the nation, the family physician, not the hospital, was the central agency of formalized medical care. But black physicians were in short supply, and this at a time when Abraham Flexner and the A M A reformist leadership were complaining that there were too many physicians.[24]

The many exceptional medical schools in Philadelphia had produced an ample but unevenly distributed supply of private practice physicians.[25] Blacks, however, accounted for only 78 (or 1.8 percent) of the 4,271 medical professionals in 1910; in 1920, they made up 2.1 percent (Table 1). The 41 black nurses accounted for only 1.5 percent of the city's nursing personnel in 1910, and 2.2 percent in 1920 (Table 2). During this period the ratio of black medical professionals to Philadelphia's black population was by far the lowest of any ethnic or racial group and, in fact, was worsening

TABLE 1
Distribution of Medical Professionals,* by Nativity and Race, Philadelphia, 1910 and 1920

Nativity and Race	1910				1920			
	No.	%	Population	Population/ Medical Professional	No.	%	Population	Population/ Medical Professional
Native white	3,544	83.0	1,080,008	305	3,740	81.0	1,290,253	345
Foreign-born white	630	14.8	382,578	607	742	16.0	392,927	530
Black	78	1.8	84,459	1,083	95	2.1	134,229	1,413
Oriental and others	19	0.4	1,963	103	50	0.9	6,375	127
Total	4,271		1,549,008	363	4,627		1,823,779	394

*Physicians, surgeons, and dentists.
SOURCE: U.S. Department of Commerce, Bureau of the Census, *Thirteenth Census of the United States, 1910* (Washington, D.C.: GPO, 1914).

TABLE 2
Number and Percentage of Trained Nurses, by Nativity and Race,
Philadelphia, 1910 and 1920

Nativity and Race	1910		1920	
	No.	%	No.	%
Native white	2,209	80.9	3,409	86.6
Foreign-born white	478	17.5	439	11.2
Black	41	1.5	87	2.2
Oriental and others	1	0.1	1	0.02

SOURCES: U.S. Department of Commerce, Bureau of the Census, *Thirteenth Census of the United States, 1910* (Washington, D.C.: GPO, 1914), vol. 4: *Population: Occupation Statistics*, table 8, pp. 588–590, and *Supplement for Pennsylvania*, table 19, p. 95; U.S. Department of Commerce, Bureau of the Census, *Fourteenth Census of the United States 1920*, (Washington, D.C.: GPO, 1923), vol. 4: *Population: Occupations*, table 2, pp. 1195–1197, and vol. 3: *Population: Composition and Characteristics of the Population, by State*, table 8, p. 857.

in comparison to whites. The ratio of medical professionals to population for whites was 1 to 305 in 1910 and 1 to 345 in 1920. By contrast, there was one black doctor, surgeon, or dentist for every 1,083 blacks in 1910, and one for every 1,413 blacks in 1920 (Table 1).

Influenced by the Progressive reform impulse, many civic activists in Philadelphia viewed this shortage of trained black medical personnel as a primary social problem that further exacerbated the situation of poor blacks.[26] Blacks reform leaders and sympathetic whites supported efforts aimed at increasing the number of black doctors and nurses in the city in two ways. One approach was to aid in fund-raising efforts for health institutions staffed by blacks and serving the black citizenry. As we will see later, this approach produced several citywide fund drives during the 1910s and 1920s to benefit Douglass and Mercy.

Another approach was to enlighten public opinion about health conditions among the black population. *The Crisis*, the official organ of the NAACP, kept close watch over Philadelphia medicine as it affected blacks. During 1912, for instance, one *Crisis* article highlighted Douglass Hospital, including photographs of the hospital's operating amphitheater, a group of its nurses, and Nathan Mossell. The magazine offered to forward any donations to the hospital, observing, "It is doubtful if the philanthropist could find a more effective method of investing his funds for the future of his fellow men than by helping this institution."[27]

Local newspapers also covered events at the city's black hospitals. The *Philadelphia Public Ledger*, the city's major liberal newspaper, published articles, letters to the editor, and editorials supporting philanthropic aid to expand the training available for blacks at the Douglass and Mercy hospitals. The *Ledger* saw the growth of black hospitals and increase in black physicians as essential measures for improving the health and welfare of black Philadelphians.[28] The *Philadelphia Tribune*, the city's most widely circulating black newspaper, also publicized the problem confronting its community's black hospitals as well as black medical issues generally. Indeed, from World War I through the Depression, the *Tribune* operated as a forum for popular and professional discussion of controversies posed by discrimination in Philadelphia's medical institutions.

Discrimination and the Self-Help Response

Race leaders and other civic reformers in early twentieth-century Philadelphia, then, confronted a twofold crisis. First, while a black medical sub-world was in place by World War I, it fell far short of meeting the expanding local needs for health care services within the local black community—a community experiencing radical population growth. In addition, a myriad of practical barriers within the city's medical institutions hindered both the numerical and the qualitative growth of black medical professionals.

Even though both black and white civic and medical leaders argued during the 1910s and 1920s, that a separate "Negro medical profession" was the best and only means for improving the health care of black city dwellers, broad problems in Philadelphia's medical life stymied measures to train more black medical professionals. Then, as now, physicians and nurses were trained and gained employment experience in four institutional settings: medical and nursing schools, hospital internships, (for physicians), hospital and clinical staff positions, and private practice. In Philadelphia through the early 1920s de facto segregation in the first two levels prevented adequate growth in the third and fourth areas.

Blacks attending the city's medical schools, among the largest and most productive in clinical innovation in the nation, were in the main a rarity. At no time between 1910 and 1925 did any substantial group of blacks graduate from the University of Pennsylvania Medical College or the Jefferson Medical College (Table 3). The latter school, which by 1924 was graduating the largest number of physicians in the country, turned out one black physician during this sixteen-year timespan. There were eight black graduates from the University of Pennsylvania Medical College, six from the Medico-Chirurgical College, six from Temple University Medical College, five from Woman's Medical College, and none from Hahnemann College. Moreover, with the exception of Temple's Medical College, there was no discernible steadying or increase in the number of black graduates at these schools. Black enrollment at Temple's medical school was relatively substantial and the number of black graduates may have actually numbered one to two each year during 1910–1925. Six blacks graduated from the Medico-Chirurgical College in the first half of the 1910s. This institution was not, however, considered to be of high academic quality. Furthermore, Medico-Chirurgical operated only through 1918, when it merged with the Polyclinic Hospital to form the Postgraduate School of the University of Pennsylvania.[29]

There were also some black graduates from the University of Pennsylvania and Temple dental schools, particularly during the war years. In 1912, William N. Hamilton received the degree of Doctor of Dental Science from Pennsylvania. Among the sixteen black graduates from the university's college and professional schools in 1917, five received D.D.S. degrees: Warren H. Collie, Robert N. Gardiner, Francis T. Jamison, Edward F. Jones, and Charles Moody. There were two more blacks, William N. Cummings and William H. Jenkins, among the dental school class of 1919. Between 1919 and 1925, Temple graduated twenty black dentists while the University of Pennsylvania had ten.[30]

While the number of black students enrolled at the city's medical and dental schools was small, it was not insignificant. Long decades of segregation in northern medical schools had preceded this period. For instance, recall that Nathan Mossell, its first black alumnus, graduated from

TABLE 3
Black Graduates Of Philadelphia Medical Colleges, 1910–1925

School	1910–1915	1916–1920	1921–1925
Hahnemann	0	NA	0
Woman's Medical College	1	1	3
Medico-Chirurgical	6	NA	—
Temple	1(8)	1(12)	4(16)
University of Pennsylvania Medical College	1	6	1
Jefferson Medical College	1	0	0

SOURCE: Yearbooks and alumni materials of these medical schools were the primary source. In addition the author surveyed two other sources. Entries on black physicians in *Who's Who in Colored America: A Biographical Dictionary of Notable Living Persons of African Descent in America, 1930–1931–1932*, ed. Thomas Yenser (New York: Thomas Yenser, 1933), were analyzed because this volume presumably contained the greatest number of black physicians who graduated from medical school during the 1910 to 1925 period. (Information gleaned from a more extensive survey of this directory appears in Chapter IV.) Also, the author reviewed year-to-year the annual summary in *The Crisis* of black students and graduates at the nation's leading black and white colleges and graduate institutions. The annual summaries by *The Crisis* sometimes did not distinguish graduating from non-graduating students. Issues of *The Crisis* surveyed were vols. 1–30 for the years 1910–1925. Specific yearbooks and alumni materials are listed below. Abbreviations are listed on pp. 209–210.

For Hahnemann: Hahnemann Medical College, *Medic, 1910* and *1921*, HHMA (1911–1920 and 1922 not available).

For Woman's Medical College: Woman's Medical College, "Negro Graduates . . . ," mimeo, Jan. 27, 1948, Medical College of Pennsylvania Collection, AWMC.

For Medico-Chirurgical: Medico-Chirurgical College, *The Medico-Chirurgeon, 1910, 1914,* and *1915* (1911–1913 not available), Van Pelt Library, University of Pennsylvania; *Who's Who in Colored America, 1930–1932*, p. 374.

For Temple: Temple University Medical Department (or College), *The Skull, 1925*, CTTU; *Who's Who in Colored America: 1930–1932*, pp. 362, 448, 461. Figures in parentheses represent the number of black students who attended Temple's Medical Department who may or may not have graduated.

For University of Pennsylvania Medical College: University of Pennsylvania Medical College, *The Scope, 1910–1922, 1924,* and *1925* (1923 not available), Van Pelt Library, University of Pennsylvania; *Who's Who in Colored America: 1930–1932*, pp. 19, 26, 73, 113, 389. These sources also revealed that, of the 1,617 graduates listed, 37 were white females.

For Jefferson Medical College: Jefferson Medical College, *The Clinic, 1910–1912, 1914–1917, 1919, 1921, 1923–1925* (data for 1913, 1918, 1920, and 1922 not available), Scott Memorial Library, Thomas Jefferson University. This yearbook had various titles through 1915.

the University of Pennsylvania Medical College in 1882, 116 years after the college's founding. In 1915, there were only thirty-one black medical students, thirty-four black dental students, and twenty-one black pharmacy students throughout all the predominantly white colleges in the North. These eighty-six students were less than 10 percent of the nation's black medical students. Most of the remaining 90 percent attended three all-black institutions: Meharry, Howard, and Leonard.[31]

During the 1919–1920 academic year, Abraham Flexner, the secretary of the Rockefeller Foundation's General Education Board, surveyed the number of black students in the nation's leading northern medical schools. In addition to the Jefferson and University of Pennsylvania medical schools, he contacted fifteen other medical schools: Yale, Tufts, Harvard, Boston University, Columbia, the University of Illinois, Northwestern, the State University of Iowa, the University of Michigan, Long Island College Hospital, the University of Minnesota, Western Reserve, Syracuse University, Ohio State, and Rush Medical College. The results reflected black enrollments as sparse as those found at Philadelphia medical schools; each of these fifteen schools had an average of two black students.[32]

The appearance of black medical and dental students in Philadelphia was also significant because it coincided with a sharp decrease in the number of the nation's medical schools as well as with an intensifying segregationist ideology gripping post-World War I American educational and hospital life. As a result of the American Medical Association's policies raising medical education standards, the number of medical schools dropped from 110 in 1905 to 88 in 1920, and 76 by 1930. By 1915, five of eight black medical schools had become extinct, and in 1923 a sixth disappeared.[33] As a result, blacks found entrance into medical training much more competitive.

Black medical school applicants also suffered from a widespread belief among whites that blacks lacked the educational ability to complete the rigorous study of medicine or that they faced too many barriers in clinical training in American hospitals to become doctors or hospital administrators in any great numbers. The general aversion of white medical educators in the city and nation toward providing medical training for blacks on an equal footing with whites was evident even among those educators who were sincerely dedicated to black medical education.[34] A key example was noted Philadelphia physician-educator John J. Mullowney. A 1908 graduate of the University of Pennsylvania Medical Department, Mullowney served for a few years as a medical missionary in Peking, China. After about a year as a Philadelphia public health inspector, he became assistant chief of the Pennsylvania Department of Health and then chairman of the department of science and professor of chemistry and hygiene at Girard College. In 1921, he was appointed president of Meharry Medical College, which was, next to Howard University, the nation's leading center for the training of black physicians. As Summerville notes, even as head of this outstanding black medical school, Mullowney "denied firmly that black people were ready to lead" in the medical education of their people. According to Mullowney, "Negroes have not yet developed many good disciplinarians or administrators nor do they seem, as a general rule, to be dextrous or as able to coordinate highly skilled actions with thoughts, nor are the majority of them blessed with impelling energy." He believed that "the white men will need to act as heads of nearly all branches of clinical medicine [at the black medical schools] for at least ten, possibly twenty years or longer." [35]

Those blacks who did attend the predominantly white schools in Philadelphia had to face racial ostracism from two sides, from those within their particular medical school and from white patients with whom they came in contact during clinical training. In the Jefferson Medical College yearbook, for instance, the picture of the sole black graduate at the school, Monroe Hinson Tunnell was captioned, "Has an appropriate name." Walter F. Jerrick, a dark-complexioned black senior in the class of 1919 at the University of Pennsylvania Medical School who went on to become a leading black Philadelphia physician was referred to as a "melanotic blonde" and nicknamed "Anthracosis" by his classmates. [36]

Furthermore, during the 1910s and 1920s, black students once admitted often faced unique academic and career pressures. The standard policy toward blacks admitted to white schools was to arrange their transfer after their first two years to black medical schools. This transfer was mandatory, first-year black medical students were told by school administrators, since the medical school could not require local affiliated, separately governed white hospitals (which prohibited black medical trainees or, for that matter, physicians) to accommodate its black students for clinical training. [37] Moreover, attrition among black students at white medical schools was high. At one school the ratio of blacks failing to graduate to those receiving their medical doctoral degree was three to one. [38]

In 1917, an incident occurred that underscored the tension between the world of black physicians, black medical students, and their militant community supporters, on the one hand, and the white medical and political establishment, on the other. The dean of the obstetrical department at the University of Pennsylvania Medical College made a request to Mossell that Douglass Hospital admit that department's black students to their maternity training, since white maternity patients at University Hospital did not desire any contact with black interns. In a conference with the school's black students along with other associates of Douglass Hospital, Mossell found that the students "declined to favor the idea of being sent away from the university to Douglass Hospital to take this part of their training" because it "savors of race segregation." Mossell and the other managers of Douglass then conferred with the dean and, in Mossell's words, "we told him that the management of the Institution [Douglass] was necessarily interested in all medical education, but no department would be opened to White students where Colored would be excluded; nor to Colored where White students would be excluded; that the Institution was not organized to encourage race segregation, but rather as a protest against it."[39]

Philadelphia blacks hailed Mossell's stand in not permitting the medical school to make Douglass Hospital "a Jim Crow Station for colored interns," but the decision placed the continued existence of Douglass Hospital in jeopardy. Shortly thereafter, the Charities Bureau of the Philadelphia Chamber of Commerce withdrew its support from Douglass Hospital, a gesture that Mossell perceived as "a definite plan . . . by certain co-ordinated charities and certain concentrated medical centers of education together with certain political influences to dominate and control the Douglass Hospital." Moreover, the Pennsylvania State Board of Charities Appropriations Committee informed the Douglass Hospital board of managers that allocation of its funds, some $22,000, was contingent upon the removal of Mossell as its chief of staff.[40]

This funding rider sent bitter ripples not only through the Douglass Hospital board of managers but also through the black community and among concerned whites as well. Dr. J. Max Barber of the board of managers announced to the Appropriations Committee the hospital's resolute refusal to oust Mossell. Dr. Charles A. Lewis, an instructor of medical social services who later made significant contributions to tuberculosis research and programs at Douglass, publicly denounced the legislature's withchhunt against Mossell as an affront to blacks in their struggle for

18

equality that proved that black Americans were denied rights enjoyed by the "cheapest immigrant or anarchist."[41]

Concerned blacks undertook their own campaign to keep the hospital afloat. In June of 1917, some two thousand black people packed into a crowded room at the hospital for a reception in Mossell's honor. According to the *Philadelphia Tribune*, they wanted to remind Mossell "that he had a host of friends who admire his leadership and the sacrifices he has made to give our people the finest hospital building controlled by colored physicians in the United States." A fund-raising committee was formed, with auxiliaries that volunteered to seek donations of at least one half of the $50,000 necessary to run the hospital through 1919. Contributions came in particularly from working-class blacks, and in October of 1919, one thousand young black women took to the streets throughout the city for a day to solicit donations. The *Public Ledger* commended the drive by Douglass fund-raisers pointing out that Douglass Hospital subsisted largely on black self-help with donations primarily from the black working poor, and it called for adequate state funding for the institution, citing the institution's history of performance:

> This hospital has put behind it in a quarter of a century a record of unselfish public service to more than 80,000 persons without racial discrimination. It has graduated eleven classes of nurses; it has given nurses to the municipal staff, and it has [during World War I] sent doctors to active service in France.

The small $50,000 allocation, they stated, "would be made to go far by those who have had a plucky uphill struggle to keep the doors ajar to all comers."[42]

The attempt by local and state funding bodies to force Mossell's resignation proved unsuccessful. In 1920, mindful of the substantial bloc of black Republican voters, one of the city and state's leading Republican power brokers, State Senator Edwin H. Vare, introduced and sponsored the passage of a resolution in the state senate that struck the anti-Mossell rider from Douglass Hospital's appropriation bill. Vare's resolution, which passed unanimously, not only restored fully the funds for the 1919–1921 period that had been withheld from Douglass due to the anti-Mossell rider;

it also required the state to advance the 1921–1922 appropriation to Douglass.[43]

Despite this triumph, we will see in later sections that the wounds between Douglass and many local political and medical authorities never really healed. In later decades, when old-line Pennsylvania bosses passed away and their machines lost their influence, Douglass became increasingly isolated and weakened by key political decision-makers and medical authorities.

The mood of militant race pride that emerged throughout black America during World War I and the early 1920s was not only evident in the Douglass controversy. A combative political spirit and "New Negro" social impulse also surfaced in other ways in Philadelphia black medical affairs. In 1920, at the University of Pennsylvania, "because of the clause prohibiting Negroes from membership in fraternities at the University," the few black medical students united with other black students at this institution to form their own campus organization. The students named their organization the "Daniel Hale Williams Surgical and Oral Society in honor of the well known Negro physician." M. Russell Nelson, a senior at the medical school, was the society's first president.[44]

Racial barriers not only beleaguered those black men who were involved in medical education at predominantly white institutions, but also severely limited opportunities for black women to train as graduate nurses. Through the 1910s and 1920s, the city and state's nursing schools were even less accessible to blacks than the medical schools. At this time, the Douglass Hospital Training School for Nurses and the Mercy Hospital Training School for Nurses were the only institutions in Pennsylvania where young black women could receive nursing education. This condition was especially crippling to Philadelphia's black hospitals because through World War II nurses were the chief source of hospital labor.[45] Thus, the lack of adequate numbers of black nurses also served to limit the capacity and, we will observe in later chapters, the long-range viability of these institutions.

While Pennsylvania hospitals had over one hundred fully or conditionally accredited training schools for nurses, only one-third of these schools required high school graduation for admission. Nonetheless, discrimination against black women in Philadelphia prevailed despite the fact that many who had high school diplomas sought admission to nursing programs. Among these graduates, according to Nathan Mossell, some had "superior

20

attainments which would elevate the standard of the nursing profession." Even in the Woman's Hospital in Philadelphia, black women were making no progress. Roberta West, a former president of the Graduate Nurses Association of Pennsylvania, wrote in 1931 that one black nurse had graduated in 1897, the second and last black nurse to graduate from this institution.[46]

Once trained and enthusiastically encouraged by community leaders to observe orderly ideals of nursing, black nurses still faced prejudice. At the 1915 commencement exercises for the Douglass School for Nurses, the Reverend W. Spencer Carpenter spoke to the graduates on the problem of racial prejudice. The popular minister sought to strengthen the young ladies' confidence: "You will find because you are colored that people will say you do not know your business. But in spite of this, you are still ready." In fact, the nursing graduates of Douglass, Mercy, and the other black nursing schools throughout the country were in increasing demand by private patients, including white people, who frequently preferred them to white nurses with similar training.[47]

An event indicative of the racial caste system pervading the city's medical life involved Philadelphia General Hospital's brief use of black nurses in the winter of 1919–1920. Because of an urgent demand for nurses during the influenza epidemic and the absence of many of its normal staff who were serving in the military, Philadelphia General hired eight black nurses, five of whom had graduated from Douglass. After working only a month or so, however, most of the nurses resigned because, according to Douglass Hospital officials, "they had been embarrassed and humiliated [by] certain discrimination perpetrated against them because of their race." Nathan Mossell cited three conditions as most aggravating to the black nurses:

> First, they had been forced to eat in separate apartments; second, they had been requested to wait on other nurses with less experience, who had come to the hospital after them; third, they had been refused the privilege of using the bus that runs, for the accommodation of the nurses and servants, from the trolley line to the institution.

About the time of the nurses' resignations, Mossell and other black medical leaders lodged a complaint with the director of Health and Charities, who oversaw Philadelphia General and the city's other municipal health facilities. As a result of this complaint, some of the more glaring discriminatory practices were eliminated; however, none of the black nurses who resigned chose to return to Philadelphia General.[48]

During the 1910s and 1920s, black women in Philadelphia were also excluded from other medical professional fields in which white women were making their first significant gains. Thirty-seven white women graduated from the University of Pennsylvania Medical College (Table 3). White women were also attending Temple University, where black women rarely obtained such educational openings during World War I. One exception was Bertha Gaskins King, who became the first black woman to own and operate a drugstore in Philadelphia after graduating with honorable mention from the Temple School of Pharmacology. Going to night school, King completed the three-year course of study in two years and was awarded the Dr. H. B. Morse prize "for the most proficient work in the class in the practice of pharmacy."[49] Her success is especially notable because so few of her sisters in the medical profession were able even to graduate. For example, even at Woman's Medical College, black women only infrequently graduated. Woman's Medical during this period was the only medical school in the nation exclusively operated for women, yet only five blacks graduated from the college between the years of 1910 and 1925 (Table 3).[50]

The black women graduates of Woman's Medical College, like their male counterparts at other Philadelphia medical schools, experienced widespread discouragement. They were considered "colored doctors," working toward a predetermined future that was worlds apart from the white medical mainstream. Perhaps most disappointing to black female physician aspirants was the unavailability of internships for black medical graduates. When, in 1914, a Pennsylvania state law was implemented that required an internship as a qualification for a license to practice medicine in the state, the city's black medical leaders like Nathan Mossell challenged the fairness of this policy.[51]

Young black students also reacted with outrage. While doing informal postgraduate work at Woman's Medical College in 1917, Dr. Isabella Vandervall, a black graduate of the New York Medical College and Hospital for Women (class of 1915) and first in her class academically, searched unsuccessfully at numerous hospitals in the city and state for an internship. That year she wrote of her frustration in an article on "Some Problems of the Colored Woman Physician," which appeared in the *Women's Medical Journal*. Highly critical of the race bar that she had run up against in

Pennsylvania, Vandervall condemned the new internship requirement. The law, she believed, victimized black women more than whites, who could occasionally gain an internship at white male-controlled institutions. According to Vandervall, the internship regulation

casts a serious reflection upon these white people—democratic and philanthropic Americans—who lavishly endow colleges and hospitals and allow colored girls to enter and finish their college course, and yet, when one steps forward to keep pace with her white sisters and to qualify before the state in order that she might do the same services for her colored sisters that the white woman does for hers, those patriotic Americans figuratively wave the stars and stripes in her face and literally say to her: "What do you want, you woman of the dark skin? Halt! You cannot advance any further! Retreat! You are colored! Retreat!"[52]

Vandervall's plight drew the attention of the larger feminist-physician community outside of Philadelphia. Shortly after her article appeared, a white female medical activist in Chicago, Emma Wheat Gilmore, wrote a sympathetic public rejoinder and cited crude race prejudice as the culprit. "One can hardly escape an impulse of keen pity for this young woman," wrote Gilmore; "[she] has qualified as a physician, but is deprived of the right to practice medicine in her resident state because she is unable to fulfill the requirements of the law on account of color prejudice." She urged Vandervall to continue sending out "a bugle blast commanding her to take up arms against the injustice she suffers." Gilmore drew a parallel between the struggle of Vandervall and other black female doctors with that of "her [white] sisters of lighter complexion. . . . The one must break down the barrier of color prejudice, the other of that tradition which limits the usefulness of her sex."[53]

The exclusionary internship policies of white-controlled hospitals in Pennsylvania plagued other talented black female physicians throughout the World War I and interwar periods. In January of 1924, Dr. Martha Tracy, the dean of Woman's Medical College, wrote to Dr. Charles J. Hatfield, executive director of the Henry Phipps Institute and a member of the Philadelphia Health Council, who was prominent in anti-tuberculosis work among blacks, concerning the school's "problems . . . in relation to finding satisfactory internship for the colored women graduating from [the] college."[54]

The most recent black woman at issue was Lillian Atkins Moore of the class of 1923. Moore was considered the best prospect as a physician in her class because of her outstanding academic achievements: she won the freshman prize in anatomy with an average of 97, was chosen the secretary of her senior class, and passed the Medical Board with a high average, completing her medical studies with distinction. She was rejected for internships because of her race at several hospitals, however, including the college hospital. Moore had submitted her application to the hospital on October 12, 1922, during her senior year. She did not receive any response until March 2, 1923, when all the interns had been appointed by the hospital. The letter of rejection read in part:

Dear Mrs. Moore:
I was a little surprised to get your letter in regard to an internship. . . . I had been told that we could not possibly undertake to give you a service here. We are all your good friends and it is a most unpleasant thing to have to tell you that just because you are colored we can't arrange to take you comfortably into the hospital. I am quite sure that most of the interns who come to us next year will not give us as good work as you are capable of doing; and I hope that if I can be of any service to you in helping you to secure an internship that you will let me help.

Yours truly
Jessie W. Pryor, M.D.
Medical Director

The College Hospital's discrimination against Moore was considered so egregious that it drew the protest of Dr. John P. Turner, a head officer at Douglass Hospital, W. E. B. Du Bois, and the NAACP. Turner attempted to pressure Tracy directly to get Woman's Medical to accept Moore, while Du Bois ridiculed the college publicly in the *Crisis*. Moore finally secured an appointment at Douglass Hospital.[55]

The racial wall in medical training at this time was virtually impossible for blacks to scale, and the sex barrier pervading medicine was also stronger than at any subsequent period in the century.[56] This barrier tended to constrict even further black female mobility in the medical fields.[57] But during this time, when no blacks, female or male, were permitted internships in Philadelphia's white medical institutions, some white women doctors, albeit few in number, were interning at several of these facilities. In addition to Woman's College Hospital, by the early 1920s, white women were allowed internships at the University of Pennsylvania Hospital, Samaritan Hospital (the Temple affiliate), Philadelphia General Hospital, and white female-dominated hospitals in the city. Also, in 1919 the Hahnemann Medical College admitted its first woman student in seventy-one years.[58]

White women in sparse but significant numbers were not only gaining medical school admissions and internships in comparison to black women, but they were also trickling into skilled employment throughout Philadelphia's hospitals. By 1919, white women were employed as the head pharmacists in eleven Philadelphia hospitals. These institutions included the Hospital of the University of Pennsylvania, the Pennsylvania Hospital, Presbyterian Hospital, Methodist Episcopal Hospital, Germantown Hospital, and Woman's College Hospital. At the Philadelphia Municipal Hospital for Contagious Diseases, five women were successfully apprenticing as "technicists" or laboratory researchers in bacteriology.[59]

The advances that white women were making in medicine both as professionals and as skilled workers were being won largely after great agitation on the part of white feminists to end sex discrimination. The effective performance of white women in civilian and military-related medical services during World War I that earned them wide respect throughout the nation enhanced their status in the health occupations.[60] In contrast, black people of Philadelphia found their patriotic war service did not bring similar results. Not only were black physicians and nurses limited to black hospitals for internships and hospital practice, but discrimination against black patients was the norm at most other hospitals, and there were even inadequate hospital resources for the care of black soldiers.[61] Throughout the 1910s and early 1920s black and white reformists tried to penetrate the divide between Philadelphia's medical institutions, but each episode of crossfire usually ended the way it began—in a stalemate. With the majority of mainstream medical institutions in the city uninterested in desegregating their training, staffing, or treatment policies, black medical professionals and their lay supporters concentrated on developing the strongest black-controlled medical institutions possible. In this area, black medical activists scored numerous successes.

Strengthening the Black Medical Community

During the 1910s and 1920s, the black community made significant and successful efforts to strengthen Mercy Hospital. In 1919, the hospital purchased a much larger site, the Protestant Episcopal Divinity School structure, at a cost of $135,000. The move placed Mercy at the service of the growing black population of West Philadelphia as well as eliminated the direct competition between Mercy and Douglass for South Philadelphia clientele. A fund drive within the lay community collected $15,000. An additional $20,000 was contributed by four black members of the hospital's board of directors, who endorsed bank notes on their homes to raise this sum. The balance of $100,000 was secured by three mortgages of $50,000, $30,000, and $20,000. Within a decade, almost all these notes and mortgages had been paid off.[62]

Like Mercy Hospital, as the 1920s unfolded Douglass Hospital experienced a tremendous surge of financial donations and political support from the Philadelphia black community. Between 1917 and 1920 spurred by the state of Pennsylvania's refusal in 1918 to make its annual appropriation of $22,000 to Douglass, some twenty-three black churches, eighteen black social clubs and fraternal lodges, and over five hundred volunteers organized into twenty separate auxiliaries raised over $17,000 for Douglass. Throughout 1920, the donations and public praise for Douglass gained even greater momentum. In its annual report for that year, the hospital's board summarized such events as follows:

February 22, 1920.—Frederick Douglass Day was celebrated at Gibson's New Standard Theatre. The Hon. Marcus Garvey was the principal speaker.

April 30, 1920.—A Queen's Rally was held at White's Auditorium. One hundred sixty-six dollars ninety-four cents ($166.94) was raised.

July 26, 1920.—A Mid-Summer Rally was held at the Olympia Theatre. Five hundred twenty-three dollars ninety-three cents ($523.93) was raised.

November 9, 1920.—Tag Day Drive. The receipts for the day amounted to $1,494.60.

November, 1920.—Senator Edwin Vare presented a resolution to the Pennsylvania State Senate demanding that the rider attached to the Frederick Douglass Hospital appropriation, requiring the removal of the Medical Director and Superintendent, Dr. N. F. Mossell, be stricken from the bill and the appropriation for the years 1919–1921 be paid as well as the allotment for the years 1921–1922. The resolutions were unanimously passed.[63]

The central importance of Douglass Hospital and Nathan Mossell to Philadelphia's black and liberal community was articulated best by the Reverend Dr. Patrick O'Connell, speaking at the hospital's twenty-fifth anniversary celebration in 1920. O'Connell stated that the politicians and health leaders who were demanding Mossell's removal and who had canceled the hospital's state funds "have undertaken an impossible task." He described Douglass Hospital as "the embodiment of [Mossell's] mind and heart, the scientific training, [and] the love of his race and humanity." He characterized Mossell as a brilliant physician and self-sacrificing hospital leader whose value to Philadelphia's oldest black hospital equaled that of General Samuel C. Armstrong to Hampton Institute and Booker T. Washington to Tuskegee Institute:

> Dr. Mossell and the hospital [have] a position in the affections and esteem of the people of this community from which they cannot be thrust out by a prejudice so virulent that it would corrupt the milk o' human kindness and restrain the tender ministries of mercy, a prejudice so ignoble that it cannot feel respect for a man and an institution devoted to the alleviation of pain and eminently successful therein; a prejudice so cowardly that it dares not declare itself, but resorts to indirection to accomplish its inhuman and unchristian end.[64]

Despite their popularity and professional achievements, the number of black medical professionals in Philadelphia barely changed between 1910 and 1920. According to census data (Table 1), the number of black doctors, surgeons, and dentists increased only from seventy-eight to ninety-five. Furthermore, these black doctors were so isolated from the mainstream medical profession that the slightest cooperation or acceptance was applauded as a major attainment. For instance, during August 28–30, 1917, the national convention of the all-black National Medical Association (NMA) of physicians was held in Philadelphia. The NMA had been formed in 1895 by black medical professionals as a result of the color bar of the American Medical Association (AMA). The 1917 meeting had been shifted to Philadelphia from the planned Memphis site because of recent lynching campaigns in Memphis. As part of the convention activities, the black doctors were permitted to attend a clinic at Philadelphia General Hospital where they viewed a gastric-ulcer operation. Later that same day, they participated in another clinic, focused on tuberculosis treatment, held at the Department of Diseases of the Chest, Jefferson Hospital. "These were unusual privileges," a black newspaper reported, "and the physicians highly appreciated them."[65]

Despite their isolation, black medical professionals of Philadelphia made "internal" professional and social advances, as well as occasional individual gains in white-controlled institutions. In 1900, black physicians in Philadelphia had organized their own separate professional association, the Philadelphia Academy of Medicine and Allied Sciences. Membership of the Academy reached thirty health professionals in 1910, including dentists and pharmacists as well as physicians. The Academy also was the city's branch of the NMA and worked with the NMA to raise the professional standards of Philadelphia's black medical community. The Academy convened meetings on medical research and clinical matters, contributed information to the *Journal of the National Medical Association* (started in 1909) and served as a forum for the city's black medical leaders to share ideas and strategies to strengthen their community stature.[66]

The general segregation between the AMA and NMA notwithstanding, the Philadelphia County Medical Society did allow black doctors to become members during the 1910s and 1920s. At a time when apparently none of the medical registries throughout the nation would accept black registrants, an occasional black entrant is also found on the Philadelphia County Medical Register.[67] But almost all the Philadelphia County Medical Society's membership flowed from the graduating classes of the local medical schools. Furthermore, the county society had a rigorous balloting and approval procedure for membership candidates.[68] Thus, black membership in the society remained infrequent. Apparently the Philadelphia society received a smaller number of blacks than other northern cities. For example, the New York City chapter of the AMA provided a much larger number and, in fact, the bulk of the association's very small national black membership through 1930.[69]

Perhaps the most celebrated black receiving membership in the Medical Society of Philadelphia during the 1910s was Dr. John P. Turner. A graduate of the Leonard Medical School, Turner had a long association with Douglass Hospital that began in 1906. He served as the president of the NMA in 1921. During the 1920–1921 academic year, fifteen years after he received his medical degree, Turner spent a year of graduate study specializing in surgery at the University of Pennsylvania. In 1935, he became chief of the surgical department at Douglass.[70]

Despite the occasional membership that black physicians like Turner were able to obtain in the Medical Society of Philadelphia, the majority of the city's black medical practitioners found an avenue for organized professional and public activities in the all-black Academy of Medicine. Academy members met monthly, and in some periods weekly, to make exchanges on medical cases. The Academy also was involved in activities to improve the health conditions of the city's blacks. On December 16, 1912, the members formed a committee chaired by Turner to campaign against the slum housing conditions throughout black sections of the city.[71] In later years, the larger Philadelphia community consulted the Academy on matters relating to the health problems of black citizens, particularly those migrating from the South. (See Chapter IV.)

In addition to the Academy of Medicine, there was a Philadelphia black dental association, the William A. Jackson Society, named after a pioneering black dentist, as well as an active branch of the all-black National Association of Colored Graduate Nurses (NACGN).[72] The growing recognition and public pride attached to black dentists within Philadelphia's black community was summarized by a prominent local black dentist, J. Max Barber. A former newspaper editor and an outspoken critic of segregation, he wrote in 1914 that the Philadelphia black dentists' growth in practical experience, civic involvement, and professionalism had made them "a power in the community, a factor of good among [their] people."[73] As for the NACGN, black nurses either trained or working in Philadelphia were instrumental in the founding (in 1908) and early growth of this national organization.[74]

Although blacks were neither sizably nor substantially integrated in the medical schools and professional circles of larger Philadelphia, they nonetheless by the 1920s had established a separate medical community. As black medical practitioners strove to accommodate to the local medical caste, they won the support of the black and local liberal presses and the black community in airing the unfairness of their experience in the medical field. This support also enabled Philadelphia's black medical leaders to expand the local black hospitals. The black medical professional's skill and trustworthiness were put to important use in the public health work for blacks conducted in Philadelphia during the early decades of the twentieth century. Indeed, opportunities in public health provided the first solid avenue that pre-World War II black physicians and nurses could take into their city's larger medical professional community.

CHAPTER II

Blacks Enter the Public Health Movement, 1910–1923

The racial division in the medical community coincided with a critical period in health conditions for Philadelphia's poor blacks. Between 1890 and 1910, thousands of black southern immigrants continued to flow into the city and its population grew tremendously. During this twenty-year timespan Philadelphia's black population leaped from 40,000 to 84,000. Moreover, infectious desease-related and infant mortality, both of which are closely associated with poverty and unsanitary living conditions, were widespread throughout these black newcomers' communities. The five leading causes of death for blacks in Philadelphia in 1910 were all infectious disorders. Tuberculosis was the leading killer, followed (in rank order) by pneumonia, diarrhea and enteritis (which killed children under two years old), and nephritis. Bright's desease (a kidney ailment) and heart disease ranked sixth and seventh, respectively. While infectious diseases were also some of the leading causes of death for white Philadelphians, these illnesses were not as prevalent among the city's whites. For example, heart disease, a degenerative ailment that traditionally afflicts mostly the middle- and old-aged, ranked as the second leading cause of death among Philadelphia whites, while diarrhea affecting two-year olds ranked only fifth.[1]

As for overall mortality rates in the city, the rate for blacks in 1910 was 57 percent greater than that of the city's native-born whites and 44 percent

31

greater than that of foreign-born whites.[2] The black and white infant-mortality rates in Philadelphia were both dropping drastically at this time. However, the substantially higher infant mortality among the city's blacks contributed heavily to this serious mortality discrepancy between white and black Philadelphians (Table 4).

Although blacks did not gain access to employment or advanced training in the city's predominantly white hospitals and medical schools, during the pre-World War I years, the white and black medical communities gradually built a most significant bridge during the World War I decade. Increasingly hazardous employment and social conditions, as well as epidemics in the city, pressured white and black medical professionals to undertake joint public health efforts. These efforts led to the emergence of public health clinics, which encouraged the involvement of black medical professionals.

The first public health clinics in which black medical personnel were permitted to work were started by the Henry Phipps Institute for the Study, Prevention, and Treatment of Tuberculosis. A private philan-

TABLE 4
Black and White Mortality Rates for Infants Under One Year Old
(Deaths per 1,000 Population), Philadelphia, 1920–1931

Year	Black	White
1910	341	153
1920	252	101
1926	134	70
1927	103	58
1928	117	63
1929	99	56
1930	100	58
1931	103	58

SOURCE: U.S. Department of Commerce, Bureau of the Census, *Negro Population in the United States, 1790–1915* (Washington, D.C.: GPO, 1918), p. 335; U.S. Department of Commerce, Bureau of the Census, *Mortality Rates, 1910–1920* (Washington, D.C.: GPO, 1923f), pp. 540–541; U.S. Department of Commerce, Bureau of the Census, *Negroes in the United States, 1920–1932* (Washington, D.C.: GPO, 1935), p. 375. Figures are not available for 1921–1925.

thropic establishment founded in 1903, this medical center was one of the few facilities in Philadelphia during the 1910s and 1920s that received political and financial support from the municipal and state health officials to aid in reducing the turberculosis crisis among blacks. Once black doctors and nurses had proven their effectiveness at the Institute's clinics during the 1910s, a few more positions became available to blacks at other public health agencies in the city.

Black Domestic Labor and the Public Health Crisis

The immediate impulse that caused the Phipps Institute and, later, Philadelphia public health agencies to seek ties with black medical personnel was the spread of tuberculosis among the black population. The disease was seen, not simply as a black health problem, but as an epidemic threatening the entire city because of labor patterns that placed the white elite at risk. As we have seen, Philadelphia blacks were heavily concentrated in the domestic service strata. In his classic 1899 study *The Philadelphia Negro*, W. E. B. Du Bois noted this condition, which he traced back to the heritage of slavery. "When we turn to . . . study the disease, poverty and crime of the Negro population," he stated, "then we realize that the question of employment for Negroes is the most pressing of the day and that the starting point is domestic service which still remains their peculiar province." Du Bois estimated that more than one-fourth of the domestic servants in Philadelphia were blacks and, conversely, that about one-third of the city's blacks were domestics.[3]

The fusion of black labor in Philadelphia to domestic service occupations remained a dominant pattern in the early decades of the twentieth century. Although large numbers of white workers in Philadelphia were able to leave domestic service work for relatively better jobs during the World War I decade, most blacks in the city remained constrained to domestic service. A 1913 study by Philadelphia's Armstrong Association found that blacks of the city "can work in but few trades." Black women, it stated, "are restricted chiefly to domestic service," while for black men "the restrictions are even more serious."[4] Faced with such limited job opportunities, and with domestic work increasingly available due to the wartime mobilization that diverted much white labor into industry and military service, the number of blacks in domestic work in Philadelphia between 1910 and 1920 grew substantially. In all eight major domestic and personal service categories, blacks were in 1910 and 1920 proportionately higher than white ethnic groups (Tables 5 and 6). Blacks worked in greatest numbers as servants and laundry workers and in fewest numbers as untrained nurses and midwives, which were included in the "domestic and personal service" work category by census enumerators. In these latter two occupations—both relatively higher-paying and more respected than other domestic jobs—native whites predominated.

In 1910, some 87.8 percent of black female laborers worked in domestic service (Table 7). Women of foreign white immigrant background were also substantially employed in domestic service, but their numbers in the domestic field declined sharply from 42 percent in 1910 to 30.2 percent in 1920. Among native whites, the percentage of females in general domestic labor was much smaller for these two periods—13.2 percent in 1910 and 9.4 percent in 1920. Whereas the absolute numbers of foreign-born white female domestic servants declined significantly between 1910 and 1920, this was not the case for black women. Their absolute number actually increased by 2,289 from 19,795 to 22,084.

Black men show both a decrease in percentage and in the number working in domestic service, from 6,483 in 1910 to 5,777 in 1920 (Table 8). This decrease no doubt was related to the wartime shift of black men into the industrial sectors. But black men comprised about the same major percentage of male domestic laborers for both 1910 and 1920—roughly 45 percent. By contrast, native white men made up a miniscule proportion of domestic labor in 1910 and 1920—1.1 percent and 0.8 percent respectively. The employment of black domestics increased markedly during this decade. Despite the decline in black male domestic workers during the 1910s, blacks in general increased their percentage in Philadelphia's domestic labor force from 36.6 percent in 1910 to 45.8 percent in 1920. Black women went from 34.5 percent of the city's female domestic workers to 46.2 percent. The ethnic group with the next greatest concentration in domestic service work was the Irish. In 1920, about 25 percent of the Irish women of Philadelphia were working in domestic service. However, this concentration was much less than that of black women, 79.5 percent of whom worked domestic service as of 1920.[5]

This pervasive and disproportionate presence of blacks throughout the

TABLE 5
Males and Females in Selected Domestic and Personal Service Occupations,
by Nativity and Race, Philadelphia, 1910

Occupation	Total		Native White		Foreign-Born White		Black	
	Male	Female	Male	Female	Male	Female	Male	Female
Total*	510,871	200,298	311,509	128,628	168,731	49,102	29,561	22,535
Charwomen and cleaners	—	1,549	—	590	—	537	—	422
Housekeepers, stewards, and stewardesses	607	4,284	297	2,694	191	1,191	132	399
Laundresses (not in laundry)	—	6,112	—	1,223	—	1,357	—	3,532
Laundry operatives	1,045	2,545	405	1,715	169	537	72	256
Nurses and midwives (not trained)	621	2,925	306	1,746	268	989	44	189
Porters (except in stores)	1,807	—	218	—	241	—	1,347	—
Servants	6,132	37,050	1,326	8,015	2,069	14,741	2,645	14,278
Waiters and waitresses	4,683	2,937	1,012	996	1,392	1,222	2,243	719

*Figure is entire employed population in Philadelphia in all occupations.

SOURCES: U.S. Department of Commerce, Bureau of the Census, *Thirteenth Census of the United States, 1910* (Washington, D.C.: GPO, 1914), vol. 4: *Population: Occupation Statistics*, table 8, pp. 588–590.

TABLE 6
Males and Females in Selected Domestic and Personal Service Occupations,
by Nativity and Race, Philadelphia, 1920

Occupation	Total		Native White		Foreign-Born White		Black	
	Male	Female	Male	Female	Male	Female	Male	Female
Total*	603,237	215,763	367,267	149,431	184,101	38,510	50,809	27,792
Charwomen and cleaners	—	1,576	—	541	—	416	—	619
Housekeepers, stewards, and stewardesses	639	4,987	298	3,145	198	1,169	139	673
Laundresses (not in laundry)	—	4,612	—	513	—	522	—	3,577
Laundry operatives	1,076	1,999	283	985	121	313	192	699
Nurses (not trained)	589	2,737	401	1,917	158	670	30	150
Porters (except in stores)	1,517	—	165	—	206	—	1,145	—
Servants	5,661	28,290	1,009	5,464	2,021	7,585	2,557	15,227
Waiters and waitresses	4,153	3,609	830	1,514	1,569	955	1,714	1,139

*Figure is entire employed population in Philadelphia in all occupations.

SOURCE: U.S. Department of Commerce, Bureau of the Census, *Fourteenth Census of the United States, 1920* (Washington, D.C.: GPO, 1923), vol. 4: *Population: Occupations*, table 2, pp. 1195–1197.

TABLE 7
Number and Percentage of Philadelphia Workers in the Major Domestic and Personal Service Occupations, by Nativity, Race, and Sex, 1910 and 1920

Nativity, Race, and Sex	1910			1920		
	Domestic Workers	Total Workers	% Domestic Workers	Domestic Workers	Total Workers	% Domestic Workers
White						
Male	3,546	311,509	1.1	2,986	367,267	0.8
Female	16,979	128,628	13.2	14,079	149,431	9.4
Foreign-Born White						
Male	4,330	168,731	2.6	4,273	184,101	2.3
Female	20,610	49,102	42.0	11,630	38,510	30.2
Black						
Male	6,483	29,561	22.0	5,777	50,809	11.3
Female	19,795	22,535	87.8	22,084	27,792	79.5

SOURCE: U.S. Department of Commerce, Bureau of the Census, *Thirteenth Census of the United States, 1910* (Washington, D.C.: GPO, 1914), vol. 4: *Population: Occupation Statistics*, table 8, pp. 588–590; U.S. Department of Commerce, Bureau of the Census, *Fourteenth Census of the United States, 1920* (Washington, D.C.: GPO, 1923), vol. 4: *Population: Occupations, table 2, pp. 1195–1197.*

TABLE 8
Philadelphia Workers in Major Domestic and Personal Service Occupations and
Percentage of Blacks, by Sex, 1910 and 1920

	1910			1920		
Sex	Total Workers	No. Black	% Black	Total Workers	No. Black	% Black
Male	14,359	6,483	45.1	13,036	5,777	44.3
Female	57,384	19,795	34.5	47,793	22,084	46.2
Total	71,743	26,273	36.6	60,829	27,861	45.8

SOURCE: U.S. Department of Commerce, Bureau of the Census, *Thirteenth Census of the United States, 1910* (Washington, D.C.: GPO, 1914), vol. 4: *Population: Occupation Statistics*, table 8, pp. 588–590; U.S. Department of Commerce, Bureau of the Census, *Fourteenth Census of the United States, 1920* (Washington, D.C.: GPO, 1923), vol. 4: *Population: Occupations*, table 2, pp. 1195–1197.

city's domestic service workforce curiously enough generated the first significant ties between black medical professionals and the larger medical community. During these early decades of the twentieth century, when most of the sick were treated and recovered or worsened at home, physicians and public health authorities were concerned that close contact between black domestics and their upper-class white employers subjected whites to an explosive health threat.[6] They feared in particular that white Philadelphia would suffer a tuberculosis epidemic.

The Tuberculosis Threat

Civic and medical leaders viewed the city's black residents, especially black domestic service workers, as a potent source for the spread of tuberculosis. Both local and national medical research and public health investigations supported this opinion. Racialist views notwithstanding, by the 1910s, medical research had publicized the association of tuberculosis with poor and congested living conditions. The disease seemed to be particularly rampant among blacks living in urban areas in poverty, malnutrition, and deficient sanitation.[7] About this time, the Phipps Institute was conducting controversial occupational studies of tuberculosis that revealed that "house-workers" had by far the highest incidence of tuberculosis.[8]

By 1915, the Philadelphia Bureau of Health began to survey occupations, race, and tuberculosis mortality. The compilations showed that house-workers and domestic servants accounted for about 25 percent of the city's tuberculosis deaths during 1915 for which occupations were known. As for race, blacks totaled about one-fifth of the deaths in these occupations. In overall mortality from tuberculosis of the lungs, blacks were dying at a rate four times higher than that of whites.[9]

These findings on tuberculosis intensified consternation among public health and social welfare leaders. In its annual report for 1915, officials of the Whittier Center, a Philadelphia social welfare agency serving blacks, cited top priorities as educational and screening programs for tuberculosis among the city's blacks. "No movement for the betterment . . . of the Negro, from a social as well as health standpoint," they stated, "demands more attention than the one having as its object the prevention and arrest of tuberculosis."[10]

The fear that black domestics were a threat to public health was also voiced by Dr. Henry R. M. Landis, a white physician who was elected vice-president of Whittier at the meeting. Landis was largely responsible throughout the war years and the twenties for popularizing the notion in Philadelphia health circles that the health of black domestics should be a key public health concern. At a meeting of the National Tuberculosis Association in 1921, for example, Landis compared the tuberculosis affl-iction of Philadelphia blacks with the plight of the people of Vienna. Living under conditions of actual starvation, Landis observed, the Viennese had a yearly death rate of 500 people per 100,000 from tuberculosis; "among the Negroes of Philadelphia in 1919 the death rate, on the same basis, was 477." And the health conditions of the city's 125,000 black residents, Landis pointed out, were not an isolated problem: "As servants, they go most intimately into many homes of the whites, and are a constant source of possible infection there."[11]

Leading black doctors in the city agreed with Landis. At the same time, inspired by the militant integrationism that characterized black urban protest during 1910s, they also believed that black domestics were a po-tential asset to the city's public health life. In an address in 1916, Nathan Mossell pointed out that most avenues of employment except domestic service were closed to black women. Douglass Hospital was severely limited

39

in the number of black interns and nursing students that it could accommodate, yet training programs there and at Mercy Hospital were the only ones available for educating blacks as nurses or interns in the entire Commonwealth. Mossell advised whites that they could help black women and the general public by laying aside their "race antipathy" and opening their hospital nursing schools to qualified blacks:

> In failing to extend equal advantages of proper medical education to colored people, the white people in authority not only rob them of a civic right . . . but their continued and forced ignorance of these medical subjects will cause these very colored people to endanger the health and happiness of their white neighbor.

Mossell strongly criticized white medical professionals who were "not adverse to employing colored people as subordinates and domestics, but [when] forced to meet a colored man as an equal, . . . become his bitterest enemy."[12]

Administrators of Mercy Hospital arrived at a measure aimed at transforming black domestics into agents of health rather than disease. Dr. A. B. Jackson, the superintendent of the hospital, announced in April of 1916 that the institution planned to initiate a "department of domestic science for women."[13] Others involved in uplifting blacks in cities like Chicago also held the view that black women had proven their skills and potential in nursing, and only needed access to formal education.[14]

Starting the Public Health Bridge: The Phipps Institute's Negro Clinic Plan

The intense public concern in Philadelphia with tuberculosis outbreaks was a reflection of broad public health fears that had been simmering throughout urban America during the Progressive era. Increased pressures of foreign immigration, black migration, and urbanization led many upper- and middle-class Americans as well as members of the medical community to view the wide range of diseases among the cities' poor as one of the most alarming signs of social erosion.[15] At the same time, city hospitals did not have clearly defined admissions and treatment policies for their nearby lower-class residents, nor was the unevenly dispersed and often expensive family physician proving sufficient for combatting the health problems of this growing urban poor population.[16] As for municipal public health institutions, they too were being overwhelmed by the mounting health hazards unleashed by industrial work life and social congestion. This vacuum in health care work was filled by the neighborhood health center movement. Throughout urban America, health centers emerged most often as components of settlement houses or similar community agencies, usually located in the European immigrants' neighborhoods. The health centers undertook campaigns to improve the health and "social hygiene" of the poor immigrants and, in some cases, served blacks as well.[17]

Extensive medical research, supported by the nation's financial magnates, paralleled the growth of these centers.[18] The Rockefeller family was in the forefront of funding medical research. The Rockefeller Institute for Medical Research in New York was established in 1901. Eight years later, the Rockefeller Sanitary Commission was set up for the purpose of eradicating hookworm throughout the southern states.[19] The Phipps Institute, initiated by Henry Phipps in Philadelphia in 1903, was based on similar philanthropic premises—the eradication of contagious diseases. A highly secretive businessman and philanthropist, Phipps was a steel magnate and a commercial partner of Andrew Carnegie. He apparently never made direct public statements regarding his reasons for establishing the Institute or the many other projects that he sponsored, including a low-income housing unit for blacks in New York City and similar projects in places as far away as India and the Transvaal, South Africa. According to the newspapers, however, he was preoccupied with "stamping out" tuberculosis and had started the Institute to make available "every device known to science for the study and treatment of tuberculosis."[20]

The Phipps Institute was the nation's first endowed center for the study and eradication of tuberculosis, and in the next three decades it would become recognized widely for its antituberculosis work among Philadelphia's black residents. During its first fifteen years, it was divided into five units: a main dispensary composed of various clinics for tuberculosis treatment and patient study; a laboratory for the investigation of infectious diseases (eventually equipped with x-ray apparatus); a sociological division (sometimes called the social service department), which was responsible for neighborhood studies and visiting nursing services; a library focusing

41

on tuberculous and infectious disease materials; and a hospital section, which had a small number of beds for patients. From 1903 through 1918 the Institute was maintained by annual appropriations of $54,000 by Phipps. In 1910, the main building of the Institute, which housed all five of the Institute's operational units, was constructed at Phipps's expense. It was located in South Philadelphia in the midst of heavily black neighborhoods, not far from Douglass Hospital. Also in 1910, the Institute became affiliated with the University of Pennsylvania. Over the next nine years, however, the university proved unable to make sizable appropriations to the Institute, and when Phipps retired from active business and his endowments to the Institute decreased, the Institute was forced to abandon the hospital section. From 1921 to 1926, however, the Carnegie Foundation provided $25,000 each year and funds from the University of Pennsylvania became substantial, allowing the work of the remaining four units, especially the laboratory and main clinic, to continue. These four units were the mainstay of the Institute's work for decades.[21]

During its first ten years of operation, the Institute's dispensary patients were overwhelmingly white, despite its location in the midst of a mostly black section of the city. The first clinic for blacks commenced in 1914 as a separate component within the main clinic. By the mid-1920s the Institute also became a co-sponsor, along with other private charitable health organizations, of black tuberculosis clinics that were located in other sections of the city with heavy black populations.

Henry R. M. Landis was the key figure in the Phipps Institute's first three decades of operation. Born in 1872 and educated at the Jefferson Medical College (class of 1897), Landis became one of the nation's leading white clinicians and researchers in the field of tuberculosis. His scholarly work included the textbook *Diseases of the Chest*, which he wrote with Dr. George W. Norris; originally published in 1917, this work had been republished in five editions by the mid-1930s. Landis also served as editor of *International Clinics* from 1916 to 1921, was a founder of the National Tuberculosis Association, and presided over the Pennsylvania Tuberculosis Society from 1928 to 1932. In addition to being the director of the clinical and sociological divisions at Phipps, he served as visiting physician at the Commonwealth of Pennsylvania's White Haven Sanatorium after 1904 and was connected with Philadelphia General Hospital, one of the nation's oldest and largest municipal hospitals, until 1909. In 1912, he began a teaching career at the University of Pennsylvania that lasted until his death in 1937. Along with these professional posts, Landis was associated for many years with the Whittier Center and was an influential board member of the Philadelphia Health Council and Tuberculosis Committee, a voluntary association that raised substantial funds through annual sales of Christmas seals.[22]

The receptiveness of Landis and his colleagues to plans for analyzing and attacking the problem of tuberculosis among Philadelphia's black citizens was an outgrowth of two factors. First was a belief in a bacterial etiology of the disease. In 1882, when Robert Koch isolated the tubercle bacillus, this bacteria was not immediately accepted by American physicians as the cause of the disease, but by the late 1890s and early 1900s, Phipps, Landis, and others in public health medicine supported the bacterial school, which was led by physician-scientists such as William Osler.[23] Second were the original studies conducted by Landis and his colleagues beginning in 1904 that established a connection between certain occupations and the incidence of tuberculosis. These were supported by epidemiological studies whose results suggested that blacks in the city were harboring tuberculosis at a critical level.[24]

The immediate inspiration for the Institute's work with black citydwellers, however, was provided by a young black physician named Charles A. Lewis. A graduate of the University of Pennsylvania Medical School (class of 1910), Lewis was a medical and political iconoclast, especially with regard to the issue of his race and tuberculosis, who went on to have a distinguished career at Frederick Douglass Memorial Hospital and led many anti-tuberculosis activities among the city's blacks through the 1950s. As a medical student at the University of Pennsylvania, he had been critical of the assumption by some medical thinkers that "Negroes were more susceptible to the devastating disease primarily because of color."[25]

That blacks would eventually disappear from the United States as a result of epidemics of tuberculosis and other infectious diseases because of the race's inherent susceptibility was, in fact, a view widely held by American scientists and sociologists before World War I.[26] In February 1915, for example, Dr. J. Madison Taylor, professor at one of the medical schools in Philadelphia, delivered an address entitled "Remarks on the Health of the Colored People" in which he maintained that blacks were susceptible to tuberculosis because they were maladapted to northern urban environments. The unique physical characteristics of blacks had evolved during the thousands of years the race had inhabited Africa prior to America's colonial settlement, and thus, according to Taylor, blacks were by heritage adapted only to the hot climate of the African lowlands. He concluded that, "in order [for] the Afro-American [to] survive or even to maintain a fair measure of health, it is imperative that he shall keep out of the big cities [and] go live in the warmer regions." Whites and blacks "will not fuse and . . . are totally unlike in racial characteristics and constitution," he stated, and "unless the colored people in a body realize these facts and adapt their forms of life in accordance with them they will disappear."[27]

Unconvinced by the popular argument from social Darwinism, after graduating from medical school, Lewis set out to raise funds that would enable him to conduct his own survey on tuberculosis. The difficulty of this task was recollected (in 1939) by Lewis and two of his acquaintances, Bernard J. Newman and Dr. Algernon B. Jackson. Newman was a leading figure in Philadelphia's social welfare establishment and, later, a member of President Hoover's White House Conference on Child Health and Protection. Jackson was a prominent local black physician. They recalled, "As this was the first attempt in the city to combat tuberculosis among Negroes no funds were available, so in order to get the work under way, the University [of Pennsylvania], through its president, contributed $50, and Lincoln University [in Pennsylvania], at which Dr. Lewis was physician to the students, $75." Lewis managed to gain supervisory sponsorship from the Phipps Institute, and the survey was made in 1911–1912.[28]

Lewis investigated a section in South Philadelphia, in particular a block bounded by Bainbridge, Fitzwater, 12th, and 13th streets that was home to several hundred people. He employed the latest public health survey methods for uncovering tuberculosis in unsanitary and impoverished city neighborhoods. These methods had been initiated by Wilbur C. Phillips, a former New York City public health official who had about this time completed similar surveys in Cincinnati and Milwaukee. Lewis believed that his study demonstrated "that the deplorable conditions under which Negroes were forced to live, because of an economic set-up that failed to net them a living wage, which in turn fostered improper nourishment, caused them to be more susceptible to tuberculosis . . . than [did] color." Though humble in scope, according to Works Progress Administration (WPA) research of the New Deal period Lewis's socio-medical study on blacks and tuberculosis "was the first of its kind in the city."[29] Current medical authorities would support the position anticipated by Lewis and the conclusion reached by Landis: crowded and impoverished conditions, rather than racial susceptibility, were the major reasons blacks had such a high rate of tuberculosis.[30] Although immunization and chemotherapy for tuberculosis would not come until the 1940s,[31] Drs. Landis and Lewis had an important impact on tuberculosis prevention and screening. Landis's perception of the origin of tuberculosis—that it was social as well as medical—was consonant with Lewis's findings. In accordance with this view, Landis implemented changes in the workings of the Institute to address better the lingering tuberculosis crisis among blacks. These concurrent measures took two forms, both of which, over the next three decades, would significantly influence tuberculosis work among the nation's blacks. First, Landis's methods differed from the largely lay-sponsored Negro Health Week campaigns initiated by Booker T. Washington in that Landis employed black physicians and black nurses to screen and treat black tuberculosis patients directly, as well as to educate blacks outside the clinic.[32] Second, while he began to add black medical personnel to the Institute's staff, Landis also attracted simultaneously a steady flow of leading medical researchers to the Institute who pursued novel research regarding social factors and racial susceptibility to tuberculosis.

Landis began to alter the staffing in the clinics at Phipps around 1914. "In the earlier period of the Phipps Institute's work," he wrote, "it was found impossible to do satisfactory work with Negroes":

Those [blacks] who came to the clinic, more or less by accident, could seldom be induced to persist in their attendance, and no considerable progress could be made with them as individuals. Moreover, the educational effort, which at the time served to bring increasing numbers of whites to the clinic, had no perceptible influence in increasing the interest of the colored people in their health.

In 1914, at Landis's instigation, administrators of the Whittier Center decided to provide the salary for a black nurse who was to be employed at the clinic of the Phipps Institute.[33]

The annual report of the Whittier Center for 1914 included an article titled "A Plea for Health," which was presented by Landis. In the report, Landis and Whittier center officials attributed widespread tuberculosis among Philadelphia's blacks to social and economic ills: "Aside from serious unsanitary defects common to all slums, the Negro dwelling in our larger cities has to contend with the additional burden of . . . the over-crowding evil." The article offered the rationale for employing a black nurse as the center's "medical social worker" in cooperation with the Institute, and it indicated that steps were being taken to obtain a black physician. Anti-tuberculosis work among blacks, the article concluded, had to be "done by colored people, for colored people." Landis and center officials expected that in the initial phase the financial assistance for this measure would come from whites, but that blacks would eventually con-tribute most of the necessary funds. They firmly believed that black self-help was the key, both in the war against tuberculosis and in improving the well-being of black Americans. "If the race is to rise," they stated in the report, "it must be through and by its own members. In no other way can it become self-reliant and independent."[34]

The first black nurse hired for the Institute was Elizabeth W. Tyler. A graduate of the Freedman's Hospital School of Nursing in Washington, D.C., Tyler had previously been employed with the Henry Street Visiting Nurse Service, a service connected with the Henry Street Settlement in New York City, which was one of the earliest neighborhood health services. Tyler began to make visits throughout black neighborhoods, particularly in an area designated by the Whittier Center "the Black Belt of Philadel-phia"—south on Broad Street below the Schuylkill River. She wrote that "on visiting the colored churches one could hear the telltale cough [and] note the symptoms in physique and carriage." Traveling from house to house she was able to persuade some black citizens to submit to out-patient treatment at the Phipps Institute.[35]

Landis and the Institute staff discovered that, as Landis put it, "Mrs. Tyler's work, from the beginning, had an appreciable influence." From 1910 through 1913, the Institute had averaged about 47 black patients a year. In 1914, "as a result of the educational efforts of the colored nurse for about six months," the number of blacks treated rose to 121. Later in 1914, two more black nurses were added to the clinic's staff through the financial support of the Philadelphia Committee of the Pennsylvania So-ciety for the Study of Tuberculosis.[36]

In 1915, Dr. Henry M. Minton, a black physician, was hired to work at the first Negro clinic of the Institute. The salary for Minton's position at the Phipps clinic was provided by the Pennsylvania State Department of Health, which supported the Institute's effort to reach greater numbers of tubercular blacks.[37] Born in Columbia, South Carolina, in 1871, Minton had completed studies in pharmacy at the Philadelphia College of Pharmacy in 1895 and established Pennsylvania's first black-owned drugstore. In 1903 he closed his drug business to study medicine, and 1906 he graduated from the Jefferson Medical College and commenced a long and prominent career as a physician. Minton was a central figure at the Phipps Institute's Negro clinic from the time of his appointment until his death in 1946. In addition to his work at Phipps, he was a member of the advisory council, and later the board of directors, of the Whittier Center. He was also the acting superintendent of Mercy Hospital from 1920 to 1944, a member of its board of trustees, and a prominent instructor among the interns of the hospital. Minton's abiding interest in the social welfare of blacks led him to serve as treasurer of the mainly black Downington Industrial School and to make studies of the social condition of Philadelphia's blacks. He became influential in both white and black medical and philanthropic circles on policy matters related to the health of black Americans.[38]

Like that of other physician-supervisors of tuberculosis clinics, Minton's work consisted of making endless decisions regarding diagnosis and treatment. Because the disease typically struck the lungs without presenting dramatic symptoms—in comparison to, for example, typhoid fever or leprosy—physicians in tuberculosis clinics had to maintain a high degree of suspicion in examining people thought to be infected. In addition to sputum cultures, Minton had to interpret both the patient's history of exposure to the disease and the physical findings derived from chest x-rays, neither of which yielded clear-cut indications of tubercle bacillus infection. Usually forced to work with only a "presumptive diagnosis," Minton and his nursing staff had time and again to make difficult decisions regarding the type and duration of hospitalization or sanatorium detention.[39]

In addition to performing his clinical duties, Minton ensured that meticulous records were kept of each patient treated at the clinic; these records provided the epidemiological data that were crucial to Phipps researchers and public health officials. Minton also supervised the training of young black physicians and nurses at Mercy Hospital, some of whom he was later able to bring into the Phipps black clinics as staff or trainees. Minton's initial work, in Landis's opinion, was of "high quality" and, like Tyler's, had "greatly improved" the Negro clinic's work with black tuberculars.[40]

Outside the clinic, Minton publicly agitated for a more comprehensive attack on tuberculosis among blacks in the city and the nation. He believed that reducing the high incidence of tuberculosis among blacks required attacking the disease from a "social as well as [a] health standpoint." Convinced that "entirely too large a number of tuberculous members of the [black] race [were] going without treatment," Minton suggested three social and clinical steps to ameliorate this situation. First, an education campaign was to be undertaken among blacks who lacked knowledge about the disease. This work was to be led by black public health nurses, who would visit families and lay groups to distribute hygienic and dietetic information and advice. Second, incipient cases were to be sought out and referred to appropriate clinics by these community nurses. Third, advanced cases were to be isolated from the community and were to be hospitalized for treatment and study. Like Landis, Minton believed that black medical professionals could fill a vital function, as exemplified by the successes attributed to Tyler's work, and he applauded the new direction in race relations the Institute had taken: "The movement appeals to me as being capable of much expansion, and as likely to result in much good."[41]

Through the early 1920s, local public health and social welfare organizations increased their support of the Institute's work with blacks. These groups provided funds for expanding the staff of the Negro clinic of the Institute, and the flow of black patients into the clinic steadily increased. In 1915, another black field nurse, Cora A. Johnson, was hired. She was salaried by the Philadelphia Health Council and Tuberculosis Committee. In 1919, 190 blacks were treated at the clinic; the following year, 245 were treated. In 1920, the Whittier Center supported the employment of another black graduate nurse, Pauline Ernst. Ernst had served as the chief social worker at Douglass Hospital from 1916 through 1919.[42]

In 1921, the Pennsylvania State Department of Health provided the clinic with two black physicians, Frank Boston and Griffin A. Saunders, to work alongside Minton. Later, Boston's primary connection was with Mercy Hospital, where he served as chief surgeon in the early 1930s. These physicians made it possible for the clinic's work to be broadened, and it was projected that 450 black patients would be treated in 1921.[43]

The Negro clinic was able to thrive despite the fact that, by the summer of 1921, the Institute's funds were all but depleted and its closing seemed imminent. In October, however, the State Department of Health agreed to provide funds for the Institute so that its effective out-patient health center and bureau of social service could be kept in operation. The Institute's financial status was further strengthened by the Phipps family's donation of $500,000 in 1920. At the luncheon where this gift was formally announced, Mayor J. Hampton Moore of Philadelphia declared: "No worthier cause can be engaged in by humanitarians than in sustaining an Institution like the Henry Phipps Institute. I do not live very far from this Institute and I constantly see people of all nationalities groping their way to this ray of light." Two members of the Institute's advisory council also heaped praise on the Institute's recent operations. One was Dr. Hermann M. Biggs, commissioner of health for New York, who extended compliments to Institute officials for the positive effect of their work on public health. Dr. David R. Lyman, the president of the National Tuberculosis Association, also paid respects.[44]

The Phipps Institute's acquisition of black medical professionals for social outreach and clinical work with blacks began to gain attention from other medical establishments both in the city and throughout the nation. "The utilizing of colored nurses and physicians," Minton wrote in 1924, "was, in the beginning, an experiment." However, Minton continued, "as the success of this plan became more and more apparent, it was realized that other groups should be given the benefit of what had been demonstrated in this experimental period."[45]

One of the first outgrowths of the Institute's "Negro clinic approach" occurred in 1918, in the Department of the Diseases of the Chest at the Jefferson Hospital in Philadelphia. After conferring with the Whittier Center, Jefferson placed a black physician "in charge of the Negro work," as Minton phrased it. The intake of black patients and the regularity of their attendance immediately began to improve. Also in 1918, the Philadelphia Committee of the Pennsylvania Society for the Prevention of Tuberculosis established an advisory committee composed of blacks, emulating the Phipps Institute's "idea of selecting Negroes to carry on . . . tuberculosis work among their own race." Minton was selected as chairman of this committee.[46]

Between 1919 and 1921, the Institute's all-black clinic led Philadelphia's other tuberculosis treatment centers in volume of black patients. Sadie T. Mossell, a young sociologist and the first black woman to receive a Ph.D. from the University of Pennsylvania, conducted a survey in 1923 that highlighted this development. Mossell's study was sponsored by the Whittier Center and published by the Phipps Institute. One of its primary disclosures was the impact black medical staff members had on the effectiveness of Philadelphia clinics in treating blacks. According to the study,

49

only two hospitals in the city, Philadelphia General Hospital and Rush Hospital, admitted black tuberculosis patients. The city's two black hospitals had no facilities for the care of tuberculosis patients. Mossell's study stated that Philadelphia General was "the only hospital where tuberculous Negroes could be admitted readily in 1921 and kept for any length of time."[47]

Mossell did not interview patients; rather, she collected treatment data at five of the eight out-patient tuberculosis clinics in Philadelphia that were open to blacks: the Phipps Institute, Rush Hospital, Jefferson Chest Clinic, State Clinic No. 21, and State Clinic No. 107.[48] Although all these facilities were located in the midst of or directly adjacent to neighborhoods with substantial black populations, the Phipps Institute led all the clinics studied in the number of new black patients examined (389). In fact, the Institute accounted for 50.3 percent of the 774 black patients examined by these five clinics (Table 9). The Jefferson Chest Clinic, which by the time of the survey employed a black nurse in addition to its black physician, ranked second. State Clinic No. 21 examined 179 blacks in comparison to Jefferson's 136, but the patient intake of the former was more than twice that of Jefferson. Black patients made up 19 percent of Jefferson's total new patients but just 12 percent of the new patients at State Clinic No. 21.[49]

TABLE 9

New Patients Examined at Five Tuberculosis Clinics, Philadelphia, 1921

Clinic	Total	White		Black		% Black
		No.	%	No.	%	
Total	4,466	3,692	83	774	17	100.0
Phipps Institute	1,288	899	70	389	30	50.3
Rush Hospital	212	195	92	17	8	2.2
Jefferson Chest Clinic	732	596	81	136	19	17.6
State Clinic No. 21	1,520	1,341	88	179	12	23.1
State Clinic No. 107	714	661	93	53	7	6.8

SOURCE: Sadie T. Mossell, *A Study of the Negro Tuberculosis Problem in Philadelphia* (Philadelphia: Whittier Center and Henry Phipps Institute, 1923), p. 24, table 9.

The use of black medical professionals had a direct influence on the rankings of these clinics with regard to black patient compliance. According to Mossell, "The Negroes in these 5 clinics showed a favorable record for regular attendance and cooperation, especially in the case of the Phipps Institute and Jefferson Hospital, where colored doctors and nurses cared for the patients." She drew special attention to the Phipps Institute. According to her findings, the "Phipps Institute with the largest staff of such doctors and nurses enrolled twice as many Negro patients as any other clinic, and the average number of visits per patient was also greater." Mossell repeatedly referred to this pattern of black patient attendance in her study in order to refute contemporary stereotypes of incompetent black medical professionals and superstitious, cowardly black patients.[50]

The Phipps Institute's Negro clinic had an impact outside Philadelphia, and particularly in the mid-Atlantic and southeastern states. At the 1921 meeting of the National Tuberculosis Association, where Landis presented a report about the clinic, Dr. M. J. Fine observed that in 1917, influenced by Landis's work, he had secured a black nurse and two black physicians for his Newark clinic. At first, Fine recounted, "we couldn't get the colored patients to come to the clinic, . . . and we have seventeen thousand Negroes in Newark." But after adding black staff, "our clinic has increased immensely." According to Fine, "the Negroes seem to take pride in coming to a white clinic: however, they do not want charity and when they come to the colored clinic they feel that it is their own." "Negro clinic work" by other medical leaders that either paralleled that of Landis or was influenced by his approach appeared in Burkeville and Norfolk, Virginia, and Wilmington, Delaware.[51]

By 1922, the Institute's staff had had eight years of experience with a clinic administered by black medical professionals, and Landis had several well-developed ideas concerning how anti-tuberculosis work among blacks could best become part of the national effort to eradicate tuberculosis. At the annual meeting of the Medical Society of New Jersey that convened on June 22, 1922, he observed that the strategic foundation for all anti-tuberculosis work had to be the knowledge "tuberculosis is, more than any other disease, a social problem and that nearly everything that relates to the health of the public is included in the battle against it, including "better housing, a knowledge of dietetics, [and] occupation problems."[52]

Since tuberculosis was associated with so many social conditions, Landis believed that work to eliminate the disease was "the source from which many other public health movements [had] been shaped." He recounted the tremendous accomplishments that had been made in this multifaceted effort since the late nineteenth century, including the founding of the Adirondack Cottages Sanatorium by Edward L. Trudeau in 1884 and the Phipps Institute (1903), both of which had aided research and therapy, and the National Tuberculosis Association (1904), which had been responsible for a wide-ranging educational movement that effectively changed popular sanitary practices as well as hospital treatment methods.[53]

Landis was concerned that, as of 1922, tuberculosis was still responsible for one-third of all the deaths of persons between the ages of twenty-five and forty-five throughout the nation. He believed that three major hurdles had to be cleared in the anti-tuberculosis campaign of the near future. One was the failure of many physicians to acquire existing knowledge of the disease and to apply it to diagnosis. If large numbers of physicians were to do this, Landis maintained, they would become a strong force for preventive medicine throughout the community: "I believe, not because I am identified with tuberculosis work, but because of my interest in preventive medicine, that every practicing physician should be identified with his local tuberculosis organization."[54]

A second area in the anti-tuberculosis movement that required improvement involved industrial conditions. Manufacturing occupations such as pottery-making and granite-cutting posed hazards to the health of workers. To Landis, these "dusty trades" seemed to "predispose the worker to infection with tubercle bacillus." Thus, means within the factory had to be devised that would "eliminate the danger from the inhalation of dust." Furthermore, conditions in the homes of other industrial workers had to be improved. In his work at the White Haven Sanatorium, Landis had encountered patients who were workers in cigar-making factories; their factory conditions were satisfactory, but the housing conditions for these poorly paid laborers were found to be "vile."[55]

The third major contemporary problem Landis saw in anti-tuberculosis work concerned the nation's black community. Because of the spiraling migration of blacks over the preceding decade from the South to the northern and western regions, in his opinion the so-called "Negro problem" was no longer a "southern problem"; it had become a national one as well. Blacks were suffering an unusually high mortality rate from tuberculosis, Landis pointed out. At the same time, because of their high concentration in occupations like domestic service and laundry work, blacks were in frequent contact with whites and could therefore increase the incidence of tuberculosis in the white population. Landis informed the doctors, "It is obvious that any tuberculosis program which fails to make provision for this phase of the problem is inefficient." "It is not a question of sentiment," he explained, "but one of necessity."[56]

Landis firmly believed that establishing clinics for blacks like the clinic at the Institute was the only successful course local medical institutions could follow in working with black patients. Having failed to reach black patients "with the ordinary means," Landis reflected, the Institute had "determined to try the experiment of using Negro nurses and physicians." Just by employing one black nurse and one black physician, the clinic had been able to increase its black patient load daily. "There can be no doubt," he commented, "that this is the solution of the problem and any community which has a large Negro population would do well to put it in force." Moreover, to him, the "Negro clinic concept" was a concrete alternative to prejudicial approaches to the problem: "The prevailing opinion is that tuberculosis in the Negro is incurable and that little can be done for [him]," but recent studies had refuted this opinion, showing "that the Negro is just as amenable to recovery in the early stages of the disease as the whites, providing he is given proper treatment."[57]

In 1922, the Phipps Institute's clinical services for blacks were expanded. To ensure the accuracy of the Institute's research and therapy on black patients, the importance of a comprehensive and detailed diagnosis was stressed in the Institute's black clinic. As a result, other diseases afflicting these patients became evident. Writing on "Non-tuberculosis Complications of Tuberculosis" in the *Therapeutic Gazette* for December 1922, Landis stated that there were proportionately more syphilis cases among Phipps's black patients than in the population at large. In this study and a related one he conducted a year earlier, Landis's purpose was not to imply that patients with tuberculosis were inherently more susceptible to syphilis but rather to call attention to a problem in diagnosis frequently encountered at the clinic. In some patients complaining of lung problems, a complex constellation of symptoms of respiratory infection were present, and it was impossible to diagnose tuberculosis as the primary source of that infection, which might be caused primarily by syphilis instead. Therefore, in addition to the black clinic for tuberculosis, the Institute had begun conducting special separate clinics for prenatal, postnatal, and syphilis treatment. Successful black patient attendance in these clinics depended, once again, on the presence or absence of black staff: "Our experience with the Negro in these special clinics was similar to that in the tuberculosis dispensary, namely, few patients [came] belonging to that race, so long as they were handled by white nurses."[58]

Indeed, patient census data cited by Landis demonstrated the marked jump in new cases at these maternal and syphilis clinics after Mercy Hospital's training school for nurses provided several black nurses to help staff the Phipps clinics. This was a mutual benefit. Landis and his medical colleagues received staff support, and these new graduate nurses gained specialized clinical and public health training that was not readily available to them at other medical institutions in the city. At the close of 1922, the Institute employed a total of six black nurses and three black physicians. Among the newer nurses was Nancy Lois Kemp, a leader among black nurses and head of the Philadelphia district of the National Association of Colored Graduate Nurses.[59]

Despite the unique link that the Phipps Institute's black clinics provided for black medical practitioners and trainees in Philadelphia and the national praise the Phipps Institute received, locally the health needs of the black community began to outstrip these black clinical resources. In the early 1920s black migration to Philadelphia began once again to intensify, and so did the spread of communicable diseases and mortality among this largely lower-class population. Between February 1, 1922, and January 31, 1923, the number of new black patients at the Phipps Institute clinics increased dramatically. In 1922, there were 192 blacks and 832 whites treated at the Institute's chest clinic, the largest clinic operated by the Institute. By the beginning of 1923, however, blacks comprised 727 and whites 1,070 of the chest clinic's new patients. A similarly rapid increase in black women and children patients occurred at the Institute's prenatal and postnatal clinics.[60]

Landis and his staff attributed the increase in black female and child attendance to the fact that "the colored work (in the clinics) is in the hands of colored nurses and physicians." But they also emphasized that the Institute's black clinics were merely scratching the surface of the problem of providing a supply of black medical professionals large enough to handle the health crisis presented by Philadelphia's black community. "The problem of dealing with the Negro (and tuberculosis) is becoming a serious one for us," he remarked in 1921. "The work has developed to such an extent that it threatens to swamp us."[61]

Both the city and state health departments saw the separate, all-black clinics of the Phipps Institute as ample and highly successful local resources for controlling the black tuberculosis epidemic. Ironically, by relying on the largely privately financed Phipps black clinics, these officials were, in effect, sanctioning inadequate and racially separated governmental health agencies in the city—agencies that could avoid spending revenues on the health needs of the city's black minority and also avoid disturbing customary racial separatism in their employment and treatment policies. In 1919, the state health department gave financial support to the Institute for general activities and additional funds for employing more black medical personnel at the Institute's black clinics. At the same time, the department made no attempt to open up existing clinics and hospitals to black tuberculosis patients or to construct new facilities for serving blacks. In 1923, in fact, the State Department of Health commenced a policy that would in effect wash its hands of Philadelphia's tuberculosis problem except for its occasional funding of Phipps's black clinics or all-black clinics conducted at Douglass or Mercy.

Indeed, the white and black leaders of the Phipps plan themselves were accommodating to the city's racially divided medical world. True, through the early 1920s, the Phipps Institute's black clinics were significant as a symbolic employment outlet for black medical professionals. Moreover, the Phipps "experiment" had countered what Landis perceived was the widespread attitude that blacks were inefficient doctors and nurses. Yet, while Landis was complimentary of black medical professionals, he neither envisioned nor argued for their employment with equal status alongside whites in interracial clinics.[62]

Landis's fears that disease among Philadelphia's blacks would become epidemic were borne out as the 1920s progressed. The black tuberculosis and pneumonia mortality rates in Philadelphia remained three to four times higher than that of the city's whites throughout the rest of the decade. This left public health officials facing only two options: expanding the black clinic plan of the Phipps Institute or mounting a major assault on black Philadelphia's health problems by appropriating substantially more resources and integrating public health institutions to treat this multitude of ill blacks. Rather than attempt to fuse the city's black and white medical communities, city officials and medical leaders chose to expand the all-black clinic approach.

CHAPTER III

The Expansion of the Public Health Bridge, 1923–1939

D uring the latter 1920s and throughout the 1930s, the concern of Philadelphia health leaders to control disease outbreaks associated with the city's growing population of southern black migrants intensified. At first, this issue preoccupied mainly private, social welfare organizations of the city. These non-profit associations, in turn, looked to the Phipps Institute to coordinate improvements in health facilities for the city's poor blacks—improvements that resulted only in small increases in clinical resources at the Mercy and Douglass facilities. By the early 1920s, black physicians and nurses were being called upon in increasing numbers to work in public health capacities, primarily under the auspices of the Phipps Institute's black clinics. By the latter 1920s and during the Depression years, when the health picture for black Philadelphians became especially grim, black medical professionals, particularly nurses, and black-staffed clinics were sought actively by the city's public health departments. Leaders of both the private charities and public health agencies came to a common understanding that black health workers were a vital tool for ameliorating the public health crisis in the black community.

The broadening dialogue between influential civic figures, philanthropists, and black medical leaders, and the great popularity and race pride throughout the black community that black medical professionals generated once they were granted limited opportunities in community health work, enhanced the general public recognition of the black medical professionals. Municipal health roles heretofore inaccessible to Philadelphia black doctors and nurses became available. Thus, another narrow, yet significant, bridge was constructed between the black and white medical worlds of the city. Spanning the gap between municipal health agencies and the black medical community dispersed throughout Philadelphia's black neighborhoods, this bridge strengthened as the Depression era unfolded.

Facing the Black Migrant Health Crisis, 1923–1924

Between 1919 and 1921, black migration to Philadelphia decreased only to surge upward again in 1922. Black newcomers were settling in Philadelphia at a rate of over 10,000 per year. By the spring and early summer of 1923, overcrowded neighborhoods and outbreaks of disease associated with the city's black migrants produced near-hysteria locally. Since other northern cities like New York and Indianapolis were experiencing similar threats, the Philadelphia crisis drew national attention. Beginning in May, editorials ran in city newspapers on the "Negro Migration Problem," and headlines proclaimed, "Exodus from South Begins," "Negro Exodus . . . Ten Thousand Come in Few Weeks,"and "Negro Congestion Menace to Health." In July, the National Medical Association described the health problems of Philadelphia's black migrants as "acute," demanding a "colossal effort" in medical and black self-help work.[1]

A Philadelphia organization representing a broad range of municipal health and welfare interests, the Migration Committee, felt the full weight of public concern. This group had been established by the Philadelphia Armstrong Association (a branch of the Urban League) and the Philadelphia Housing Association during World War I at a time when the stream of in-migrating blacks had strained housing reserves throughout the city.[2] In 1923, the Committee, which included representatives from housing, welfare, employment, and health organizations throughout the city, tried to coordinate their operations to attack social and public health problems stemming from the heavy migration. In doing so, they generated a brisk public debate between white and black health advocates and professionals, the first such debate in the city's history.

57

The Migration Committee was headed by Bernard J. Newman, executive director of the Philadelphia Housing Authority. In hopes of gaining greater support from social welfare establishments throughout the city, as well as acquiring some policy directions, Newman conducted an extensive survey of the housing and social conditions of the new migrants.[3] Information was solicited from dozens of black and white leaders of welfare institutions that serviced Philadelphia blacks, including H. W. Parker and M. J. Earle, the heads of two of the city's black YMCAs and YWCAs respectively, Richard R. Wright Jr., black business leader and church activist, Henry M. Minton and Nathan Mossell, and local black newspaper editors.[4] The report, which covered the one-year period ending on June 30, 1923, revealed serious problems.

First, southern blacks were migrating to Philadelphia in phenomenally high numbers and at a time when the city was in the midst of a severe housing shortage. In 1923 alone, the Committee approximated that some 10,500 black newcomers had arrived. This number comprised about one-third of the city's average population increase for all races. Records of the previous decade showed that the average annual increase in the black population from 1910 to 1920 had been 4,977. Thus, the committee pointed out, there had been a better than 200 percent increase in the growth of the black population in the year 1922–1923.[5]

The Migration Committee also found that living conditions for these poor migrants, who settled mostly in the black neighborhoods of South and West Philadelphia, were unspeakably bad. The Committee's study covered 931 properties and 1,282 blacks who had recently arrived in Philadelphia from the South. Landlords subdivided single- and two-family units and crammed tenants into these structures regardless of the disastrous psychological and hygienic effects on the occupant:

> One four-room house was found occupied by four new families, one family consisting of a man, his wife and six children. Another six-room house was found with five families, and within two weeks the house next door, which had been occupied by one family, had increased to three-family occupancy. Above a small West Philadelphia garage a migrant rented a single room for herself, an adopted son, three married children, and their children, making a total of 16 persons.[6]

The Migration Committee's report authorized four subcommittees, each charged with pursuing measures to alleviate a particular aspect of the migration problem: "Health Program for Philadelphia," "Labor and Housing Opportunities in Pennsylvania Towns to Help Absorb the Excess Migrants," "Housing Accommodation," and "Publicity."[7]

The health subcommittee, composed of Harvey Dee Brown of the Philadelphia Health Council, Mrs. Edmund Stirling of the Inter-Racial Committee civic group, Prentice Murphy, and Henry Minton, now a consultant to the municipal children's bureau, proposed to enlist the cooperation of the Department of Health in a campaign to enlighten the public about health hazards and sanitation measures. A "Health Week" campaign was promoted throughout the city. Furthermore, the subcommittee exchanged information and recommendations with the Health Bureau on specific measures to prevent the spread of communicable diseases such as smallpox that were likely to arise from congested housing. Particular focus was placed upon new black migrants, and the subcommittee planned to conduct its work with respect and "due caution so as not to offend the sensibilities of the Negro population of the city."[8]

The subcommittee on health met with Bernard J. Newman and Dr. Norman Taylor, acting director of the city's Department of Public Health. The meeting resulted in three measures, all of which attempted to encourage the city's newly arriving blacks to seek medical care and, at the same time, to compel landlords to eliminate glaring health hazards. First, at the subcommittee's insistence, the Department of Public Health compiled a list of the hospitals and clinical facilities providing free treatment to blacks. The subcommittee urged health and welfare organizations throughout the city to utilize the directory in "giving special attention in their work to the incoming Negro population." They also forwarded the list to all real estate agents having substantial dealings with the black population, to employment agencies that recruited black laborers, and to industrial plants where blacks were employed.[9]

As a second step, the subcommittee sought to borrow nurses from the Metropolitan Life Insurance Company to alleviate the special health problem presented by the black migrants. In computing policies on the basis of "mortality experience," Metropolitan systematically collected data that compared rates of mortality and morbidity from individual diseases, frequency of accidents, nature of epidemics, and population changes between black and white Americans. Once the company had written policies for poorer clientele, it provided its policyholders with family health literature or nursing care and medical examinations. By 1920, it had established a nationwide network of special agents and nurses to survey the health status and to improve the health practices of its policyholders. Although Metropolitan had about twenty nurses in Pennsylvania at this time, it did not honor the Migration Committee's request.[10]

Third, the subcommittee solicited the help of the Academy of Medicine and Allied Sciences. This request met with more success. Headed by Dr. John P. Turner, its secretary, the Academy sent a communique to all ministers of black churches and to all black fraternal and social organizations on the importance of preventive health practices, especially vaccination. During Health Week, supported by the state and city health departments, the Academy also used motion pictures—at this time a most advanced medium—to reach an estimated 75,000 people. In addition, according to Minton, "seventy physicians and nurses spoke in many churches on Health Sunday. Thirty large industrial plants massed their employees at lunch hour and they were given health talks by Negro physicians and dentists. Many large mass meetings were held and thousands of pieces of health literature were distributed." The inspiration behind this campaign was not purely the migration health issues, but racial pride and elevation generally. "We feel that to give the Negro a new vision, a new hope," Turner wrote of the campaign, "is to aid him to reduce his mortality through the consciousness that he must not [be ill] just because he is a Negro."[11]

In the winter of 1923, as the Migration Committee report circulated through municipal and social welfare circles, an outbreak of smallpox struck the black migrant community and thrust the Public Health Department into harried action. Between December 1922 and June 1923, city medical inspectors were forced to quarantine forty-two different districts, covering a total of 303 city blocks. Some 28,000 citizens, including several thousand black residents, were vaccinated.[12] Dr. James G. Cumming, the chief medical inspector, reported that for the year ending December 31, 1923, sixty cases of smallpox had been uncovered, as compared to twenty-seven for 1922 and three for 1921.[13]

The fact that a smallpox epidemic of such magnitude occurred as late as 1922–1923 was worrisome. Other mid-Atlantic cities like New York and Baltimore had experienced their worst bouts with smallpox back in the late nineteenth century, between the late 1860s and the early 1890s. The historic Milwaukee epidemic had taken place in 1894–1895. Everyone agreed that the epidemic originated among recent black southern migrants. According to Cumming, "the increase in the number of cases for 1923 is directly attributed to the unusually heavy influx of the colored population from the South during this same period."[14]

Public health officials blamed the epidemic on the migrants themselves. "All these [smallpox] cases have been imported cases," one of the chiefs of the Bureau of Health wrote to Minton during the crisis:

> These people have come from Georgia, North Carolina, South Carolina, and Virginia. [Only] some live in crowded houses, while in others the conditions were good . . . In conversation with many of these people, when asked why they had not been vaccinated, their reply invariably was that they had never been asked to be vaccinated.

Dr. Walter S. Cornell, the director of medical inspection for the public schools, also lamented the lack of vaccination among the recent migrants: "If our native [white] Philadelphians were as a class unvaccinated smallpox today would be epidemic in the city," he commented. But the disease had been confined mostly to the new black arrivals in the city. Despite the "work and anxiety" that the outbreak had caused the Health Department, "in a city of two million people, no native Philadelphians have contracted smallpox."[15]

The Migration Committee agreed that the outbreak was largely confined to recent black migrants, and to the poverty and ignorance in which they lived, but it interpreted that fact differently. One house where seven cases had been discovered, it pointed out, had thirty-eight occupants; another seven cases occurred in a house with forty occupants; in a third household of equal size there were eight cases. To the Committee, inadequate inspection and education facilities were partly responsible. On July 11, 1923, the Committee held a special meeting with Norman Taylor to try to convince him that the small size of the Health Department's inspection staff was a primary stumbling block to improving the living conditions of migrants and controlling the spread of disease among them. Since 1909, the number of housing inspectors had stood at five, but in the interim nineteen years, Philadelphia's population had increased by nearly 400,000 and about 75,000 new houses had been constructed. Many of these houses were now crowded tenements. The Committee urged the City Council to pass a measure providing the Department of Public Health with more inspectors.[16]

Despite an exchange of letters and a series of meetings with public health department heads throughout July, the Committee was unable to convince city officials of the need for long-term measures. Perhaps fearing a backlash among the city's landlords, City Council failed to appropriate any funds to increase the number of inspectors.[17] The Health Department limited its response to the smallpox crisis to immediate quarantine efforts: "Most intensive and extensive quarantines were carried out in 1923 to control smallpox in Philadelphia; this disease was entirely confined to Negroes."[18] It offered to assist in disseminating information about health services, and it made occasional public statements about the seriousness of the health problems afflicting Philadelphia's blacks, but it failed to seek any substantial new health care facilities or inspection personnel, responding instead with a superficial rearrangement of its already limited health care resources. As long as communicable disease outbreaks did not affect white Philadelphians, city officials saw no need for increased public health efforts.

One immediate and significant outgrowth of the smallpox crisis, however, was the establishment of a new vaccination clinic at Mercy Hospital, which the Bureau of Health requested as part of its effort to address the current virulent outbreak.[19] This cooperative contact with one of the city's black hospitals was a significant first step in bringing these black institutions and their personnel into a more professional relationship with white health institutions. Since the city and state health departments remained unwilling to commit substantial new resources for black health care, they were forced to build additional links with black medical professionals and to expand black clinics.

By the beginning of 1924 the Migration Committee had disbanded. The Committee had been an ad hoc arrangement of concerned social welfare leaders and black medical professionals, not a formal extension of local government or the large health institutions of the city. Consequently, once the Committee completed its survey of the black migrants and its subcommittees had gotten their work underway, its head, Bernard Newman, discontinued the group.[20] But in its short period of operation, the Committee had contributed to bringing the smallpox epidemic under control. It also brought much more public visibility to the medical needs of blacks and paved the way for additional black medical professionals to work in the black health clinic network.

In the wake of the Migration Committee's and Academy of Medicine's public campaigns, for the first time in the city's history, its health officials began to focus seriously on the city's stake both in the smallpox outbreak and in the tuberculosis problem that was still devastating the black community. Although from 1915 to 1925 overall tuberculosis mortality in Philadelphia had dropped about 43 percent, the death rate for blacks declined by only 28 percent and yearly stayed from three to four times higher than that of whites. By 1925, blacks comprised only about one-tenth of the city's population but suffered one-fourth of Philadelphia's tuberculosis deaths (Tables 10 and 11).

In August 1923, the Pennsylvania Department of Public Health complicated the city's health care problems. The Department had been supporting ten tuberculosis clinics in Philadelphia. State legislators from counties outside the Philadelphia area, who had been agitating aggressively for fiscal conservatism, naturally felt that they were being overtaxed to support these clinics. Therefore, when a study of the city's tuberculosis problems conducted under the auspices of the Philadelphia Health Council

TABLE 10

Death Rates from All Forms of Tuberculosis (Deaths per 1,000 Population), by Race, Philadelphia, 1900–1928

Year	Total	White	Black
1900	239.6	197.6	448.2
1905	237.5	—	—
1910	216.8	198.7	444.0
1915	184.6	163.7	437.5
1920	137.3	118.9	353.7
1925	106.1	81.9	315.9
1928	84.4	84.0	300.9

SOURCE: Nathan Sinai and A.B. Mills, *A Survey of the Medical Facilities of the City of Philadelphia, 1929: Being in Part a Digest of the "Philadelphia Hospital and Health Survey, 1929"* (Publications of the Committee on the Costs of Medical Care, No. 9; Chicago: University of Chicago Press, 1931), p. 178.

TABLE 11

Tuberculosis Death Rates, by Nativity and Race, Philadelphia, 1925

Race and nativity	No.	%	Est. population*	Deaths/ 100,000
Native-born white	1,083	51.5	1,399,525	77.4
Foreign-born white	430	20.5	431,537	99.6
Black	542	25.8	148,464	365.1
Unknown	46	2.2	—	—
Total	2,101	100.0	1,979,526	106.1

*As of July 1, 1925.
SOURCE: Nathan Sinai and A.B. Mills, *A Survey of the Medical Facilities of the City of Philadelphia, 1929: Being in Part a Digest of the "Philadelphia Hospital and Health Survey, 1929"* (Publications of the Committee on the Costs of Medical Care, No. 9; Chicago: University of Chicago Press, 1931), p. 181.

and Tuberculosis Committee recommended that it would be more efficient and economical to let the municipality handle the complexities of maintaining local anti-tuberculosis facilities and medical personnel, the state health department withdrew support from the clinics. In the words of Dr. Ward Brinton, head of the Bureau of Health's newly created tuberculosis division, this retreat left the city "practically with an entirely inadequate provision for handling tuberculosis."[21]

Management of the black tuberculosis crisis in Philadelphia was compounded by the lack of state sanatoria willing to accept the city's black tuberculosis victims, as well as the severe limitations on black patient care within the hospitals located in the city (see Table 12). Although the state maintained three large sanatoria at Mont Alto, Cresson, and Hamburg— with a total bed capacity of 1,600—there was no provision for accepting severely ill (and, therefore, highly infectious) tuberculosis patients from Philadelphia in these institutions. These sanatoria were structured primarily to serve the populations of their respective counties, and rarely or never accepted blacks. The Mont Alto Sanatorium did not have any black patients through the 1920s and was not listed among institutions that served blacks in a 1925 Pennsylvania Department of Welfare survey of the social welfare needs of the Commonwealth's black citizens. This sanatorium was located in southcentral Franklin County, which in 1920 had a population

TABLE 12

Blacks in Pennsylvania Tuberculosis Sanatoria, 1914, 1919, and 1924

	1914			1919			1924		
Sanatorium	Total Cases	No. Black	% Black	Total Cases	No. Black	% Black	Total Cases	No. Black	% Black
Cresson	1,067	10	0.9	1,123	23	2.0	1,016	39	3.8
Hamburg	397	30	7.6	1,230	79	6.4	826	71	8.6
Mont Alto	—	0	—	—	0	—	—	0	—

SOURCE: *Pennsylvania State Manual, 1925–1926* (Harrisburg: Pennsylvania Bureau of Publications, 1926), pp. 358–359; Pennsylvania Department of Welfare, *Negro Survey of Pennsylvania* (Harrisburg, Pa.: The Department, 1928), p. 84.

of 62,275, only 2.3 percent (1,475) of whom were black. The Cresson Sanatorium was located in Northampton County in northeastern Pennsylvania, another county that had an almost negligible black population—749 (0.05 percent) blacks out of a total 153,506 people in 1920.[22]

The state's new policy toward Philadelphia clinics mandated that beds in these institutions be made available to appropriate cases from the city. However, the immense shortage in Philadelphia's tuberculosis treatment facilities, the generally poor conditions of its public health resources, and restrictive racial practices in these sanatoria and other existing health facilities made this a moot gesture. As early as the spring of 1922, a Phipps Institute study estimated that the city needed an additional 2,500 hospital beds for tuberculosis treatment. The inability of social reformers to obtain more medical inspectors in the city's public health department during the smallpox crisis and the shortage in tuberculosis treatment facilities were just two symptoms of the much broader economic frailty of this department. In a survey of the municipal health departments conducted in 1923 in the nation's one hundred largest cities, the United States Public Health Service pointed out the severe underdevelopment of Philadelphia's public health resources. Among the nations' twelve cities with populations greater than 500,000, Philadelphia ranked eighth in per capita expenditures for essential health services. Out of all one hundred municipalities canvassed, Philadelphia stood seventy-eighth in such expenditure.[23]

The in-patient facilities for black tuberculosis patients throughout the city were woefully limited. Sadie Mossell estimated that, for 1921, 900, or less than 25 percent, of the 3,800 blacks with tuberculosis were treated at any type of tuberculosis clinic or hospital. Only Philadelphia General Hospital accepted black patients, and those consumptive blacks who were in-patients at General were usually in the last, near-fatal stage of their infection. Sixty-seven percent either died or were hospitalized for at least a year. Segregated practices in the city's hospital facilities had given rise to a black institution, Jackson's Sanatorium, which was opened in 1921 but seems to have survived no more than a year.[24] Since Mercy and Douglass hospitals had no clinics for tuberculosis treatment, there were no alternative, black-controlled facilities to cope with the surge in the number of ill and diseased within the city's black population.

Black Clinics, Black Nurses, and the "Negro Health Bureau"

The Pennsylvania Department of Health had, in effect, constrained Philadelphia to rely upon its already severely limited Public Health Department to control tuberculosis. Forced into hurried action by the state's new austerity policy, the city's director of public health appointed a committee to assess ways of managing the tuberculosis problem. The twenty-two-member, all-white committee was composed mostly of Philadelphia hospital administrators and medical school professors. This committee had a much more narrow focus than the Migration Committee. Whereas the Migration Committee had sought a community-based and social reformist campaign to ameliorate the sanitary, environmental, and class causes of the tuberculosis crisis, the administrative and medical specialists focused primarily on the treatment policies and clinical resources for medically screening and identifying tubercular individuals. Its key resolution was that the Public Health Department promptly establish the Division of Tuberculosis, which, in turn, the City Council authorized on August 30, 1923. Dr. Ward Brinton was named the Division's Chief.[25]

On September 15, when the state officially relinquished its operations in the city's tuberculosis clinics, the Division of Tuberculosis undertook their management. In addition to operating ten clinics, the Division organized two new clinics, one at the Rush Hospital and the other at Douglass

Hospital. The facilities of the Division of Tuberculosis were intended to serve those sections of the city not being reached by the Phipps Institute.[26]

According to Brinton, the Division had selected Douglass Hospital because it was a black-run hospital serving blacks. He explained that the decision had been based on the previous success of black clinics operated by the Phipps Institute and Jefferson Hospital's Department for Diseases of the Chest, which functioned in affiliation with the Phipps Institute, the Philadelphia Health Council, and the Whittier Center.[27] Thus, the Division's initial policy assumed that black medical professionals would be most effective in attending to black patients. In upcoming years other public health agencies throughout the city would also follow this policy.

The start of the vaccination clinic at Mercy and the tuberculosis clinic at Douglass signified the entry of a small number of black professionals into public health agencies. By March of 1924, the Douglass Tuberculosis Clinic, for one, employed two black physicians and two black nurses. Patient attendance was described as substantial. In January 1924 the Division of Tuberculosis hired two black nurses, Charlotte Carr and Catherine Worthy, both graduates of the Douglass Hospital Training School for Nurses.[28]

Earlier in the same year that the Douglass facility was established, another tuberculosis clinic had been opened in the northern section of the city. This clinic, the Ridge Avenue Center (or "Health Clinic No. 3"), located at 20th Street and Ridge Avenue, was one of three facilities serving blacks that made up the so-called "Negro Health Bureau," a network of black health centers organized by Henry Landis and the Phipps Institute to help fill the gap in tuberculosis screening and treatment facilities in the city's black sections. Under the collective sponsorship of the Philadelphia Health Council, the Phipps Institute, and the Whittier Center, and supervised by Henry Minton, the Bureau included the black clinics of the Phipps Institute (Health Clinic No. 1) and Jefferson Hospital (Health Clinic No. 2).[29]

The Ridge Avenue Center was a success from the beginning. Its number of black patients rose so rapidly that after a month it became necessary to increase the number of clinic days and borrow workers from the Phipps Institute to assist with the heavy patient load. The Center was in the midst of a growing black community of recent migrants. The black nurse who worked in the nearby public school that the clinic served described it as "entirely colored, pupils and teachers, and . . . in the center of a congested

Negro population." She pointed out that there were 2,000 area youngsters enrolled in public schools as of October 1, 1924, but that an additional 2,500 area school-age children were not attending school. These out-of-school children were particularly vulnerable to communicable diseases since their health was not being screened by either the school nurse or the Ridge Avenue Clinic nurses.[30]

In October of 1924 the combined personnel of the three Negro Bureau clinics numbered eleven doctors and at least seven nurses, all of whom were black. The work of the nurses was particularly impressive. On the average they made a total of 134 home visits per month. This was accomplished even though transportation then often meant walking or riding the trolley. Furthermore, the clinics were normally open only part time.[31]

Minton had particularly strong opinions about the value of the black medical professionals and the Negro Bureau's health work. In line with the general New Negro mood of urban black America nationwide, he saw black public health workers as compatriots in an increasingly self-reliant racial movement. Writing on "Negro Physicians and Public Health Work in Pennsylvania" in a 1924 issue of *Opportunity*, Minton described what he perceived was an intrinsic relationship between black medical workers and the black community. "There is in the Negro race today a growing sense of racial consciousness," he stated, "which makes these people feel proud of any creditable work that is propagated by members of that race— and to the same degree of pride there will exist an interest in this [public health] work." Medical sociologists stress that bonds of trust between health professionals and patients are generally more likely when health personnel have racial-ethnic characteristics and gender or social values in common with those of their patients. Minton sensed correctly that such a phenomenon governed the success of the black clinics he supervised. "There is one thing about the employment of Negro physicians and nurses in the anti-tuberculosis crusade which has been impressed upon me," he wrote. "It had given to the colored community a group of their own men and women who, representing a great movement, are regarded as authorities and as such are welcomed into their churches, lodges, clubs, public gatherings, and by their newspapers, that they may bring a message."[32]

Minton estimated that Philadelphia's 150 or so black physicians were ministering efficiently to 75 percent of the 150,000 blacks residing within the city. As for black nurses, he predicted that they would gain in prominence because of their excellent record of performance. In conclusion, Minton urged that black physicians and nurses be consulted and employed on all health matters involving Pennsylvania black communities. He also called for liberal support of the black hospitals in the state.[33]

As the Negro Bureau expanded its personnel and reputation, black nurses began to find employment with some of the city's official public health agencies. By November 1, 1924, four nurses—all products of black nursing schools—had worked for the Division of Child Hygiene. They included two Douglass nursing school graduates, Mary B. Tucker and Camilla McArthur, Eleanor Selah, a graduate of Freedman's Hospital in Washington, D.C., and Carolina Still, a Lincoln Hospital (New York) graduate. About this time there were also two or three black nurses on the staff of the Visiting Nurses Association. On May 1, 1927, one additional black nurse was hired by the VNA. She was Christiana L. Thomas, a graduate of the Mercy Hospital Nursing School.[34]

The Board of Education also hired black nurses. In 1923, Cora Nicholson, a graduate of the Douglass Hospital Training School, became a public school nurse. The following year, a similar position was filled by Louise Antoine, a graduate of another black nursing school, the Provident Hospital Training School for Nurses in Chicago. Nicholson was in charge of the Durham, Smith, and Logan schools, while Antoine covered Hane, Singerly, and Reynolds. All six of these schools had virtually all-black enrollments.[35]

Although unable to attend the city's and state's nursing schools and excluded from working in Philadelphia's large white hospitals, Philadelphia's number of black nurses were still increasingly in demand in public health work or at Mercy and Douglass hospitals.[36] In fact, by the mid-1920s, public health nursing was a much more important field for trained black nurses in Philadelphia than for the city's white nurses. On January 1, 1924, the National Public Health Nursing Organization conducted a census of public health nurses throughout the United States. The census covered public health nurses for units of state and city governments, such as boards of health and boards of education, as well as for non-governmental nursing services, such as the American Red Cross, the National Tuberculosis Association, and the Metropolitan Life Insurance Company. The census showed that Philadelphia had 281 public health nurses out of the

961 for the entire state of Pennsylvania, and that 27 of these nurses were black. While only one in twenty white nurses worked in the public health field, slightly more than one-fourth of Philadelphia's black nurses were in public health work.[37]

In January 1927, Landis assessed the performance of black public health nurses of Negro Health Bureau. At this time, the Bureau had twelve black doctors and ten black nurses. His remarks appeared in the *Child Health Bulletin* and covered the black nurses' work in fields other than tuberculosis work. He pointed out that, while the black nurse was beginning to receive her due recognition in tuberculosis work, her effective activities in other health fields were going unnoticed. He recounted his experience with the other clinics at Phipps—that is, those for prenatal and prophylactic care— as evidence of the black nurse's all-around abilities. For the first years of their operation, the special prenatal and prophylactic clinics at Phipps had been used only by white patients, and administrators assumed that black women were uninterested in seeking treatment for themselves or their children. As soon as a black nurse had been placed in charge of prenatal and prophylactic clinics that specifically welcomed blacks, however, the number of black patients had grown rapidly. In fact, Dr. Landis reported, the black prenatal clinic had grown larger than the white clinic.[38]

Black public health nurses also disseminated public information on preventive health practices. "The educational value of these nurses is great," Dr. Landis stated, "and they can arouse an interest and a desire for a knowledge of health matters among their own people that the white nurse cannot create." He believed the success of black nurses with black patients was irrefutable: "Just why this should be so is difficult to understand; nevertheless it is a fact . . . that where the white nurse fails the colored nurse succeeds."[39]

Dr. Landis predicted an increased demand for black nurses in black communities and decried the obstacles that black women faced in getting into nurses' training programs. Once a black received the basic nurse training, "as a rule, post-graduate work is not possible," he said. He called for some foundation to provide educational funds for both prospective black nurses and physicians.[40] His plea would be answered, but not by the predominantly white medical and nursing institutions in the region. Instead, once again charitable lay organizations throughout the city would rally to the cause of black health improvement, this time by forming an immense campaign to strengthen Mercy Hospital's nursing school.

The Lingering Black Health Crisis, 1927–1928

Even though in the mid-1920s the employment of black medical professionals and a small network of black clinics had come to be looked upon by most of Philadelphia's medical authorities as the answer to reducing infectious disease among the city's blacks, overall public health programs for blacks were still proving inadequate. In 1927, the Division of Tuberculosis reported that the rate of tuberculosis mortality among blacks was very high. For Philadelphia's approximately 167,000 blacks, there were 454 recorded deaths due to tuberculosis, a tuberculosis mortality rate of 271 per 100,000. The report called this rate vastly higher than the rate for the city's white population, which was 85 tuberculosis deaths for every 100,000 of their number. But the report referred to the poor health of blacks as, in effect, a different and distant problem, recommending no corrective measures other than another study. It even implied that blacks' relatively poorer health resulted from the black race's being fundamentally more predisposed to tuberculosis than whites.[41]

During 1928, medical authorities again expressed grave concern over the ill health of blacks and its implications for the health of Philadelphia's white citizens. A statistical summary of the tuberculosis incidence for blacks and whites was given by the Division of Tuberculosis in 1928. This ward-by-ward survey found that there were 508 reported deaths from tuberculosis among the city's blacks in 1928. These figures translate into a death rate for blacks about four times higher than the rate prevailing among Philadelphia's whites.[42]

Medical authorities established that for every death from tuberculosis there were nine living tuberculosis cases. Based on this formula, the Division officials warned that there was reason for alarm. It meant that in Philadelphia there were currently "almost 5,000 Negroes suffering from active tuberculosis who are employed in our homes as cooks, maids, child nurses and who are working side by side with the whites in factories, mills, stores or attending our public schools and who are potent factors in the spread of tuberculosis." For this reason, the report urged that more antituberculosis work be conducted among the city's black population.[43]

The fear of blacks as tuberculosis carriers was reinforced by a tendency by some health officials to accept racialist explanations for blacks' susceptibility to tuberculosis. The Division report echoed this notion as explaining why "the mortality from tuberculosis among Negroes is much greater than among the white population living in the same localities under the same conditions."[44]

The renewed consternation in 1928 within the Tuberculosis Division and Bureau of Health over a public tuberculosis threat posed by blacks resulted in the establishment of another special clinic, in addition to the daily Douglass Hospital facility, the City Tuberculosis Clinic, a night clinic for blacks at the Woman's Medical College Hospital.[45] Unlike the Negro Health Bureau clinics, this municipal clinic was staffed by whites. For a number of years, the poor had been treated in the clinics of the Woman's Medical College main hospital, as well as in its Barton Dispensary, and as a result, blacks were not resistant to attending the clinic. The City Tuberculosis Clinic was not a new, autonomous facility, but rather it was a program built into existing seriously overtaxed clinical facilities. In mid-1928, the medical director of the Woman's College Hospital, Dr. Florence K. Polk, reported that demand for services at the clinic greatly exceeded the limits of space and personnel. The clinic operated only on a part-time basis, beginning at 6:00 P.M. on Mondays and Fridays and at 3:00 P.M. on Tuesdays. Even so, during the period from June 1, 1928, through May 31, 1929, its large caseload involved 2,360 patient visits.[46]

In December 1928, the tuberculosis clinics of the Woman's College Hospital and the Douglass Hospital were assessed by the Division of Communicable Disease, Tuberculosis Section. They were described as heavily attended and as conducting excellent work. However, the report emphasized that study of the citywide tuberculosis problem strongly indicated that there should be other clinics established for blacks in those sections of the city where they were most concentrated; however, just exactly which Philadelphia institution would provide these clinics was not mentioned.[47]

Fortifying Black Medical and Nursing Resources

In 1928, as sentiment among community and public health leaders intensified regarding the health of black residents, a broadly based campaign emerged to strengthen Mercy Hospital's nurses' training program. Over the decades, although burdened by limited and inadequate physical accommodations, the school had become known nationwide as one of the most important centers for the training of black nurses.[48] It attracted an annual student body of about thirty-five to forty women from as far away as Texas and Missouri, as well as the West Indies.[49] As with many nursing schools associated with black hospitals and other financially weak hospitals, the residence quarters of Mercy's nurses were grossly undersized and poorly ventilated.[50] As a consequence, in 1928 the school was threatened with losing its accreditation from the Pennsylvania State Board of Examiners for Registration of Nurses. If this accreditation were to be terminated, Mercy graduates would be severely limited in the number of local and out-of-state hospitals that would hire them.[51]

During the spring of 1928, Mercy Hospital officials decided to initiate a major fund drive similar to the one in 1919 as a means of building up its nurses' training and service resources. During the 1920s hospital campaigns were not only vital means for obtaining funds for both capital expansion and operations but were also highly publicized social movements by urban ethnic groups to reinforce their group cohesion and sense of community health.[52] Both the urgency of the situation at Mercy and support for the board's idea of a fund-raising drive were seconded by leaders in public nursing and medical schools of the city.

Two persons in particular, S. Lillian Clayton, president of the State Board of Examiners and director of nurses at Philadelphia General, and Katherine Tucker, general director of the Visiting Nurses Association of Philadelphia, lent their reputations to draw attention to the financial needs of Mercy Hospital. In May 1928, Clayton and Tucker submitted statements to the Mercy's board president, Rev. Henry L. Phillips, in support of the board's idea of a fund-raising drive for the hospital's nursing program. Clayton stated that, based on her direct contact with Mercy Hospital over the past six years, "I know of no finer body of young colored women than that which is yearly graduated from this School of Nursing." If the nursing school were to lose its accreditation because of the "sadly inadequate" nurses residence, Clayton believed it would be a "sore blow" not only to Mercy nursing graduates "but also to the colored people [in general] since there are so few endorsed institutions in which colored women may take up the study of the nursing profession."[53]

By June 1928, a number of white health officials, politicians, and philanthropists joined with Mercy board and staff members including Phillips and Minton, and prominent black professional leaders in what was becoming a highly organized national campaign to establish a new three-story nurses' home and to strengthen the nursing school. This citywide campaign committee of ninety-four members set $200,000 as its financial goal. Key blacks serving on the committee included Dr. Leslie Pinckney Hill, Eugene Rhodes, John C. Asbury, and Edward W. Henry. Hill had been president of Cheyney State College when it became a fully accredited black teachers' college. An ardent Republican and a close political ally of local philanthropist and U.S. Senator George Wharton Pepper, Rhodes had become the assistant U.S. attorney in 1926. Asbury, a state representative from 1921 to 1925, and Henry were attorneys and both eventually became magistrates.[54]

From its inception the campaign was vigorously supported by the Chicago-based Julius Rosenwald Fund. By now one of the nation's most influential philanthropic institutions, the Rosenwald Fund had decided in the late 1920s to place a high priority on health care for black Americans. Between 1928 and 1944, it contributed over $1.7 million to black hospitals and other medical facilities, helping to upgrade black medical personnel, to make budgetary and equipment improvements, and to implement studies and research projects on health problems that seemed particularly hazardous to blacks during the years between World War I and World War II. In this period of consistent segregation in health care institutions and public ignorance surrounding the severity of health care problems that faced blacks, the Philadelphia campaign workers, black health personnel, and larger black community were highly appreciative of the Fund's support.[55]

The concerns of the campaigners were set forth in its promotional publication, *For the Health of a Race*, a compendium of statements, data, and photographs that stressed the pivotal need to expand Mercy's nursing resources. Though recognizing the effect of the housing situation on black health problems, the booklet also stressed the need for black physicians, surgeons, and nurses. While there were many among the black American community seeking to learn these professions, the campaigners admitted, few institutions were open to them.[56]

The committee's statement reasoned that strengthening separate black institutions would ameliorate the health problems of Philadelphia's blacks. This position echoed ideas proposed earlier by the Phipps Institute in organizing the Negro Health Bureau, as well as the pragmatic racial accommodationism of Booker T. Washington and his chief financial backers, large northern philanthropic foundations involved in health and education projects among blacks. The publication emphasized: "Within the race there are great possibilities for a well-organized and highly successful future, but this race cannot be expected to solve its manifold problems without training—education." The campaigners argued that blacks had to develop and extend their established collegiate and medical facilities so that they could, in the end, solve their own local and national problems.[57]

The campaign group also referred to a recent statement by Edwin R. Embree, president of the Rosenwald Fund, that they felt summarized the urgency of the black health care situation. Embree had argued that whites had a stake in resolving the public health problems of blacks simply because "Jim Crow Laws have never successfully been set up for the germs of tuberculosis, pneumonia, typhoid or malaria." Blacks were so widely dispersed throughout America, Embree wrote, that it would be pure fantasy for white Americans to ignore health facilities for blacks. The nation's black medical and nursing schools should be fully supported and expanded. Their graduates could, in turn, serve in clinics, schools, and homes of the black communities throughout the country.[58]

The Mercy Hospital campaign statement detailed the depressed health levels of blacks in Philadelphia and throughout America, noting that the death rate of blacks was 34 percent higher than that of whites, even higher in urban areas. In Philadelphia, the rate for blacks was twice that of whites. In 1927, for each 100,000 people in the two racial groups, there were 1,038 deaths of whites and 2,138 deaths of blacks.[59]

The campaign plea quoted the Armstrong Association as saying that each year there were 135 black medical graduates, yet only 65 internships were available to them. Five of these internships were provided by Mercy. Except for the Mercy and Douglass programs, no opportunities for nursing for blacks existed in the city. Between 1924 and June 1928, two black hospitals in Philadelphia had graduated eighty-nine nurses. This achievement was commended by the Armstrong Association in light of the nearly nil integration of the country's white nursing schools.[60]

The Campaign Committee called its efforts to raise $200,000 for Mercy nursing facilities a campaign that aimed at a "chance, not Charity." It looked particularly to businesses employing significant numbers of blacks to become donors. The statement predicted that the "horizons" of "opportunities" for Mercy Hospital were on the brink of great expansion. The nurses' school, it emphasized, would serve the nation as well as Philadelphia.[61]

This campaign was significant as a meeting ground of converging social attitudes that were deeply anchored in pre-World War II Philadelphia and the nation at this time. First, like most American health authorities during this period, the campaigners believed that the "two worlds of medicine," one for whites and the other for blacks, would remain an unalterable reality. Second, campaign leaders argued that it was in the self-interest of white Americans to facilitate a supply of black medical personnel and health care resources to lessen the spillage of black illnesses into the white community. Thus, that a cross-section of the city's social elite, traditionally one of the most conservative in America, rallied around the cause of Mercy Hospital in union with prominent blacks in the city is not surprising. This cry for measures to prevent cross-racial epidemics had worked effectively for Phipps Institute leaders over a decade earlier, and it still appealed to the city's elite during the twenties. Finally, while pragmatic accommodationism on matters of race relations was the social and political philosophy that united both groups, black campaigners were particularly enthusiastic since the Mercy drive represented an outlet for the collective racial spirit of self-help that pervaded black communities through the mid-1920s in the forms of New Negro consciousness and Garveyism.[62]

The campaign proved to be financially successful. Some $319,568 was raised, making possible the construction of a new nurses' home as well as a power plant and laundry unit. Writing of the new facility in a letter to the president of the Rosenwald Fund, Minton said, "We feel that it fills every demand of a modern Nurses' Home without extravagance." He closed this same letter on a hopeful note: "The future looks bright, and we are trying in every way possible to raise the standard of our institution."[63]

While the city's influential whites and prominent blacks had played a major role in initiating the drive, ultimately it received greater support from ordinary black citizens, who were both dependent on and appreciative of Mercy's services. In its annual report of 1928, Mercy's board of directors pointed out that the many black fund-raisers who took to the field raised over 50 percent of the donations. At the close of the drive, more than 1,110 black campaign workers, as opposed to about 220 whites, had been counted. The black group had secured 6,214 subscriptions at an average of $25.94 per subscription. The white campaign group raised $158,492 from a much smaller group of white subscribers (873) with an average subscription of $181.54.[64]

Although significant in itself, in terms of the general citywide shortage of black nurses and public health resources, the success of Mercy Hospital must be seen as a limited one. Douglass, the city's other black nursing school, was sinking, suffering from the political disfavor of local and state government as well as the large charitable funding institutions of the city as a result of the unpopularity of Nathan Mossell's earlier activism. Two fund-raising campaigns undertaken by the Douglass Hospital in 1928 did not reach their goals, and although the construction of new housing for nurses was underway, Douglass was unable to finance its completion. The inadequacy of the nurses' quarters became the main cause for the school's loss of state approval in 1928.[65]

Moreover, by the early 1930s, it became evident that fund drives and even foundation grants were an inherently weak, sporadic financial base for black health care institutions.[66] Fortunately for Douglass supporters, just at the time when their hospital needed government-funded programs more than ever, the city's public health department also needed to extend its services to black residents whose overall ill health threatened the city's public weal. Thus, during the Depression decade, although Douglass nearly closed down completely, it managed to survive by virtue of its value to the municipality's overall public health community. In fact, not only did the pressure to contain the diseases afflicting the Philadelphia black community force linkages between the city health agencies and the black hospitals, but it also led to wider use of black medical personnel by these agencies.

Surviving the Depression

The Depression intensified the protracted crisis in the health of Philadelphia's blacks and, like the black migration episode of 1923, resulted in greater ties between white public health authorities and the black medical community. The so-called Negro Health Bureau's facilities, Mercy and Douglass hospitals, and black public health professionals were all called upon by city health officials to restrain infectious disease menaces within the expanding, poverty-ridden black community. In the year of the Great Crash (1929) white unemployment in Philadelphia reached 9 percent compared to 15.7 percent for blacks; by 1932 the jobless rate reached a shocking 39.7 percent for whites and 56 percent for blacks.[67]

As for the health status of Philadelphia blacks during these years, the traditional discrepancies became even more extreme. In 1930, the black population of Philadelphia numbered 189,363, or 10.7 percent of the city's residents. The number of deaths attributed to tuberculosis reported for blacks was 582 as opposed to 1,587 for whites. Thus, the death rate for blacks was approximately five and one-half times greater than the white rate. There had been 126 fewer deaths among whites from tuberculosis in 1930 than in 1929, but 47 more deaths for blacks.[68] In comparison to the nine other major cities with the largest black populations, Philadelphia ranked in the middle in both tuberculosis and pneumonia mortality rates for its black residents. Southern blacks who had come to Philadelphia to improve their lives were more likely to die from tuberculosis in their new home than in southern cities like Birmingham, New Orleans, Baltimore, or Washington and more likely to succumb to pneumonia in Philadelphia than in Memphis or Birmingham (Table 13).

The Division of Tuberculosis in 1930 referred to the problem among blacks as very grave. For not only were disease rates for blacks inordinately high, but also facilities for treating blacks with advanced cases of tuberculosis were largely unavailable. In Philadelphia and in the rest of Pennsylvania, the division found racial prejudice so strong that "these people are not well received in existing sanatoria and many institutions exclude them entirely." Calling for a sanatorium to treat black people exclusively, it noted that several large cities had already established such institutions. The Division warned that, "unless adequate facilities for the prompt isolation and treatment of these cases can be developed, tuberculosis among the Negroes and its spread through them among the whites, cannot be effectively controlled."[69]

In 1930, the Division operated two day clinics and one night clinic for blacks. A summary of the operations of the Douglass Hospital appeared around 1930 in the publication *Philadelphia—World's Medical Centre*. Written by Dr. Alfred Gordon, a white physician, it described the work done at the Douglass Chest Clinic for the Department of Health as "fundamental to the health of the population."[70] Yet the few clinics supported by the Department of Public Health by its own admission were not adequate to deter fundamentally the citywide tuberculosis vulnerability of blacks. The Division of Tuberculosis praised its clinics for blacks as having done

78

TABLE 13
Tuberculosis and Pneumonia Death Rates in Ten Cities with Largest Black Population (Ranked), 1920 and 1930

Rank	City	1920 Black	1920 White	Rank	City	1930 Black	1930 White
Tuberculosis							
1	Washington, D.C.	216	74	1	Birmingham	172	27
2	St. Louis	249	69	2	Baltimore	218	58
3	Birmingham	260	47	3	Washington, D.C.	228	55
4	Memphis	260	87	4	New Orleans	231	92
5	Baltimore	285	98	5	Philadelphia	232	53
6	Philadelphia	291	100	6	Chicago	233	43
7	New Orleans	316	144	7	Memphis	236	54
8	New York City	NA	NA	8	St. Louis	252	35
9	Chicago	NA	NA	9	New York City	263	55
10	Detroit	NA	NA	10	Detroit	325	46
Pneumonia							
1	Birmingham	289	120	1	Chicago	137	67
2	Baltimore	325	161	2	Memphis	155	85
3	Chicago	341	152	3	Birmingham	187	82
4	Memphis	344	147	4	Detroit	190	76
5	New Orleans	348	127	5	Philadelphia	192	80
6	Washington, D.C.	352	130	6	Washington, D.C.	219	86
7	Philadelphia	388	176	7	New York City	221	98
8	New York City	396	177	8	St. Louis	253	109
9	St. Louis	400	193	9	New Orleans	283	94
10	Detroit	744	209	10	Baltimore	308	114

SOURCE: U.S. Department of Commerce, Bureau of the Census, Negroes in the United States, 1920–1932 (Washington, D.C.: GPO, 1935), "Vital Statistice—Mortality," pp. 454–455.

commendable work in its 1930 annual report, but was forced to admit that additional in-patient and out-patient clinics were desperately needed in areas that had high concentrations of black residents.[71]

The situation was conspiring to resurrect panic about the safety of white Philadelphians. The publishers of *Philadelphia—World's Medical Centre* wrote that the work of the Negro Health Bureau and the Philadelphia Health Council and Tuberculosis Committee was "needed not only for the sake of the Negro people, but also in the interest of the health of the city as a whole." They feared that "the wide employment of Negroes throughout the city, frequently in occupations involving personal service and the preparation and handling of food, renders the problem of tuberculosis among them peculiarly a community problem."[72]

By 1932, the Division of Tuberculosis was maintaining "six daily and one night-clinic for colored people." This number apparently included the clinics of the Negro Health Bureau and one new day clinic started at Mercy Hospital. The division judged the work of these clinics as quite efficient. Although the mortality from tuberculosis dropped slightly throughout the city during 1932, and black mortality was down from 1930, it was still over four times higher than white. According to the Division, a better distribution of clinics had begun to enhance anti-tuberculosis work, and, for this reason, they expected "much betterment by placing of our colored clinic in the Mercy Hospital."[73]

Yet the following year the tuberculosis mortality among blacks began to worsen, with 473 deaths recorded. Shortages in clinical and long-term care facilities for blacks throughout Philadelphia were again receiving publicity. The Tuberculosis Division report for 1933 called the tuberculosis problem of blacks in Philadelphia and similar cities "a very serious one." The division emphasized an acute need for separate black health care facilities. Once more, the Health Bureau recommended a sanatorium and other in-patient facilities devoted exclusively to the treatment of black people.[74]

The authorities of the Tuberculosis Division cited three reasons for segregating the proposed facilities for Philadelphia's tuberculosis victims—reasons that illustrate clearly how racial caste and intraracial dynamics governed health policy in the city at this time. First, their experience indicated that black and white patients did not get along well when being treated at the same institutions, and because tuberculosis treatment required many days and months of hospitalization, the authorities assumed that racial antagonism would surface among black and white recuperating patients. Second, noting that "many existing sanatoria and [medical] institutions exclude [blacks] entirely," the division favored a laissez-faire approach to this long standing policy of segregation. Third was the unmatched success that black doctors and nurses had with stimulating black patients to comply with therapeutic regimens. In new black clinics, the report stated, "the immediate supervision and management should be colored as there seems to be better co-operation between the patient and the authorities when they are both colored." The division feared that unless prompt treatment and adequate isolation facilities be developed for blacks, "tuberculosis among the Negroes and its spread from them to whites can never be controlled."[75]

While during 1932 one concrete effort was made to develop a separate facility at Douglass Hospital for a small number of black in-patients, this clinic took more than two years to materialize because Douglass itself was barely surviving. In 1932, a private donor agreed to finance floor renovations and five new beds at Douglass for tubercular blacks. However, the deep-seated feud between many members of the state assembly—an assembly that was now splintering the old Republican machine—and Nathan Mossell, who at the of seventy-seven was still the medical director of Douglass, resulted in the hospital's losing its state appropriation for 1932. Also during this same year Douglass failed the minimum standards required by the State Welfare Department for certifiable internships and nursing training. Thus, staff morale was low and turnover high since the graduates of these training program at Douglass were not licensed to practice anywhere in Pennsylvania.[76]

The financial distress of 1932 at Douglass was temporarily relieved by the private donation, but, in 1933, the situation worsened. The board of directors reported that in early June of 1933 "the electric current was turned off for unpaid bills and other creditors threatened." At this point, the staff and officials at Douglass threw in the towel on the Mossell issue. During the World War I years, the younger Nathan Mossell had been enthusiastically supported by a loyal professional staff and board, as well as an energetic, relatively prosperous black community. Now time and Depression conditions had washed away Mossell's official leadership of Douglass, although respect for his long-standing professional leadership strengthened. On June 19, 1933, Dr. Charles Lewis, now the vice-president for the hospital's board, convened an emergency meeting. He explained that the influential tuberculosis authority, Dr. Lawrence Flick, had agreed to help Douglass meet its financial crisis on the condition that Douglass officials yield to the state assembly's will that Mossell be removed from any official connection with the hospital's operations. With Mossell present, the somber gathering required and accepted his resignation. The board resolution accepting the resignation stipulated that, in recognition of his thirty-eight years of leadership, all of the hospital's literature would still carry Mossell's name as founder and director emeritus. The resolution also provided him with an ample pension as well as repayments for money he had loaned the hospital over the years.[77]

With Mossell now retired, Flick authorized the White Haven Sanatorium Association to provide about $6,000 to Douglass to maintain ten additional beds at the hospital for consumptives. A statewide sanatorium for whites headed by Flick, White Haven was located in rural Luzerne County and received generous funds from Philadelphia philanthropists. This support that Douglass received from White Haven offset the reduced state allocation that began to flow once Mossell was replaced. Combined, these public and private funds were enough to keep the hospital solvent.[78]

In fact, even during this dismal phase for Douglass Hospital, the small tuberculosis section was effectively operated and monitored. The floor for tuberculosis patients at Douglass was reserved for the most severe cases. Only people having the symptom of tubercle bacilli in the sputum, a clear-cut indication of a highly infectious individual, were admitted. Prior to July 1933, 67 patients, who the doctors at Douglass suspected had exposed an additional 368 family members, were admitted. The Douglass hospital Board explained that hospitalizing the most severe cases would spare many others from the disease and, eventually, the overall tuberculosis rates would drop. The hospital's administrators thought highly of their anti-tuberculosis program, which they interpreted as a new milestone in a forty-year movement to develop isolation facilities for tuberculosis patients. "Being staffed as we are by well-trained and conservative physicians, dentists and nurses, although handicapped by lack of funds, the work done and the results obtained compare favorably with the best hospitals in Philadelphia," the board wrote in May 1934.[79]

Despite its success, the tuberculosis program at Douglass was too small to have a fundamental impact on the overall battle against the tuberculosis public health crisis. Throughout the middle and late 1930s, the Division of Tuberculosis complained repeatedly about the high tuberculosis mortality among blacks and advertised the minimum improvement in facilities that alleviation required. Yet the Division was unable to support its good intentions. In 1936, it reported, "tuberculosis in the colored race continues to be a great responsibility," and in the same report it acknowledged that the opening of an additional chest clinic for screening tuberculosis was to be postponed. Unable to procure new city-sponsored resources, and with the Phipps Institute's black clinics now seriously overburdened and the Institute's overall resources for tuberculosis screening and personnel curtailed, the Division sought to rezone city districts in order to give black patients residence eligibility at other clinics. But this effort also met with failure since clinics newly zoned to receive black patients were themselves overtaxed.[80]

The agencies of the Philadelphia Department of Public Health during the 1930s had no plans to hire large numbers of black medical personnel or to implement major health programs in the city's black sections. However, the persistent tuberculosis outbreak among the city's increasing black population, and racial barriers in virtually all private and state-owned health accommodations, combined to force their hand. By the close of the thirties, the heads of the local public health agencies brought small but noteworthy numbers of black nurses and doctors onto their staffs. The Division of Child Hygiene had three black nurses employed by 1939. That year three black nurses could also be found on the staff of the Division of Tuberculosis; these nurses were Hattie Reynolds, Dorothy Ferguson, and Catherine Worthy. Also, both of these divisions had at least one doctor in affiliation, and Louise Antoine and Cora Nicholson were still employed as nurses with the city's school system.[81]

As for private-sector health service, by 1939 the Negro Health Bureau employed one field supervisor and seven nurses, all of whom were black registered nurses. The supervisor was Bertha Bryant and the nurses were Elinor Turner, Cleo C. Hudson, Margaret Campbell, Sophia S. Purnell, Nancy L. Kemp, Bertha Lee, and Margaret H. Brisbane. With the exception of Lee and Kemp, trained at out-of-state black nursing schools, all were graduates of the Mercy Hospital Training School. Besides Christiana L. Thomas, who had been appointed in 1927, the Visiting Nurses' Association had hired Marie Sherman on March 1, 1934, Kate B. Lee on March 1, 1938, and Frances Taylor on September 15, 1938. All were graduates of the Mercy Hospital nursing school.[82]

Despite these employment gains, the overall situation for black nurses in Philadelphia worsened when the Douglass Hospital finally closed its nursing school around 1936, eight years after it had lost its accreditation with the Board of Examiners. The Douglass Hospital Nursing School was one of the nation's oldest black nursing schools, and, at its closing, had approximately three hundred graduates. Many, if not most, of its more recent graduates were in "institutional work, public health nursing, school and social service work, etc.," according to the Douglass boards.[83] Its financial problems and closing was no small factor in contributing to the gradual decline in the number of black nurses in Philadelphia in the 1930s and 1940s.

Throughout the Depression decade, the incorporation of black medical professionals into public health activity is clear evidence that health, social welfare, and municipal leaders in Philadelphia had entered an irreversible stage in race relations within the public health sphere. No longer could these leaders wholly ignore the black community's health crisis because it overlapped inextricably with the health aspirations of the white community of the city. Yet the public health work of black medical practitioners of interwar Philadelphia was but one dimension of their overall role in this city's medical life. The majority of Philadelphia's black doctors and nurses, as well as dentists and pharmacists, were still working in private practice or in their own enterprises within the black community. As was the case in public health medicine, racial segregation greatly limited their education, distribution, and professional activity at a time when American medicine was undergoing increased technical specialization. In response to the widespread racial discrimination, typical black medical professionals of interwar Philadelphia could cultivate no particular ties with the white medical establishment. Instead, these black medical workers strove to sustain their own professional universe and institutions, which ranged from hospitals to retail drugstores.

CHAPTER IV

Status Without Power: Black Medical Professionals Through the Outbreak of World War II

A lthough the admission of black professionals into public service medicine was symbolically important, and critical to improving health care in the city's black neighborhoods, most of Phila- delphia's black medical professionals remained separated from the mainstream medical community. Roughly 90 percent of the city's black doctors were not connected with public health clinics; most of them were in private practice. Like other black professionals such as dentists, hospital staff members, and pharmacists, they were virtually invisible to the larger health care community. Their working lives were interwoven with their self-contained professional networks and neighborhoods, and they con- centrated on treating the common illnesses of the city's indigent blacks, who usually had no other avenue for medical care. The conditions they dealt with—accidental injuries, childbirth, dental problems, and so on— posed no threat to the city's larger public health the way communicable disease outbreaks did.[1] As a result, despite their popularity and influence within the black community, as well as their important role in the city's public health efforts, Philadelphia's black medical professionals lagged behind the larger medical professional community in education, training, and professional accomplishment.

Black medical practice throughout ordinary neighborhoods reflected the racial separateness pervading Philadelphia during the Depression. Black churches, black fraternal lodges, black YMCAs, and segregated black child welfare institutions all displayed what Philadelphia's leaders called "voluntary segregation."[2] But the city's racially divided public health system, social institutions, and youth services bespoke not just a desire by whites, at least, to live among their own but a peculiar economic isolation and spatial diffuseness that was coming to characterize the city's developing black ghetto. Unlike Chicago, Detroit, and New York (with its Harlem section), Philadelphia's black community was fragmenting well before 1940 into three predominantly lower-class areas, all with pockets of slum conditions (Map 1).[3]

During the 1920s and 1930s, South Philadelphia, the city's traditional black population center, whose hub was Douglass Hospital, changed from a black working-class and professional section into a generally impoverished one. "During the 'Great Migration' to Philadelphia between 1916 and 1930," as John Bauman has noted, "the city's black population rose over 13 percent to 219,599, and most of these newcomers crammed the ancient bandbox rookeries of the . . . [southern] sections of the city." By 1930 the center of the city, once the workplace for South Philadelphia's black domestic and service workers, had become an area of white-collar occupations that in general excluded blacks. A similar expansion of poverty occurred in West Philadelphia near Mercy Hospital. In this formerly multiclass black section southwest of Strawberry Mansion, one-family homes were transformed into crowded multifamily quarters for the migrant black poor. Finally, an estimated 90,000 blacks resided in North Philadelphia, a section covered with innumerable factories and warehouses. But black residents found few jobs in this surrounding industrial center. Lacking employment income and affordable safe housing, many of the black poor of Philadelphia became dependent on the new, largely federally funded public assistance handouts. They lived crowded together in dilapidated tenements, hoping that public projects would finally be built to relieve the housing shortage.[4]

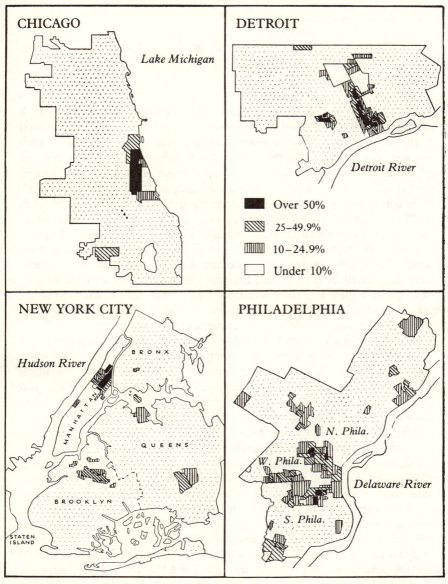

CHICAGO

Lake Michigan

DETROIT

Detroit River

■ Over 50%

▨ 25–49.9%

▥ 10–24.9%

☐ Under 10%

NEW YORK CITY

Hudson River

BRONX

MANHATTAN

QUEENS

BROOKLYN

STATEN ISLAND

PHILADELPHIA

N. Phila.

W. Phila.

S. Phila.

Delaware River

MAP 1

Distribution of Black Population According to Census Tracts in Philadelphia, New York, Detroit, and Chicago, 1940

SOURCE: Adapted from E. Franklin Frazier, *The Negro in the United States* (New York: Macmillan, 1957), p. 255. Based on the *Sixteenth Census of the United States, 1940*, "Population and Housing."

Black Medical Professionals:
The Race's Elite

In this largely working-class, poverty-ridden, and racially separate black community, the black medical professionals in private practice or involved with the two black voluntary hospitals generally held positions of high esteem. The great prestige ascribed to black doctors, dentists, nurses, and pharmacists throughout the city's interwar black community is indicated by surveying the occupations of those Philadelphia blacks listed in *Who's Who in Colored America* (Table 14), which appeared every three years from 1925 through 1944 (and later reappeared in the 1950s).[5] In 1927, there were sixty-seven Philadelphians listed in *Who's Who in Colored America*, and in 1938, sixty-five. "Doctors" was the most frequent entry in both years. Physicians comprised 43 percent of these prominent black Philadelphians in 1927; eleven years later they constituted an even larger percentage—roughly 48 percent. Indeed, Carter Woodson in his 1934 study *The Negro Professional Man and the Community* deemed the black physician "the most important professional element in the negro race."[6]

The high prestige accorded black doctors in Philadelphia and elsewhere does not mean that they were invariably patronized by black community members. In Southern black communities there were often few black professionals available, and in many circumstances, in the North and South, blacks doubted the skills of their professional "race men" and insisted upon employing white doctors, lawyers, bankers, and so forth. Yet in cities such as Philadelphia, Chicago, and Baltimore, which experienced tremendous interwar growth in their urban black populations, traditional professional services were not readily accessible to poor blacks. Consequently, it was black medical, legal, and educational professionals who were more frequently called upon to serve the black community.[7]

While black doctors in Philadelphia, like those in similar cities, were influential and highly respected within their own community, they experienced chronic problems in comparison to the larger body of Philadelphia physicians. A quantitative analysis of their educational and professional attainments, based on biographical data in the AMA directories and *Who's Who in Colored America*,[8] reveals large discrepancies between black and white Philadelphia physicians in medical education, internships, hospital affiliations, membership in professional associations, and professional practice and specializations, as well

TABLE 14
Occupations of Prominent Black Philadelphians, 1927 and 1938

Occupations	1927	1938
Doctor	29	30
Clergyman	13	10
Lawyer	4	6
Dentist	5	3
Bank president/businessman	3	3
Teacher/principal	1	4
Editor	1	2
Funeral director	1	1
YMCA official	1	2
Manufacturer	0	2
Fraternal officer	2	0
Author	1	0
Musical composer	1	0
Druggist	1	1
Magistrate	1	1
College president/professor	2	0
Graduate nurse	1	0
Total	67	65

SOURCE: *Who's Who in Colored America: A Biographical Dictionary of Notable Living Persons of Negro Descent in America, 1925–1927*, ed. J.C. Boris (New York: Who's Who in Colored America, 1927), and *Who's Who in Colored America; A Biographical Dictionary of Notable Living Persons of African Descent in America, 1938–1940*, ed. Thomas Yenser (New York: Thomas Yenser, 1942).

as interesting sidelights on the group I call "eminent black physicians." (A description of the survey methodology can be found in Appendix A.)

The Educational Barrier

A key factor underlying the shortage of black physicians in Philadelphia was the limited availability of medical education. Since the latter half of the nineteenth century, particularly in the South, blacks had been restricted primarily to attending the nation's black medical schools.[9] This pattern also prevailed in Philadelphia (Table 15). In 1925, 1929, and 1938, 60 percent, 58 percent, and 64 percent of graduates came, respectively, from black medical schools. This agrees with the figures in Dr. Julian H. Lewis's national survey done in 1932, which concluded that over 69 percent of America's black physicians were black medical school graduates, and in Woodson's 1934 survey (of a limited sample), which placed this proportion at 60 percent. Dr. Numa P. G. Adams, whose survey was nationwide and exhaustive in scope, established a figure of 83.8 percent for 1936.[10]

The percentage of Philadelphia's black doctors who attended black medical schools, as opposed to white medical schools, was somewhat lower for the 1929 physician group. The same drop can be expressed another way by calculating the ratios of black to white medical school graduates. In 1925 this ratio was 1.49; in 1929, 1.33; and in 1938, 1.77. This development can be accounted for if we analyze these three groups of black physicians in terms of the years in which they graduated. Table 16 shows that the peak in the number of blacks graduating from white medical schools in all three physician groups occurred during 1911–1920. Of the 110 black physicians in Philadelphia between 1925 and 1938 who were white medical school products, most (43) had attended those white schools in the World War I decade (period III). The number of graduates of black medical schools was lowest for all three groups in 1925, when 43 had attended black medical colleges, most of whom graduated during period

TABLE 15

Number and Percentage of Black Philadelphia Physicians, by Predominant Racial Composition of Medical School Attended, 1925, 1929, and 1938

Type of School	1925		1929		1938	
	No.	%	No.	%	No.	%
White	29	40	42	42	39	36
Black	43	60	56	58	69	64
Total physicians	72		98		108	

SOURCE: *American Medical Directory: A Register of Legally Qualified Physicians of the United States* (Chicago: American Medical Association), vols. for 1925, 1929, and 1938.

TABLE 16
Type of Medical School Attended by Black Philadelphia Physicians, by Period of Graduation, 1925, 1929, and 1938

Type of Medical School	1882–1900 (I)	1901–1910 (II)	1911–1920 (III)	1921–1930 (IV)	1931–1937 (V)	Total
Black						
1925	7	19	11	6	—	43
1929	6	19	12	19	—	56
1938	7	12	11	21	18	69
Total	20	50	34	46	18	168
White						
1925	4	8	13	4	—	29
1929	5	9	14	14	—	42
1938	2	8	16	9	4	39
Total	11	25	43	27	4	100

SOURCE: *American Medical Dictionary: A Register of Legally Qualified Physicians of the United States* (Chicago: American Medical Association), vols. for 1925, 1929, and 1938; *Who's Who in Colored America: A Biographical Dictionary of Notable Living Persons of African Descent in America*, ed. Thomas Yenser (New York: Thomas Yenser, 1942), vol. for 1938–1940.

II. In 1929, of 56 graduates of black schools, most graduated during periods III and IV, and in 1938, of 69 graduates, most graduated during periods IV and V. Of all 168 black physicians in Philadelphia from 1925 to 1938 who were black medical school graduates, a majority (96) completed study in periods II and IV, far fewer in period III.

The relative rise in the number of those black Philadelphia physicians who had attended white medical schools during 1911–1920, and the concomitant low number of black medical school graduates during this same period has a two-sided explanation. One, as we saw in Chapter I, was the comparative liberalization of admissions policies toward blacks among predominantly white medical schools during the World War I period. Although this usually meant that these schools admitted only one or two black students per entering class, it was a gain over strict segregation.

But the primary reason for the dip in the number of black medical school graduates during 1911–1920 was the closing of black medical schools. As Table 17 shows, nearly one in five of Philadelphia's black doctors during 1925 who had attended black medical schools had gone to Leonard Medical College or the University of West Tennessee Medical Department.[11] By 1938, only one in ten black medical school graduates was an alumnus of Leonard or West Tennessee. Located in Raleigh, North Carolina, Leonard was the nation's third oldest black medical school. It was founded in 1882, but closed in 1915 during the aftershock of the Flexner Report on Higher Education. Likewise, all-black West Tennessee, located in Memphis, did not recover from severe limitations in operating resources and the Flexner policies for re-standardization of medical education. It ceased operating in 1923.[12]

By 1938 two larger trends are evident that bespeak a deepening segregation in medical education and an overall decline in the number of the city's black physicians. First, the number of black physicians contributed to Philadelphia by the city's medical schools between 1929 and 1938 was declining. Medico-Chirurgical College had closed in 1918. The University of Pennsylvania, Jefferson, Hahnemann, and Woman's Medical College all had fewer black alumni practicing in the city during 1938 than in 1929 (Table 17).[13] Second, the supply of black physicians in Philadelphia was becoming increasingly, indeed overwhelmingly, dependent on the two surviving black medical schools—Howard and Meharry. In 1929 nearly 49 percent of the black medical practitioners in Philadelphia were graduates of these schools, and in 1938 over 57 percent (Table 17).

TABLE 17
Medical Schools Attended by Black Philadelphia Physicians,
1925, 1929, and 1938

Medical School	1925		1929		1938	
	No.	%	No.	%	No.	%
Black						
Howard	32	44.4	41	41.8	55	50.1
Meharry	3	4.2	7	7.1	8	7.4
Leonard	7	9.7	7	7.1	5	4.6
W. Tenn. M.C.	1	1.4	1	1.0	1	0.9
Pred. White (Phila.)						
Univ. of Pa.	10	13.9	11	11.2	10	9.2
Temple	9	12.5	13	13.2	15	13.8
Jefferson	3	4.2	3	3.0	2	1.9
Medico-Chirurg.	3	4.2	3	3.0	5	4.6
Hahnemann	1	1.4	2	2.0	1	0.9
Woman's M.C.	1	1.4	4	4.0	0	0
Pred. White (Other)						
Col. Phys. & Surgs. (Mass.)	1	1.4	1	1.0	1	0.9
American M.C. (Mich.)	1	1.4	1	1.0	1	0.9
Univ. of Mich.	0	0	2	2.0	0	0
Univ. of Toronto (Canada)	0	0	1	1.0	1	0.9
Queens Univ. (Canada)	0	0	1	1.0	0	0
Univ. of Ill.	0	0	0	0	1	0.9
Harvard	0	0	0	0	1	0.9
Col. Phys. & Surgs. (N.C.)	0	0	0	0	1	0.9
Total	72	100.1	98	99.4	108	98.8

SOURCE: *American Medical Directory: A Register of Legally Qualified Physicians of the United States* (Chicago: American Medical Association), vols. for 1925, 1929, and 1938. Percentages do not total 100 due to rounding.

The decline in black student enrollment in Philadelphia's medical schools during the 1920s and 1930s was part of a nationwide trend. During the nine years between 1927–1928 and 1935–1936 the number of black medical students in the United States dropped from 497 to 371.[14] This decrease occurred despite the fact that American medical schools were enrolling increasing numbers of students.[15] The outright institutional segregation practiced in Southern medical schools barring blacks from admission and the de facto segregation that predominated in most northern medical schools no doubt had minimized black enrollment.[16] Yet these practices were only the most obvious barriers. There were other more pervasive socio-economic and educational factors that compounded discrimination at the admissions stage to constrict opportunities for blacks even further.

One cause was the economic barrier to medical education. Most black youths during the interwar decades were from poor families. The vast majority of their parents were unskilled laborers, sharecroppers, or domestic servants who were unable to assist their children with the cost of medical studies.[17] According to Dr. Numa P. G. Adams, dean of Howard Medical School, the chief "supplier" of black medical school graduates from Philadelphia, and a prominent advocate of racial equality in the medical field, writing in 1937, each year forty to fifty of the students admitted to Howard, and an equal number at Meharry, were unable to attend because of financial problems. Even those blacks who managed to undertake medical studies had to wrestle with financial constraints. Most did part-time work to help finance their studies. As a result, according to Adams, the average black medical student "does not have sufficient time for study, for necessary collateral reading in the medical library, for reflection and recreation."[18]

In addition to financial disadvantages, a second socio-economic factor hindered black youths from attending medical school. This was the prevalence of second-rate segregated public education for blacks. The graduates of urban ghetto or rural public school systems for blacks during the interwar period usually received less than adequate scholastic preparation for strenuous pre-medical and medical studies.[19]

A third factor was the constant rise in the standards of medical school programs and medical practice. This development accelerated especially in the late 1920s and 1930s, at the same time that the number of medical schools was being reduced. The result was often to intensify the first two problems: students needed higher and higher levels of academic preparation, and they also needed more funds, since it usually required from seven to ten years' training (beyond high school) before a doctor could even start to practice.[20]

It is not surprising that it took substantially more time for a black person to obtain a medical degree than it did for a white (Table 18). Whites were significantly younger than blacks when they graduated from medical school. In the 1925 and 1929 survey groups, over 15 percent of the white physicians but less than 6 percent of the black physicians were medical school graduates by the age of 23. Within the 1938 group, 18.2 percent of the whites and only 5.6 percent of the blacks had completed medical school at either 22 or 23 years of age. Overall, whites tended to graduate in their early twenties, while blacks generally graduated in their mid-twenties or thirties.

The fact that black physicians in Philadelphia through 1938 were generally older than the city's white physicians was, therefore, the result of a constellation of barriers. These included serious social and educational handicaps prior to the medical training period, and then the difficulties of locating medical schools in the nation that would admit them. The limited black enrollment at Philadelphia medical schools was, in particular, of grave consequence to the city's health services as a whole. This becomes evident when one examines more closely the relationship between the location of medical education and characteristics of the city's physician workforce.

As Table 19 indicates, the overwhelming majority of the city's white physicians were graduates of Philadelphia medical schools. In 1925, 444, or 88.8 percent of the 500 hundred white physicians in the sample, were graduates of city medical institutions. Four years later 457, or 91.4 percent of the 500 white physicians sampled, had been educated in Philadelphia. The 1938 group showed little change from the patterns of the twenties. That year 510, or 85 percent of 600 white physicians sampled, were products of Philadelphia medical institutions. The regularity of this pattern for the three samples clearly indicates that, by the beginning of World War II, nearly nine of every ten white physicians in the city had been educated at Philadelphia medical schools.

By contrast, we saw in Table 17, most of the city's black doctors had to attend medical schools outside Philadelphia and, in fact, outside the state of Pennsylvania. In 1925, 62.5 percent of the black physicians in Philadelphia had been educated outside the state; in 1929, 63 percent; and in 1938, 68.4 percent. Thus, while Philadelphia medical schools were the

TABLE 18
Philadelphia Physicians, by Age of Graduation from Medical School, 1925, 1929, and 1938

| | 1925 | | | | 1929 | | | | 1938 | | | |
| | White | | Black | | White | | Black | | White | | Black | |
Age	No.	%	No.	%	No.	%	No.	%	No.	%	No.	%
20	5	1.0	0	0	7	1.5	1	1.0	3	0.5	0	0
21	28	5.8	2	2.7	19	4.1	3	3.1	24	4.2	2	1.9
22	51	10.6	1	1.4	47	10.1	1	1.0	50	8.5	2	1.9
23	56	11.7	4	5.6	64	13.8	5	5.2	57	9.7	4	3.7
24	80	16.7	6	8.3	80	7.2	6	6.2	68	11.6	4	3.7
25	64	13.3	7	9.7	73	15.7	9	9.3	101	17.2	11	10.2
26	50	10.4	9	12.5	60	12.9	13	13.4	103	17.5	14	13.9
27	31	6.5	6	8.3	42	9.0	12	12.4	54	9.2	19	18.5
28	19	4.0	8	11.1	25	5.4	11	11.3	36	6.1	14	13.9
29	15	3.1	8	11.1	14	3.0	7	7.2	22	3.8	11	10.2
30	15	3.1	7	9.7	22	4.7	9	9.3	14	2.4	7	6.5
31	9	1.9	0	0	10	2.2	0	0	10	1.7	1	0.9
32	8	1.7	2	2.7	12	2.6	3	3.1	10	1.7	2	1.9
33	11	2.3	5	7.0	7	1.5	5	5.2	12	2.0	5	4.6
34	8	1.7	3	4.2	7	1.5	3	3.1	8	1.4	2	1.9
35	8	1.7	1	1.4	8	1.7	4	4.1	4	0.7	2	1.9

TABLE 18, *continued*

| | 1925 | | | | 1929 | | | | 1938 | | | |
| | White | | Black | | White | | Black | | White | | Black | |
Age	No.	%	No.	%	No.	%	No.	%	No.	%	No.	%
36	2	0.4	1	1.4	1	0.2	1	1.0	4	0.7	1	0.9
37	3	0.6	0	0	3	0.6	2	2.1	5	0.9	2	1.9
38	2	0.4	0	0	2	0.4	0	0	1	0.2	0	0
39	5	1.0	0	0	3	0.6	0	0	0	0	0	0
40	2	0.4	0	0	3	0.6	0	0	1	0.2	0	0
41	2	0.4	0	0	1	0.2	0	0	1	0.2	0	0
42	1	0.2	0	0	0	0	0	0	0	0	0	0
43	1	0.2	1	1.4	1	0.2	1	1.0	2	0.3	2	1.9
44	0	0	0	0	0	0	0	0	0	0	0	0
45	2	0.4	1	1.4	0	0	0	0	0	0	0	0
46+	2	0.4	0	0	1	0.2	0	0	0	0	0	0
Total	480	99.9	72	99.9	465	109.9	96	99.0	587	100.7	108	100.3

SOURCE: *American Medical Directory: A Register of Legally Qualified Physicians of the United States* (Chicago: American Medical Association), vols. for 1925, 1929, and 1938. Some physicians' ages are not given. Percentages do not total 100 due to rounding.

TABLE 19
Medical Schools Attended by White Philadelphia Physicians,
1925, 1929, and 1938

Medical School	1925		1929		1938	
	No.	%	No.	%	No.	%
Philadelphia						
Univ. of Pa.	153	30.6	157	31.4	169	27.1
Jefferson	120	24.0	119	23.8	127	21.2
Hahnemann	56	11.2	52	10.4	73	12.2
Woman's M.C.	26	5.2	24	4.8	27	4.7
Temple	21	4.2	40	8.0	74	12.3
Medico-Churg.	68	13.6	65	13.0	47	7.8
Total Phila.	444	88.8	457	91.4	510	85.0
Out-of-state	49	9.8	36	7.2	77	12.8
Foreign	7	1.4	7	1.4	13	2.2

SOURCE: *American Medical Directory: A Register of Legally Qualified Physicians of the United States* (Chicago: American Medical Association), vols. for 1925, 1929, and 1938.

backbone of the city's white physicians stratum, black physicians in about two of every three cases were "migrant professionals."

Lewis's 1935 survey on the number and geographic distribution of the nation's black physicians demonstrates that by the mid-1930s there was a strong connection between the availability of medical education for blacks in certain locales and the number of black physicians found practicing in those locales. Lewis found that Washington, D.C., had almost twice as many black physicians (271) as did New York (151), although the latter city had a black population three times larger than the former. He attributed this discrepancy to the location of Howard Medical School in Washington. Likewise, the city of Nashville, Tennessee, home of Meharry Medical College, had 77 black physicians among a black population of about 40,000 while New Orleans, with a population of approximately 130,000 blacks, reported just 50 black physicians.[21]

On the whole, the failure of the medical schools in Philadelphia and Pittsburgh to educate any substantial number of blacks during the late 1920s and 1930s had broad negative effects.[22] Such de facto segregation in Pennsylvania contributed to making it the worst state in the North in terms of the ratio of black physicians to black population. In Lewis's survey of the northern states that had black populations of 30,000 or more according to the 1930 census, Pennsylvania's ratio of 2,552 black residents to every one black doctor placed it last, behind Illinois (991), California (1,081), Massachusetts (1,114), Indiana (1,417), Michigan (1,448), New Jersey (1,498), Kansas (1,896), and New York (2,281). In fact, according to Lewis's estimates, four southern states and the District of Columbia had better black population/black physician ratios than Pennsylvania. As for the absolute number of black physicians, Pennsylvania's total (169) was lower than that of five southern states, as well as that of the District of Columbia.[23]

Those black doctors who practiced in Philadelphia just before World War II were not able to assimilate into the larger professional community. They found employment in the city's segregated public health system or opened offices in the black community as general practitioners, dependent on their own resources and usually associated with black hospitals. Their isolation from the larger medical community is demonstrated by the difference in patterns in internships and hospital affiliation, association membership, and the types of practice and specialties between Philadelphia's black and white physicians.

Internships and Hospital Affiliation

The first hurdle that medical school graduates had to clear in building a successful career was the internship. Once voluntary, by the early 1930s the internship was mandatory in Pennsylvania for medical licensure.[24] Moreover, not only was the internship a requirement for professional certification, but it along with residencies were extremely important as springboards into professional association upon which other local academic and employment opportunities could be built. On the basis of internship or residency performance, a new physician could earn consideration for other positions not only at the hospital where he or she was working but throughout the larger web of hospitals in the city.

Prior to World War II, on the other hand, internships for black physicians in Philadelphia's predominantly white hospitals were out of the question. Among the black doctors listed in the AMA's 1925, 1929, and

1938 directories who were interning, two were at Mercy in 1925, four were at Mercy and five at Douglass in 1929, and five were at Mercy in 1938.[25] None were interning at white hospitals.

Interns formed a significant and increasing supply of the city's white physicians through 1938. In 1925, 24, or 4.8 percent of the 500 white physicians sampled, were interns in the city's hospital establishment. On this basis, we can estimate that there were about 165 white interns in Philadelphia medicine that year (i.e., 4.8 percent of all of the city's 3,430 white physicians). Four years later the number stood at 43, or 8.6 percent of 500, with 319 white interns estimated citywide (8.6 percent of 3,714). In 1938, of 600 white physicians there were 52 interns, or 8.6 percent, with an approximate total of 350 white interns (8.6 percent of 4,112) in the city that year. And while the number of internships for white doctors was growing in Philadelphia, the number available for blacks was declining and so was the overall proportion of black interns within the city's black medical community. Only 2.7 percent of the city's 72 black doctors held internships in 1925, 7.1 percent in 1929, and 4.6 percent in 1938, all at Mercy and Douglass hospitals.

After they had completed their internships, it was of utmost value to physicians to establish an association with a hospital. Through hospital affiliations doctors continued their medical education, found colleagues for clinical consultation, and had access to costly equipment and medical team services.[26] Aside from opportunities at black hospitals, however, staff positions and medical school professorships, like internships, were off-limits for black physicians in Philadelphia. Among all the black physicians listed in the *Medical Directory* for 1925, 1929, and 1938, only one is listed as having an institutional affiliation. He was Dr. Earl F. Hawkins, who was entered as an affiliate of the Philadelphia Hospital for Mental Disease in 1938.

By contrast, the larger white physician community of the city shows an ever-increasing level of affiliation with hospitals and medical schools. The number of white residents in Philadelphia hospitals was about the same between 1925 and 1938; there were 12 for the 1925 sample group (of 500) and 15 for the larger 1938 sample group (of 600). The proportion of medical professors increased, from 9.2 percent (46) in 1925 to 10.5 percent (63) in 1938. The percentage of white physicians who were hospital staff members also was growing, from 2.6 percent (13) in 1925 to 3.3 percent (20) in 1938. Lastly, the number of white doctors in Philadelphia associated with military medical institutions such as the United States Naval Hospital and the United States Veterans Bureau was on the rise from 7 in 1925 to 12 in 1938.

To be sure, much of the information that would tell us about the actual affiliations of Philadelphia black physicians was omitted by the *Medical Directory*. As we have already observed, many black doctors were employed at public and neighborhood health clinics throughout the city during the interwar decades. These doctors would have been considered part-time staff and thus would have been excluded from the *Medical Directory*, which lists only medical administrators and staff members of these clinics, who would have been white. But many of the city's black doctors had full-time connections with Mercy and Douglass hospitals. While Douglass held only conditional accreditation during the 1930s, Mercy was a fully accredited institution. Yet the *Medical Directory* makes no reference to the dozens of affiliations Philadelphia black physicians had with Mercy as governing board members, administrators, or full-time medical (or "house") staff members. Indeed, neither Mercy nor Douglass was recognized as a full-fledged entity, according to this AMA compilation. This omission was congruent with the prevailing attitude among much of the American public as well as in the medical community that "real" medicine was found only at predominantly white hospitals and medical schools.[27]

Another reflection of the tendency of black physicians to be separated from the medical status quo and to form their own self-help groupings is found in patterns of association membership. An example is the Philadelphia County Medical Society (PCMS). The PCMS, membership in which was open to all licensed physicians, served as the city's affiliate of the American Medical Association. It provided such services as medical forums, achievement awards, publications, and lobbying campaigns for its members. In the 1925 white physicians groups, 304, or 60.8 percent, were members of the PCMS. The 1929 group had 287 members in the Society, or 57.4 percent. A larger percentage of the 1938 white physicians group, 57.6 percent (346), were members.

By contrast, black physicians in the city had much lower PCMS membership rates. In 1925, 15 of Philadelphia's 72 black doctors, or 20.8 percent were PCMS members. That is, in 1925 blacks made up less than one percent of the estimated 1,900 members of the Society.[28] In 1929, 25 of the 98 black physicians, or 25.5 percent, were members, and in 1938, of 108 black physicians, 39, or 36.1 percent, were members. Thus, between

1925 and 1938, while approximately 60 percent of white physicians were PCMS members, black physicians' membership in the Society grew from 21 to 36 percent.

Although membership in northern county and state medical societies like the PCMS was open to all without regard to race, blacks apparently joined largely as a matter of formality. Asked about the experience of black members in the PCMS around 1935, one black physician remarked some years later, "Oh yea, you could get in all right. There was nothing to keep you from getting in, but because we had our own society here and because you didn't feel you would be very welcome in the Philadelphia County, there was a tendency to stay in your own society and not bother with the County."[29] Furthermore, the miniscule black membership had no influence in associations like the PCMS on matters like the selection of speakers, planning of conferences, and general policies.[30]

Since Philadelphia's black GPs confronted strong barriers when attempting affiliation with the predominantly white hospitals, and lacked clout in the predominantly white professional associations, it is not surprising that, particularly in North Philadelphia, they repeatedly "turned inward" and expanded their own array of voluntary associations and group practices.[31] In October 1936, black GPs in North Philadelphia formed a special branch of the all-black Philadelphia Academy of Medicine and Allied Sciences. This organization was called the North Philadelphia Medical, Dental, and Pharmaceutical Council. Founded by Dr. Arthur H. Thomas, a young Howard University medical graduate and former Mercy intern, and Dr. Wilbur H. Strickland, also a Howard Medical School product, its primary concern was "the matter of adequate hospitalization for our people." Given the fragmented, trifold character of Philadelphia's black inner-city community (Map 1), and the limited distribution of health facilities available for black physicians, the emergence of this North Philadelphia organization is understandable. Black physicians of South Philadelphia had access to Douglass Hospital for in-patient care for their referrals. West Philadelphia black physicians could rely on Mercy Hospital, and also Philadelphia General, where by 1936 about half the patients were black (separately treated).[32] But black physicians practicing in North Philadelphia had no such resources. They had to collaborate on locating speciality and in-patient services for their patients. By 1939, the North Philadelphia Medical Council had about thirty-five members, who cooperated to try to provide medical services that were not readily available to black North Philadelphians at the predominantly white hospitals in that area.[33]

Besides these local branches of national groups, Philadelphia's black physicians comprised the heaviest concentration of members in the all-black Pennsylvania State Medical, Dental, and Pharmaceutical Association (PSMDPA). A list of this organization's membership for metropolitan Philadelphia contained fifty-one physicians, forty-eight dentists, and six pharmacists.[34]

Specialized Medicine

The limited opportunities for black physicians in Philadelphia to expand and diversify their professional knowledge and practice is most evident in the area of specialized medicine. Specialization represented the highest level of technical training and authority within the medical profession. The emergence of specialization was concomitant with the expansion of biomedical science and clinical investigations throughout the international medical profession. During the 1920s leading American physicians and medical scientists formed societies and academies, or "colleges," for the purpose of advancing particular branches of medical practice. This led to organized graduate education in various specialty areas under AMA regulation. By 1933 certifying boards of the AMA had been created for such specialties as otolaryngology, obstetrics and gynecology, dermatology, and pediatrics.[35]

On the whole, Philadelphia physicians, like those nationwide, were becoming increasingly specialized in their fields of practice throughout the 1930s. The training of the average general practitioner in the 1920s and 1930s became outdated, and the GP was supplanted by the new specialist-physician schooled in the latest medical diagnostic and thereapeutical techniques. Between 1923 and 1940 the number of specialists rose nationwide from 15,408 to 36,880 in the sixteen major specialties.[36]. Philadelphia's white physicians were among the pacesetters of this trend, unlike the city's black physicians, who made little professional growth in the areas of specialized medicine.

A physician was considered a specialist by the AMA if he or she held membership in a recognized state specialty association of the AMA, held membership in a national or interstate specialty society endorsed by the

AMA, or was a professor or assistant professor of a specialty at an accredited medical school. Based on these standards, over 36 percent of Philadelphia's white physicians in 1925 were specialists.[37] This proportion dropped to slightly above 34 percent in 1929 before rising to 41 percent in 1938. These levels all appear to have been above the national average and attest to the superior concentration of advanced medical educational centers in Philadelphia.[38]

Of the black doctors in Philadelphia during 1925, only 8 percent (6) practiced a specialty. In 1929 this figure was about 14 percent (15), while in 1938 it was just over 18 percent (20). Most of these black specialists practiced on a part-time basis. In fact, there was no fully certified black specialist in Philadelphia in 1925, and only two in 1929—Dr. W. Harry Barnes, a 1927 diplomate of the American Board of Otolaryngology and evidently the nation's first black board-certified specialist, and Dr. Egbert T. Scott, who was certified in surgery. In 1938 there were only two additional black certified specialists. These were Drs. Frank E. Boston and Frederick D. Stubbs, both diplomates in surgery. Since it was estimated that there were fewer than twenty-five black certified specialists throughout the entire country, Philadelphia was unusual for having even this small group, all of whom were leaders in the city's black hospitals or clinics.[39]

Such a small number of full-time and part-time black physician-specialists is a gauge of the very few opportunities available to blacks for postgraduate medical study or membership in specialty societies prior to World War II. Those blacks seeking postgraduate training during the late 1920s and 1930s sometimes were able to do so under special arrangements, during the summer months and on the premise that they would be returning to the black hospital or medical school. Up to 1930, in fact, most black doctors desiring preparation in a specialty had to go to Europe for training. Thus, by 1938 any type of postgraduate instruction that black doctors obtained at such institutions as the universities of Pennsylvania or Chicago was considered an advance.[40]

The leading specialties for the city's white physicians were ophthalmology and otorhinolaryngology (Table 20). Besides surgery and obstetrics/gynecology, internal medicine was one of the most frequent areas of specialization for white physicians, ranking third in 1938. Among Philadelphia's few black specialists, most were certified in surgery or obstetrics/gynecology. None were in opthalmology or otorhinolaryngology in 1925 and 1929, and only two in 1938. Nor were any black specialists found in

TABLE 20
Black and White Philadelphia Physicians, by Specialization,
1925, 1929, and 1938

Specialization	1925		1929		1938	
	White	Black	White	Black	White	Black
Ophthalmology/ otorhinolaryngolofy	52	0	40	0	50	2
Internal Medicine	20	0	17	0	37	0
Surgery	28	2	37	4	38	6
Obstetrics/gynecology	25	2	24	4	26	5
Psychiatry/neurology	6	0	8	3	22	1
Pediatrics	18	0	9	2	21	2
Urology	9	0	9	0	7	0
Orthopedic surgery	2	0	2	0	5	0
Pathology/bacteriology	4	0	4	0	4	0
Dermatology/syphilology	5	0	3	0	6	0
Anesthesiology	1	0	0	0	2	0
Radiology/roentgenology	6	2	5	0	8	1
Other	6	0	13	2	20	3
Total	182	6	171	15	246	20

SOURCE: *American Medical Directory: A Register of Legally Qualified Physicians of the United States* (Chicago: American Medical Association), vols. for 1925, 1929, and 1938.

the fields of urology, orthopedics, radiology/roentgenology, pathology/bacteriology, dermatology, or anesthesiology.

The specialties of surgery and obstetrics/gynecology in which Philadelphia black doctors were most frequently found had the least degree of professional regulation in the 1920s and 1930s. They also usually required fewer financial and educational resources to learn and apply. Those specialties that necessitated extensive laboratory facilities and highly trained research assistants for study and application such as internal medicine, otorhinolaryngology, and urology were simply impracticable fields for black physicians to pursue, given the prevailing intellectual discrimination and financial barriers. By the 1930s the professional identities of the laboratory-oriented specialties were older and rigidly defined, and, consequently, that

105

much more exclusive. As Rosemary Stevens has stated: "Just as there were moves to stem the supply of physicians by upgrading standards and limiting the number of students in the medical schools, so the creation of standards for specialties [was] expected to limit their number."[41]

Furthermore, whereas fields like ophthalmology and otolaryngology had the oldest specialty boards in medicine, surgery and obstetrics/gynecology were often practiced by general physicians without regulation. Almost one-third of all major surgical work done by general practitioners in 1934 was for gynecological ailments. Indeed, the movement toward establishing a specialty examining board in obstetrics and gynecology was aimed at eliminating the untrained GP surgeon.[42]

Thus, by pursuing surgery and obstetrics/gynecology, Philadelphia's black physicians in 1938 had generally followed the lines of least resistance. For one thing, these two specialties were the most accessible, given the seriously limited opportunities for blacks in postgraduate medical education. Moreover, black physicians concentrated on the more primary, care-oriented specialties as opposed to the secondary care "sub-specialties." Whether they treated their patients in the home, in the office, or at the city's black medical facilities, the generally lower health status of black Philadelphians required black physicians to be prepared to treat a large variety of severe disease symptoms and injuries. Besides, the low economic status of most blacks in Philadelphia meant that demand for expensive specialty services was simply not large enough to support a black physician who decided to train in such fields, regardless of any racial barriers.

With so few black specialist physicians in the city, Douglass and Mercy hospitals had to establish alternative means for giving their physicians exposure to the new specialized medical advances. Mercy annually organized "clinical lectures" for its staff given by prominent specialists from Philadelphia's predominantly white medical schools, hospitals, and clinics. At first, these lectures occurred only intermittently, but by 1933 Mercy had found that it would have to launch an extensive lecture program if its staff were to keep abreast of the rapid developments within the specialties.[43] The hospital's clinical lecture program for 1934 covered all the major specialties as well as public health and dentistry (Appendix B).

The attending staff at Mercy also benefited from instruction given by the institution's "consulting staff." Like the lecturers, this group was composed of high-minded white physicians who were specialists at predominantly white medical schools and hospitals in the city. In 1934, for instance, Mercy had a total of thirteen consulting staff members in the fields of medicine, surgery, gynecology/obstetrics, pediatrics, otorhinolaryngology, neurology, orthopedics, and ophthalmology.[44] Indeed, black general practitioners throughout the city found it imperative to develop some type of reliable contact with such consultants. Segregated in-patient policies often made it difficult for black GPs to have their seriously ill patients admitted to the hospital for long-term or specialized treatment. If immediate full admission was possible, the physician (lacking official admitting privileges) lost the patient's patronage altogether if he or she did not have any influence at the admitting hospital. Through contact with such conscientious persons as those serving on Mercy's consulting staff, however, admission for specialized therapy for black patients could sometimes be arranged and the black GP could remain involved in the case.[45]

Individual black GPs in Philadelphia also developed unique means for learning specialties in spite of institutional discrimination. In 1936, Dr. Arthur H. Thomas, then president of the city's all-black Academy of Medical and Allied Sciences, and Dr. Earl F. Hawkins organized the Hinton Reading Club, named after William A. Hinton, the black physician in Boston who created the Hinton Test for syphilis diagnosis. The Hinton Club had about one dozen members and, according to Thomas, had as its objective "the creation of accredited, recognized specialists in every field of medicine represented among its membership." Each member was given ten years in which to become a certified specialist in his or her particular field. On the basis of these common goals and group support some of the members managed to locate and successfully complete certain postgraduate courses. By 1939, Dr. Russell F. Minton had completed three graduate courses in radiology at the University of Chicago. Another, Dr. Farmer, had completed a six-week course of graduate work in general medicine at Harvard.[46]

The Elite Black Physician

We can supplement our statistical portrait of Philadelphia's black physicians before World War II with a social and professional profile of the city's eminent black physicians. Many of these physicians were first-generation southern migrants. Of the twenty-four for whom birthplaces are given in the 1938 *Whos'Who*, twelve were born in the South, six were native Philadelphians, three were from other northern parts, and three were foreign-born. The twelve doctors born in the South came from Virginia, North and South Carolina, Kentucky, Mississippi, and Georgia. So, like many black Philadelphians, their residence in the city was probably a result of their own or families' attempt to find opportunity in the urban North.

By far the most distinctive feature of Philadelphia's eminent black doctors was their immersion in the black medical and lay community. They lived in homes located in black neighborhoods, and most had their offices in a front room or on the first floor. Twenty-five of the twenty-nine Philadelphians listed in 1927 were associated with Mercy or Douglass hospitals, or with the black public health clinics. Although by 1938 only ten, or a third of the total, had similar affiliations, the drop does not mean that Philadelphia's eminent black physicians were largely falling away from black community orientation. In fact, between 1927 and 1938 their membership in black associations increased. Among the 1927 group, thirteen belonged to the NMA, seven to the Academy of Medicine, and four to the Clinico-Pathological Society. As for the 1938 group, there were twenty-one memberships in the NMA and seven each in the Academy and the Clinico-Pathological Society.

Outside of their professional organizations, black doctors were active in local fraternal and social organizations. The Pyramid Club, for example, was a black social club to which many eminent black physicians belonged. Founded by a black physician, Dr. Walter F. Jerrick, the club was a center where black doctors mingled with blacks from businesses. These doctors were prized because of their financial power and social influence in the black community. Douglass S. Dore, perhaps the city's most prominent black salesman during the 1930s, sold them refrigerators; others sold them suits and other products. Each popular doctor was estimated to have as many as four hundred patients to whom he could make purchasing recommendations. Because black businessmen through the 1930s were restricted from serving whites, either in customers' homes or by soliciting them to come to their business offices, the friendship and trust of these black doctors was of inestimable value to them.[47]

Just as black entrepreneurs relied on eminent black doctors to enhance their business affairs, the doctors depended on black fraternal orders not only to enhance racial self-sufficiency and social life but to build practical contacts among new, ongoing, or former patients. The growing importance of membership in fraternal organizations is indicated by a comparison of specific memberships for 1927 and 1938. There were two memberships in the Elks in 1927 and eighteen in 1938; ten in the Masons in 1927 and sixteen in 1938; two in the Knights of Pythias in 1927 and eight in 1938; eleven in the Alpha Phi Alpha fraternity in 1927 and sixteen in 1938; and three in Alpha Kappa Psi in 1927 and four in 1938. Only two organizations lost members: the Sigma Pi Psi fraternity went from four in 1927 to two in 1938, and the Odd Fellows went from five in 1927 to four in 1938. All these black fraternal orders had long histories and a strong influence in black social life.[48] Moreover, several of the black physicians among those listed served as officers in the organizations. Others functioned as the medical examiners for their lodges.

Woodson's national study of black professionals is most instructive on the matter of the black physician's ties to black fraternal orders. He too discovered a strong connection between the two groups. Seventy-five percent of the physicians he investigated in 1934 held membership in a fraternal order, 71 percent of whom acted as officers. Woodson found that fraternal organizations served both as a social outlet and as an economic connection for the black physicians with the black lay public. Black doctors in the South had the most involvement with black fraternal groups, according to his study. Thus, Woodson concluded that the more stringent the social and economic racism in a particular city or region, the more black professionals and businesspeople needed to rely on black social groups.[49]

The last observation suggests that Philadelphia race relations were not as far removed from the southern experience as we might at first presume. Consequently, Philadelphia's eminent black physicians demonstrate an ability to show their race that they could achieve in the so-called "white world." Compared to the average black physician in the city, those selected as eminent evidenced a higher rate of attending white medical schools, as well as membership in predominantly white medical associations. In 1927 fifteen were graduates of predominantly white medical schools. In 1938 eighteen had attended white medical schools, while thirteen had gone to black medical schools. Thus while the bulk of Philadelphia's black physicians were increasingly black medical school products, the eminent ones were among the decreasing number of blacks attending predominantly white schools.

Although the eminent black physicians had higher rates of membership

109

in black medical associations when compared to the average black physician in the city, several of them were also members of the County of Philadelphia Medical Society and the AMA. There were fifteen members of the former organization both in 1927 and 1938. This means that roughly one in two of the eminent black physicians were members of the Society, a rate that equaled the average rate of membership for the city's white physicians and was higher than the average black membership, which we have seen was about one in three. Moreover, the AMA membership of the two eminent black physician groups increased from nine to fourteen over the eleven-year timespan.

Dentists, Nurses, and Pharmacists

Like black doctors immediately preceding World War II, black dentists in Philadelphia had declined in professional status with respect to their white peers. Furthermore, the number of black dentists coming into the city had decreased. According to census returns, Philadelphia had 47 black dentists in 1920 and 101 in 1930. But the dental professions was one of the occupations hardest hit by the financial crisis touched off in 1929.[50] The Depression put many of the city's black and white dentists out of business.

When WPA researchers interviewed black dentists throughout the city in 1939 regarding their progress and problems in the field, they found that between 1929 and 1939 there had been a noticeable decrease in the number of black dentists practicing in Philadelphia. "Some have left to practice elsewhere," the researchers wrote; "some have changed to another line of endeavor." The researchers tied the decrease to a lowering in the demand for dental services that had occurred despite the fact that during this same period the city's black population had grown tremendously. They concluded that "economic adversity, the expense of dental education, and the subsequent outlay for equipping an office have been motivating factors" in the decline of the profession. Another cause was the competitive success of white dentists. Many white dentists benefited from the negative reputation of certain black dentists in the city. Still others, according to WPA research, used unscrupulous advertising to attract black patronage.[51]

The 1940 census does not give statistics on specific professional occupations by race, but only on professionals in general. Therefore, the exact rate at which black dentists left Philadelphia or went out of business during the Depression period cannot be calculated. Judging by national trends, however, which also reflect the traumatic impact the financial crisis had on black American dentists, the attrition was considerable. The dental school of Howard University had graduated the largest number of Philadelphia black dentists by the late 1920s and 1930s, but in 1937 Dr. Russell A. Dixon, dean of the dental school, predicted that at best the number of black dentists for 1940 would only equal the 1930 level.[52]

The Depression had the twin effects of bankrupting many black and white dentists and of creating insurmountable economic barriers to low-income black and white students who wanted to go to dental school. Moreover, as Dixon noted, the rapid rise in educational standards also tended to limit the number of blacks gaining access to the profession. Beginning in the World War I decade, requirements for entrance into dental school and practice had stiffened from a high school diploma and two full academic years of dental school to a diploma and three years of dental school, which was later raised to four years. Still later, this was changed to one year of college for entrance, and, in 1937, to two full years of college for entrance and four years of dental school.[53]

As was the case with black medical students, the number of black dental students nationwide also dropped sharply during the 1930s. Black students enrolled in all dental schools fell from 213 in the 1928–1929 academic year to 61 in 1938–1939, a drop of about 75 percent. This decline was far greater than the decline in white dental students, whose numbers fell from 7,987 to 7,347 during the same timespan.[54]

The extension of more licensing requirements as well as the growth in dental research and technical innovations made segregation in the various aspects of the dental profession that much more crippling for Philadelphia's black dentists. Except for an occasional student at the city's dental schools, black dentists had no affiliation as teachers, administrators, or researchers.[55] Most of the city's black dentists were produced by Howard and Meharry dental schools. Dean Dixon's description of the situation facing blacks in the dental profession during the 1930s is applicable to the situation in Philadelphia: "Each extension of formal requirements has acted not only as an agent to retard the flow of new blood into the field, but it has served also as an inhibitory factor, limiting the number [available] who could cope with the [black public's] new demands."[56]

Like Philadelphia's black doctors, however, the black dentists relied upon associations and clinics formed within their own circles to remain abreast of new currents in dentistry, gain first-hand clinical experience, and devise ways to make limited advances in the higher, more exclusive branches of the profession. Both Mercy and Douglass hospitals maintained dental clinics. During the 1930s the all-black Jackson Dental Society was very active. In fact, in 1930 its membership donated an entire dental clinic to the out-patient department of Mercy Hospital. No other organization of dentists in Pennsylvania had ever made such a contribution. The benefit was reciprocal. According to the hospital's biennial report of 1934, the Mercy dental clinic was providing members of the Jackson Society with "the facilities of a hospital for clinical research." At the same time the dentists were making general examinations of the mouths of all ward patients in the hospital.[57]

Another association that emerged from within Philadelphia's community of black dentists was the Odonto-Chirurgical Society. This organization was established in 1927 and was most active during the Depression and World War II. Among its charter members, and later its president, was Dr. Sylvester B. Smith, a Howard Dental School alumunus. The Society's purpose, according to Dr. H. J. Greene, a leading member, was to support the "professional development" of its members. The most important requirement for membership in the Society was the submission of a case study actually encountered and treated by the applying dentist. "Papers setting forth some phase of the profession as it pertains to Negro dentists are read at meetings," said Greene. He called the organization uniquely valuable to its members "in that it carries on where the school left off."[58]

By 1939 the Jackson and Odonto-Chirurgical societies had a combined membership that totaled over one-half of the black dentists practicing in metropolitan Philadelphia. This far exceeded the number of those with membership in the Philadelphia County Dental Society or the American Dental Association (ADA). Dr. Ferdinand S. Upshaw, a black dentist interviewed in 1939, stated that some members of both of the black societies sought to become affiliated eventually with the ADA. Before they could be admitted to either the Philadelphia County Dental Society or the Pennsylvania State Dental Society, however, it was necessary for them to leave the black societies. As of 1939, according to Upshaw, about fifteen black Philadelphia dentists were members of the ADA. Most likely a much larger number of the black dentists were members of the all-black National Dental

Association. We know that in 1936 forty-eight of the city's black dentists were members of the State Medical, Dental, and Pharmaceutical Association. According to the WPA researchers in 1939, the two local black dental societies and the PSMDPA, along with the Mercy and Douglass dental clinics, were building greater respect and patronage for black dentists throughout the city.[59]

Between 1925 and 1939 black nurses in Philadelphia experienced the same limitations in professional growth as had black physicians and dentists. We have focused on their public health activities in earlier chapters. Like the city's black physicians and dentists, however, their overall number and professional opportunities outside of public health medicine were greatly restricted prior to World War II. This resulted from the same educational and economic developments that limited the black medical and dental practitioners: the ever-increasing standards in training and practice requirements and the economic depression, which placed great handicaps on poor black prospective nurses.

The nursing profession started to become more exclusive in the mid-1920s when the opinion spread that poorly trained nurses were being overproduced. In 1926 the Committee on the Grading of Nursing Schools, which functioned in the same way as had the Flexner investigation some years earlier, instituted more rigid requirements in nursing education throughout the nation. Weak nursing schools that were operated by small hospitals were the primary targets of these new standards, and many became defunct. Between 1926 and 1936 the number of nursing schools dropped from 2,155 to 1,478, a decline of about 31 percent. Among the institutions that closed were many of the black nursing schools, including Douglass Hospital's school of nursing, which lost accreditation in 1928.[60]

The decline in black nursing education prevented many blacks from entering the profession. Moreover, the Depression jolted large numbers of trained and untrained black nurses into unemployment or into other occupations. In 1920 black nurses comprised about 2.2 percent (87) of Philadelphia's 3,936 graduate, or fully licensed, nursing force. The proportion declined in 1930 to about 1.9 percent (153) of the 7,866 nurses in the city. But in both these years, more of Philadelphia's black nurses were found in the "untrained" category—that is, nurses who had been educated in non-accredited nursing programs. In 1930 there were 150 blacks among the city's 2,737 untrained female nurses, and 156 among the 2,172 in 1930. Even though the untrained nurse was disappearing, later to reappear as

113

the "licensed practical nurse," black nurses were just over 5.3 percent of those in Philadelphia during 1920 and 7.1 percent of their number in 1930.[61]

There were several reasons for this. The poor quality of many nursing schools in the 1920s and early 1930s led to the overall replacement of student and untrained nurses in hospital ward work by graduate nurses.[62] Thus, the general numbers of untrained nurses declined. On the other hand, blacks were still restricted to attending black nursing schools, which were usually operated by small black hospitals and were most often unable to meet the clinical requirements of the National League for Nursing Education for certifiable nursing education. A great proportion of black nursing school graduates were refused recognition by the League.[63] Therefore, although the general number of untrained nurses was in decline, this was not the case among blacks.

Discrimination in nursing education and employment, as well as the devaluation of black nursing school education, did not prevent black nurses from making vital contributions to the city's health services for blacks. We have already examined in detail the relatively large number of the city's black nurses found in the public health field during the interwar years. The majority of the city's other black nurses were working at Douglass and Mercy hospitals.

Like the black doctors and dentists in Philadelphia, the black nurses maintained a close-knit circle of association and self-help. The Douglass Hospital Nurses Alumni Association was still active in 1939, despite the nursing school's closing a few years earlier. According to Halvina B. Eve, R.N., the Association kept in touch with its members, aided the hospital in its financial drives, and furnished a room for it.[64] Indeed, by the time the Depression took hold, it had become traditional for the undergraduate and graduate nurses of both Douglass and Mercy hospitals to contribute money or labor to help sustain their institutions. The lasting attachment that the black nurses developed for their hospitals is illustrated in this passage from the class history of the Mercy nursing graduates of 1934:

We wished to be a good class, for our good and for the good of our school. We wished to do some piece of work that might be of material value to our institution as well as to ourselves. Hence, in December, 1931, a series of events were planned by the class to raise money to paint the first floor halls of the hospital. Candy sales, fairs and dances were given, as well as donation bags being sent far and wide to bring in contributions for our cause. On March 14, 1932, we were capped, and it was this night that we presented the big surprise to all. One-hundred and twenty-five dollars were given to Dr. [Henry] Minton as our tribute.[65]

Also active in the city during the 1920s and 1930s was the local chapter of the National Association of Colored Graduate Nurses. In the late 1930s this organization was headed by Lillian Paxon. Other more informal groups were also maintained among the city's black nurses. Nurse Eve remarked that through such groups black nurses "keep informed of matters peculiar to them, and at the same time are enabled to straighten out problems pertaining to their profession."[66]

Black pharmacists also had an important part to play in the overall health care of Philadelphia black communities. For them, as for the city's other black medical professionals, the 1930s was a trying period. Pharmacy has been referred to as the "incomplete profession" because it has not received the high prestige of the other medical professions.[67] Nonetheless, it has been a particularly important medical field to the city's poor populations. Traditionally, because the American poor could not afford the cost of treatment by physicians they have tended to treat themselves.[68] Consequently, patent medicines sold at pharmacies have been quite popular. In Philadelphia, which was the center of a constant influx of poor black migrants as well as a large blue-collar white population, pharmacies were widely dispersed. Between 1920 and 1930 some twenty black pharmacies were started in the city. These, combined with a few other black pharmacies previously established, comprised about 2 percent of the 1,537 drugstores operating in Philadelphia in 1930. This small percentage was roughly commensurate with the national figure on black employment in the drug industry.[69]

There were a number of reasons for the emergence of black pharmacies in the late 1920s and 1930s. Most drugstores reflected the ethnic and racial character of their particular neighborhoods. All-white neighborhoods tended to have drugstores with all-white employees. It should also be recalled that during this period segregated fountains and lunch counters were legal or customary. These factors tended to exclude black pharmacists or other black drugstore workers from employment in white drug enterprises prior to World War II.[70] They also made it necessary for blacks to set-up their own neighborhood drugstores.

Like the city's other black medical professionals, the black pharmacists organized themselves and in 1924 founded the Cooperative Retail Druggists Association. Its original function was to make wholesale purchases for member druggists to increase their profits and allow customers the lowest possible prices. In 1929, however, this policy was abandoned, and the Association's objective became solely that of scientific exchange. Through the 1930s the group met monthly at the Marion Tea Room. Many Philadelphia black pharmacists were also active in the PSMDPA. In 1936 at least six held membership in this organization.[71]

Despite the enthusiasm that many black pharmacists brought to their profession, it was perhaps the weakest wing of the city's black medical professional core. During the 1920s and 1930s the overwhelming majority of drugstores in the nation were operated by one person or a single family. This was another factor that contributed to the growth of "start-up" black-operated drugstores in black neighborhoods of Philadelphia. But the small size of these enterprises also made them susceptible to ruin when under financial stress. In fact, the Depression caused many of the city's black pharmacies to collapse.[72]

The inadequate number of black pharmacists and auxiliary drug workers through the 1930s made the health care situation worse than it had been for Philadelphia blacks. Both black neighborhoods and the black medical community especially needed all available pharmaceutical services. Yet, as had occurred in the other professional fields, the twin effects of the elevation of standards and the Depression greatly reduced black employment in the pharmacy field. Between 1927 and 1941 the national average of blacks graduating from pharmacy schools dropped from an estimated 52 a year to about 19. In 1935, for example, Dr. Roscoe Henry established a drugstore specifically limited to filling prescriptions from physicians. Considered a precedent for the race, it lasted only one year, largely due to the unavailability of trained black staff or clerks necessary for this type of pharmacy.[73]

Despite the dismal educational and business atmosphere, black pharmacists maintained a significant presence in the city at the close of the 1930s. It was estimated that in 1939 there were eighty black pharmacists in the city. Half owned or managed drugstores and about twenty-five of these stores compared favorably in appearance and operation with the better white ones.[74]

Toward a Politics of Confrontation

Generally, the achievements of black medical professionals within their communities are all the more remarkable given the socio-economic blight that settled over black Philadelphia during the Great Depression. Finding themselves in the midst of a city where the socio-economic wall of race was thickening, and confronted daily with multitudes of the black poor with serious health and social needs, black medical activists at the end of the 1930s sustained their intra-racial professional associations, but they publicly no longer expressed the New Negro's self-pride. Instead, they reflected what leading historians of this period describe as a "bitter psychological and sociological realism" that pervaded popular black thought during the 1930s and into the World War II years.[75]

No one expressed the outrage of the political impotence of black medical leadership with more articulateness and fire than Dr. Virginia M. Alexander. A graduate of the Woman's Medical College (1925), Alexander had grown up in North Philadelphia's black community and developed a singular life goal—to become an effective doctor for that community. Like the few other black graduates of Philadelphia medical schools during her day, she traveled out of state (to Kansas City, Missouri) to complete her internship. She returned to Philadelphia in 1927 to start general practice in her first and only office, which was located in the 2100 block of West Jefferson Street, in the middle of a poor North Philadelphia neighborhood.[76]

She soon found that for an effective practice she needed not just training and talent but constant vigilance. In a 1933 article devoted to Alexander, *Crisis* magazine reported that she spent "an endless amount of time following her patients to hospitals, checking on her diagnosis both medical and surgical, standing by her patients when operated upon and visiting them afterwards." She had found that such surveillance was necessary to ensure that her patients were not mistreated while they were hospitalized at predominantly white facilities. According to the article, this practice by doctors like Alexander, more than any other approach, helped insulate

117

the black physician–black patient relationship from "increased practices of segregation and discrimation in most if not all of the hospitals of Philadelphia."[77]

Due to the popularity of her practice and the acute need for female-infant clinical care in her community, Alexander reduced her general practice to obstetrics and gynecology. She converted her three-story home-office into the Aspianto Health Home for in-patient care and later a well baby clinic. With her patient load reaching unmanageable proportions and her interests in public health study and activism growing, she brought in as her protegé another OB-GYN specialist, Helen O. Dickens, a native Ohioan. The two developed a partnership at Aspianto that lasted until Alexander's death in 1949.[78]

Alexander became a close associate of W. E. B. Du Bois and was strongly influenced by his scathing insights into the political crisis confronting the Depression-era black community. In an attempt to strengthen her expertise in dealing with the range of health and social problems she confronted daily in her clinic, she also undertook intensive study of public health and in 1937, she received a master's degree in this subject from Yale University's Graduate School of Medicine. In the early 1930s, she began working with the race relations units of the American Friends Service Committee. This Quaker, Philadelphia-based organization was a consistent liberal force in the city, agitating for social welfare programs for the needy, international pacificism, and an end to racial discrimination. Their strategy for social and political change stressed investigative research into social ills and publications to increase community awareness, interracial conferences, and legal and electoral campaigns to counter political conservatism and prejudice.[79]

In 1937, Alexander unleashed one of the strongest public indictments of racial segregation in Philadelphia since the late 1910s, when Nathan Mossell and his Douglass colleagues had protested against segregated internships. At the Institute of Race Relations, a meeting held annually since 1933 by the Friends Service Committee at Swarthmore College, she commenced a study of the health problems of residents of North Philadelphia. She and her co-researcher, George E. Simpson, published their findings and conclusions in 1937 in a statement that documented the severe health crisis afflicting black North Philadelphians and faulted the inadequate medical services in this section of the city. The study pointed out that black physicians in South and West Philadelphia could rely on Douglass and Mercy to provide hospital services for patients they referred and could also, if necessary, treat their patients there since the doctors often were formally affiliated with these institutions. Moreover, black North Philadelphia doctors did not have access to such facilities; from 1932 to 1937 three hospitals in North Philadelphia (Women's Hospital, Woman's College Hospital, and the Northwestern General hospital) had relocated to other areas of the city. Hospitals that did remain in North Philadelphia usually treated black patients and professionals on much less equal terms than whites. According to Alexander, some hospitals had separate clinic hours for black patients, some had "special Negro wards," some refused black maternity cases or encouraged delivery in the homes by student doctors, and, in some cases, there was a lack of follow-up work on black patients.[80]

Alexander's study identified the obstacles facing black medical professionals and black hospitals. It pointed out that at the three municipal hospitals in Philadelphia each year more than fifty physicians received appointments as interns, residents, or staff, over four hundred student nurses were admitted to the nursing schools, over two hundred graduate nurses were employed as supervisors or head nurses, and more than two hundred doctors had privileges of staff membership, "but not a Negro physician, student nurse, or graduate nurse is admitted in any professional capacity to any of these three city institutions." The study noted that "efforts on the part of Negroes to obtain internships, admission to the nurses' training school, clinic, or staff appointments have been made from time to time for many years," but "no influence, political, civic, racial, philanthropic, religious, or otherwise, has been able to alter this situation."[81]

The report foresaw great problems facing municipal leaders and the black public if either relied strictly on Mercy and Douglass. "The two Negro hospitals in Philadelphia perform a valuable service," it remarked, but "even if these hospitals were wholly ideal and equalled the best hospitals in physical structure and equipment, professional personnel, and public approval, their 270 beds could not begin to meet the health needs of 235,000 Philadelphia Negroes [or] the North Philadelphia area."[82]

Alexander and her survey team recommended that a large "interracial health center" be established in North Philadelphia. Such a center should provide "less expensive and more accessible, more complete, and more sympathetic medical and dental care," "more opportunities for the continued training and professional development of Negro physicians," "health education for adults and children," and "recreation." Only through a newly equipped, fully integrated health facility could the medical providers (black and white) adequately serve the medically needy black masses of North Philadelphia. No such interracial clinic resulted from Alexander and Simpson's study. But between 1937 and 1940 three black doctors were appointed to the staff of Philadelphia General.[83]

A summary of this survey was published by the National Urban League in 1937 in *Opportunity* with the comment that the problem of hospital services in North Philadelphia unveiled by the study could "be found in nearly every American city." Thus, the 1937 study put the political and medical leadership of Philadelphia on notice to expect a new militancy on the part of the city's black health leaders. Public challenges by black medical leaders to post-World War I segregation in health care had occurred earlier in New York City and Cleveland.[84] But in Philadelphia it was not until the Alexander-Simpson study that local voices were raised publicly against the problem of discrimination in the city's health facilities. From this point, public exposé and confrontational politics would swell, and repeatedly triumph, with each ensuing decade.

By the outbreak of World War II, black medical leaders in Philadelphia were not only publicizing their displeasure with segregated medical training avenues, rigidly discriminatory hospital services, and municipal apathy toward these issues but were urging their colleagues and lay activists to take on health segregation directly. In June of 1940, Dr. Frederick Douglass Stubbs, a Harvard Medical School graduate (1931), one of city's most respected black physicians, and a nationally prominent surgeon, agitated for a direct political assault on discrimination in Philadelphia's medical institutions. In an address at the Health Session of the Thirty-First Annual Conference of the NAACP held in Tindley Temple, a popular black church, Stubbs decried the poverty that prevented most blacks from obtaining adequate medical services. "We are literally prostrate at the foot of the economic ladder," he observed, "and we must realize that health care can be bought just exactly like every other commodity by and large."[85]

Stubbs also denounced the plight of black medical professionals. Citing statistics to show that medical training and employment opportunities for blacks had actually become more restricted in recent years, he spoke against racial "prescription in internships, nurses' training and staff membership." To demonstrate the pivotal importance of political struggle in eliminating discrimination in health care employment, he described how he was able to intern at the municipal hospital in Cleveland during 1931–1932 only after a bitter political confrontation in which Cleveland's three black city councilmen nearly had the director of health fired. As for Philadelphia, Stubbs criticized municipal health leaders who "flatly refused any consideration of a situation where a Negro physician might find it necessary to examine a white patient. . . . Actually, white patients in large municipal hospitals usually prefer the Negro physicians because his very presence usually implies that he must be unusually efficient to even be there." Stubbs urged every branch of the NAACP to put on their agendas both the issue of improving access to medical services for low-income blacks and the problem of removing barriers preventing black doctors and nurses from working at public hospitals and any other health facilities that received public funds.[86]

The picture conjured up by Stubbs and Alexander reflected a black health care environment that was hard-pressed and inadequate. In almost all instances, the city's black medical professionals labored in racially segregated neighborhoods and workplaces, as they had done in the 1910s and early 1920s. By 1939 a significant number of black physicians, perhaps 10 percent, and black nurses, about 25 percent, were working in black public health clinics, but the majority were in private practice throughout the three main black residential sections of the city. As described by National Medical Fellowships, a foundation to enhance the growth of minorities in medicine, "to a greater degree than the case of his white confreres, the average Negro physician became a general practitioner, isolated professionally and serving a low-income group."[87] This detachment left black professionals in private practice vulnerable to economic ills; as observed earlier, the businesses of many black dentists and pharmacists in the city did not survive the Depression.

Philadelphia blacks had still experienced almost no educational and professional growth in the four major medical professions. In fact, the number of black medical, dental, nursing, and pharmaceutical students had declined both locally and nationally. Education of the city's black physicians and dentists came increasingly and more exclusively from Howard and Meharry, and black nurses in the city had been restricted to attending local or out-of-state black nursing schools. Black professionals continued to rely upon their own professional associations, strong black community ties, and any types of consultantships available with white medical experts in order to sustain their self-efficiency and growth in the various health fields. In particular, the black medical institutions nurtured local black medical achievers as these professionals prepared to take up the challenge of modernizing their hospitals and desegregating the predominantly white ones.

The isolated status of Philadelphia's black medical professionals fit in with the overall segregated social patterns prevalent in the city prior to World War II. In Philadelphia, as in the South and most of the North, the "two worlds of medicine," one white, one black, persisted. After America became involved in the Second World War, however, this isolation was no longer publicly unquestioned by blacks. Both nationally and locally, black Americans increasingly demanded full educational, employment, and political equality as growing numbers of their youth streamed into the armed services. As the activism of Alexander and Stubbs indicated, no longer was the black Philadelphia medical professional content with social prestige within the black community but political impotence in the affairs of the larger citywide medical community.

122

PART TWO

Changes, Social and Medical

Blacks, Health Care, and the New Mass Hospital Through World War II

Three patterns characterized Philadelphia's black medical professional community immediately preceding World War II: their lag in entry into medical training and research; their isolation from the city's major hospitals and medical schools; their dependence on black hospitals and self-help associations and, concomitantly, their close ties to the black community. But blacks were becoming increasingly vocal in their criticism of the racial barriers in medicine. During the decade following the start of the war, a growing tide of black political activism, as well as momentous medical technological and urban socio-economic changes, would begin the irreversible rupture of Philadelphia's "two worlds of medicine." Ironically, the pressures for the integration of the medical profession and health care also gradually dissipated the black medical community.

Between 1910 and 1940, Philadelphia's black population had nearly tripled. This increase largely stemmed from an influx of working-class blacks from the urban and rural regions of the South: between 1935 and 1940, 69.9 percent of the migrants were southerners. Moreover, poor health and slum living conditions were widespread among these newcomers.[1] As in other major northern cities, with the outbreak of World War II, this new black community benefited from the expanding economy by finding employment in the service sector, in defense industry work, and in military service.[2]

125

Fundamental changes also occurred in the city's medical establishment. The expanding technology and range of services of the city's larger hospitals greatly increased the employment of blacks in non-professional hospital occupations. Significant growth in the availability of hospital and clinic treatment for blacks in Philadelphia increased the contacts of black patients with Philadelphia's major medical institutions. Helped along by, and helping, these social and economic changes was a growing national movement for black political equality that inspired both the medical and lay black communities of Philadelphia.

Efforts for Equality in Health Care Widen

Given the large numbers of black Americans being called into military service, as well as the increased contact of blacks with discriminatory treatment practices in the city's hospitals and clinics, racial barriers in the medical professional sphere were bound to touch off criticism by black medical leaders and their supporters.[3] More than in any previous period, during World War II, the full span of medical education and employment barriers as well a the health service needs of blacks became a central theme in civil rights agitation in Philadelphia and throughout the state.

Among those who denounced unequal medical resources for blacks were the younger physicians involved in improving Mercy and Douglass hospitals. In preparation for seeking government funds for the Mercy-Douglass merger during 1939, Russell Minton, F.D. Stubbs, and Arthur Thomas toured seventy hospitals nationwide that largely served blacks, and concluded that "the medical situation of the Negroes in Philadelphia at that time was by far the worst of all cities visited, with perhaps the exception of New York City."[4]

The lay black community also expressed increased concern over better medical care, as was evident in the recurrent articles on the subject that appeared in the *Philadelphia Tribune* throughout 1939. The newspaper repeatedly criticized the limited number of black medical professionals—for instance, the dearth of blacks with academic degrees in public health, a situation that left the city with no qualified blacks available to be district health officers. On the other hand, the paper pointed out improvement in black health care when possible, praising appointments of a few blacks as health bureau aides, for example. In one long *Tribune* article, Minton discussed the breadth and importance of medicine to human progress.[5]

Another manifestation of popular concern throughout the black community over the health crisis was the social survey conducted by the Works Progress Administration (or Works Project Administration). Between 1938 and 1941 the WPA worked on a statewide social, economic, and cultural survey of Pennsylvania's varying ethnic and racial groups. As offshoots of this comprehensive Pennsylvania project, the WPA financed in-depth investigation of the black communities of Philadelphia and Pittsburgh.[6] The researchers for these two urban black community studies were local black journalists, social welfare workers, and writers. The Philadelphia investigation included interviews with dozens of blacks in medicine. The tone of racial pride and political militancy that characterized black America as it entered World War II pervades these interviews and the overall final report. The Philadelphia black community's traditional intense concern about health problems and race achievement in the health field was being transformed increasingly from an internal or ethnocentric priority to public claims and protestations along the lines of Alexander's and Stubb's declarations.

The most comprehensive and publicized investigation of blacks and Philadelphia hospitals was conducted by the Pennsylvania State Temporary Commission on the Conditions of the Urban Colored Population. This commission (hereafter referred to as the Urban Commission) was established in 1939 by Governor Arthur H. James and the state General Assembly in imitation of the commissions on black conditions set up by the states of New York and New Jersey. The Urban Commission functioned through two legislative sessions—1939–1941 and 1941–1943. Its fifty members were drawn mainly from among Pennsylvania's leading black educators, politicians, and welfare workers, including E. Washington Rhodes, U.S. congressman from Philadelphia; attorney Homer S. Brown, U.S. congressman from Pittsburgh; Dr. Leslie Pinckney Hill; Mrs. Maude B. Coleman of the Pennsylvania Department of Welfare; and Herbert E. Millen, a Philadelphia judge. The executive director was the noted anthropologist Dr. Lawrence Foster of Lincoln University.[7] The Urban Commission implemented a multifaceted sociological analysis and policy review in an effort to improve the obviously unequal socio-economic and political conditions plaguing blacks in Pennsylvania. Utilizing data from Pennsylvania state welfare, law, and health agencies, it conducted careful research into six major areas of black life: housing, health, crime and delinquency, education, employment, and interracial contacts and civil rights. Since the Urban Commission's work did not conclude until 1943, however, and the results of the research were not published until that time, we will analyze its investigation into medical conditions a bit later on.

The Expansion of Hospital Care for Blacks

The concern of black medical leaders, civil rights proponents, the black press, and the lay black community with racial equality in the medical profession coincided with broad changes in hospital admission practices and financing. Although Mercy and Douglass accounted for a substantial portion of black admissions, most hospitals in the city had traditionally admitted blacks to varying degrees depending on the predominant ethnic and social characteristics of the controllers and patients of the particular institution.[8] Philadelphia's largest hospital, Philadelphia General, the municipal hospital, was mandated specifically to care for the indigent. When the black population of the city began to multiply swiftly after World War I, those hospitals that had customarily treated blacks found their services in even greater demand. For one thing, poor blacks were usually not able to afford the services of private physicians.[9] For another, these impoverished blacks, like other poor Philadelphians, were more often afflicted with illness and injuries as a result of unhealthy environmental, housing, and work conditions.[10]

In addition to increased demand, hospitals faced economic pressures to admit blacks. During the interwar period, Philadelphia hospitals had grown increasingly dependent on state aid for their financial viability. Beginning in the late 1920s a Pennsylvania Supreme Court decision refused public aid to hospitals operating as strictly sectarian institutions. Moreover, the policy required hospitals to "earn" state funds in proportion to the number of free days of care it provided. The State Department of Public Welfare effectively monitored this regulation by sending its newly trained medical social workers into hospitals to verify patient service records.[11] Also, in response to their various mandates, Philadelphia General and voluntary hospitals in the city that had teaching and or university components provided at least examinations and clinical services for virtually all persons seeking them regardless of ability to pay.[12]

Under such circumstances, blacks became a more hospitalized sector than any other racial group in the city. During 1929, when blacks comprised only about 7 percent of Philadelphia's residents, they had reached about 14 percent of patients found in the city's hospitals on any given day.[13] By 1941, when Philadelphia blacks were about 13 percent of the total Philadelphia population, health authorities estimated that they made up as much as one-fourth of the patient load citywide.[14]

One other important aspect of the growing presence of black patients throughout Philadelphia's predominantly white facilities was the opening of many tuberculosis treatment facilities to blacks, a change that took place between 1939 and 1941. In response to what the local Tuberculosis Association official called in 1941 "the magnitude of the tuberculosis problem among [local] Negroes," most of the tuberculosis clinics run by hospitals in the city, including the two large clinics operated by the city-owned Philadelphia General Hospital and the Philadelphia Hospital for Contagious Diseases, started admitting increased numbers of blacks. During 1941, blacks constituted 31 percent of the 4,527 patients under diagnostic and treatment clinic care at the twenty-seven tuberculosis clinics around the city. Moreover, they made up slightly over 44 percent of an additional 12,647 patients at these clinics who were examined but not tuberculous or were under treatment for other ailments. Three of the state-operated sanatoria—Cresson, Hamburg, and Mont Alto—also opened their doors to Philadelphia blacks during the early 1940s.[15]

The New Mass Hospital

Another facet of changing race relations within Philadelphia's medical life was the entrance of hundreds of blacks into the non-professional hospital work fields. By the beginning of World War II, the hospital had become technologically transformed to accommodate greatly expanded demands for treatment. After the Depression, the rising cost of medical care had caused an upsurge in third-party hospital payment plans by government, labor unions, and insurance companies.[16] A growing multitude of middle-

and lower-class Americans who were receiving such coverage generated an unprecedented demand for medical care.[17]

To meet this demand, hospital administrators had to locate an increased supply of low-wage labor. This labor was needed to perform the expanding non-professional or allied health care work in the hospitals. For the first time, significant numbers of black laborers, who had traditionally been confined to domestic service in private homes or service establishments like hotels or restaurants, were hired in the city's major hospitals.

This influx of black non-professional labor into Philadelphia hospitals during the 1940s was not merely one aspect of a historic and rapid "sweeping in" of blacks to previously segregated industries that had lost many of their white employees to military service.[18] Actually, the entrance of blacks into skilled and semi-skilled employment fields within the war production industries was generally a slow process.[19] Moreover, the general employment rates in the state's and nation's heavy industries rose only as these industries were converting to produce armaments and civilian goods related to the military effort. By contrast, health care employment rates were consistently high both immediately before and after the start of the war (Table 21). The labor demand in Philadelphia's health care establishment during the late 1930s an 1940s was, in fact, "self-embodied." It was a demand for both professional and non-professional labor arising from the spiraling growth in the size and personnel structure of hospitals, and it stretched deep into the local black labor supply.[20]

From the late 1930s, the tendency by the majority of private GP's to perpetuate their own individually housed practices waned, and the delivery of medical care in Philadelphia and other cities became progressively centralized around the hospitals.[21] As Kenneth Boulding stated shortly after World War II: "Monopolistic restriction under the guise of high professional standards has been so great that it has resulted in the development of a number of subprofessions [that] undercut the regular medicos in the sickness market."[22]

In effect, these innovations in the hospitals of Philadelphia and similar cities undermined the practicability and profitability of individual private practice outside the walls of the hospital. The growth in hospital affiliations of Philadelphia's physicians, which we noted, occurred between 1925 and 1938 increased through the 1940s.

The GP's were replaced by new "mass hospitals" that resulted from a tremendous growth in government and consumer expenditures for hospital

TABLE 21

Total Labor Force and Health Service Labor Force Employment and
Unemployment, by Sex, Philadelphia, 1940

	Employed		Unemployed		% Unemployed*		
Labor Force	Male	Female	Male	Female	Male	Female	Total
Total							
White	441,667	187,581	69,332	22,267	13.6	10.6	12.7
Black†	43,419	31,031	20,926	8,942	32.5	22.4	28.6
Total	485,086	218,612	90,258	31,209	15.7	12.5	14.7
Health							
White	8,276	11,798	328	633	3.8	5.1	4.6
Black†	869	890	94	110	9.8	11.0	10.4
Total	9,145	12,688	422	743	4.4	5.5	5.1

SOURCE: U.S. Department of Commerce, Bureau of the Census, *Sixteenth Census of the United States, 1940* (Washington, D.C.: GPO, 1943), vol. 3: *Population: The Labor Force: Occupation, Industry, Employment, and Income*, pp. 94–95.

†Listed as "Non-White" in census. Black Americans comprised over 99 percent of this category in Philadelphia.

*Percentage (%) unemployed is calculated across rows. The unemployment rates for both black and white (male and female) in the Philadelphia health services were substantially lower than the general unemployment rate for the city.

care. Collectively, these institutions served a huge clientele of all socio-economic classes. Such institutions were characterized by both steadily enlarging physical plants and expanding and highly differentiated personnel hierarchies, including enlarged food service and laundry facilities, as well as power plants, which had to be continuously operated because of the twenty-four-hour-a-day nature of hospital services. Treatment "productivity," which experts defined as the number of patients seen per time period, was immensely increased.[23]

The appearance of the mass hospital supplanted not only the community-based private-practice physician but also the neighborhood health centers. Because medical procedures and equipment were growing more complex and needed more labor to tend them, both the public and private health sector practitioners and insurers no longer considered the neighborhood clinic an adequate apparatus for delivering primary care. Instead, these health care providers invested more and more funds in the larger hospitals, which seemed to have unlimited potential to operate more efficient and comprehensive out-patient and emergency programs.[24] Tuberculosis treatment programs in Philadelphia, for instance, were no longer operated at neighborhood clinics; instead Philadelphia General and dozens of large voluntary hospitals in the city received state contracts to provide such services. Also, since all of Philadelphia's hospitals were receiving larger reimbursements from the state for treating indigent patients,[25] and since, as a result, most of the city's hospitals now admitted poor black patients, the "Negro Health Bureau" concept became dysfunctional. The Bureau's small group of black professionals gradually entered full-time positions throughout various city or state-sponsored public health services.[26]

It cannot be overemphasized that as the physical and functional character of the hospital grew, personnel was likewise expanded. As economist Harry I. Greenfield remarks, "the demand for medical care [was] predominantly a demand for personal service," which was "provided directly by people . . . rather than indirectly by machines, and it [was] for this reason that the medical care industry [was] sometimes characterized as 'labor intense.'" During the post-Depression years, changes in American family life caused a marked decline in the use of domestic service workers to perform physical care and hygienic tasks in the household; at the same time the ill and childbearing were more frequently being placed in the hospital. Simultaneously, the labor needs within the new mass hospital expanded particularly for non-professional health service personnel. Medical administrators and planners developed new employment hierarchies that entailed greater numbers of workers, such as x-ray technologists, physical therapists, licensed practical nurses, nurses aides, dietetic worker, and orderlies.[27]

Blacks Enter Hospital Employment

In light of the growth in the institutional and functional character of Philadelphia hospitals, a new and much larger role was evolving for black labor in non-professional health care employment. The data on Philadelphia's labor force for 1940 indicate that the extraordinarily high unemployment rates consistently found among the black population were, like those of whites, substantially lower in the health industry. Although the health care industry was much smaller than the city's major industries, this data still suggest that unskilled black labor was being brought into the hospitals at a more rapid rate than in other industries.

The 1940 federal census for the first time included the general occupational category "medical and health service" workers. This inclusion in itself indicates the newness of allied health occupations within the nation's labor structure. Moreover, this data provides our first glimpses into the racial, sexual, and cross-occupational character of this labor.

As shown in Table 21, during 1940 the unemployment rate for the city's total labor force was 14.7 percent, with men having a significantly higher rate than women. Among the city's roughly 100,000 black workers, about 20,000, or 32.5 percent, of the men and 22.4 percent of the women were out of work. On the other hand, white male unemployment stood at 13.6 percent and white female unemployment at 10.6 percent. For workers in the health services, however, the rate was substantially lower. Only 5.1 percent of this labor force was unemployed: 4.6 percent of the white in this industry and 10.4 percent of the blacks were without employment.

There was a basic reason for these relatively low unemployment rates in the health industry. According to Table 22, professional workers, primarily doctors and nurses, formed over one-half (14,630) of the total health care employment (21,833). This group is a characteristically small, highly trained, and rarely unemployed element of the American workforce.

Health care labor formed less than 4 percent of the approximately 703,000 workers in the city during 1940 (Table 21). Overall, blacks comprised less than one-tenth of the relatively small health care labor segment in Philadelphia despite the fact that they made up about one-sixth of the general workforce. While blacks were only trickling into the professional levels of the health care industry, they were beginning, however, to flow disproportionately into the non-professional or auxiliary levels of health care employment. According to tabulations for 1940, nearly seven out of ten white men in the health industry (or 69.1 percent) were in professional occupations (Table 22). Moreover, slightly less than two of ten white men (or 16.2 percent) were in service work. The remaining one-tenth were craftsmen or skilled, operative, and clerical workers. On the other hand, about six of ten black men in the city's health industry (62.3 percent) were service workers. Only about three in every ten black male health workers (27.0 percent) were professionals.

TABLE 22

Major Health Industry Occupations in Philadelphia, by Race and Sex, 1940

Occupation	White		Black		Total	
	Male	Female	Male	Female	Male	Female
Professional and semi-professional	5,719	8,494	235	182	5,954	8,676
Clerical	258	1,476	135	45	271	1,521
Operatives	302	296	38	64	302	360
Protective	71	1	0	0	71	1
Service	1,341	1,496	541	591	1,882	2,087
Laborers	123	4	33	4	156	8
Skilled	449	11	9	0	458	11
Occupation not reported	13	0	0	4	13	4

SOURCE: U.S. Department of Commerce, Bureau of the Census, *Sixteenth Census of the United States, 1940* (Washington, D.C.: GPO, 1943), vol. 3: *Population: The Labor Force: Occupation, Industry, Employment, and Income*, pp. 121–124.

Black female health labor evidenced an even greater concentration in the service occupations. Whereas over seven out of ten white women (72.6 percent) worked in professional occupations, primarily nursing, only about two of ten black women (20.4 percent) had professional employment. In service work, however, the ratios were roughly reversed. Only about two of ten white women were in service occupations; nearly seven of ten black women (66.4 percent) were concentrated in the service jobs.

Prior to the latter 1930s, most forms of hospital work were traditionally off limits for blacks. As we saw earlier, the non-professional personnel of a hospital usually reflected the racial and ethnic character of the hospital controllers and neighborhood. With the emergence of the mass hospital, however, blacks were hired by hospital administrators because they were the cheapest and most productive surplus labor available.[28] In fact, black labor was becoming pivotal to the city's health care industry. Table 23 indicates that about 18 percent of all male health service workers in Philadelphia were black, as were 11 percent of the operatives. Black women were 19.1 percent of the female health service workers, and 17.8 percent of the female operatives.

There can be little doubt about the sources for the city's black non-professional health care labor. They came from a pool of unskilled and semi-skilled workers whose prior work experiences had been limited to domestic and personal service. The race and employment figures for the three industries with the largest concentrations of black employees, and for the health care field, are represented in Table 23. In keeping with the traditional employment patterns for blacks in Philadelphia, all three industries—domestic/personal services, food trades, and eating and drinking—revolved around various forms of domestic or personal service.

TABLE 23
Black and White Employment and Unemployment in Philadelphia
in the Health Industry and Three Other Industries
with the Highest Black Employment, 1940

Industry	Employed		Unemployed		% Unemployed		
	Male	Female	Male	Female	Male	Female	Total
Health services							
White	8,276	11,798	328	633	3.8	5.1	4.6
Black	869	890	94	110	9.8	11.0	10.4
Total	9,145	12,688	422	743	4.4	5.5	5.1
Domestic/personal services							
White	2,050	10,790	561	1,610	21.5	13.0	14.5
Black	2,472	19,776	984	5,195	28.5	21.7	22.5
Total	4,522	29,566	1,545	6,805	25.5	18.7	19.7
Food trades							
White	84,404	37,069	10,471	5,139	11.0	12.2	11.4
Black	8,019	1,694	2,174	440	21.3	20.6	21.2
Total	92,423	38,763	12,645	5,579	12.0	12.6	12.2
Eating and drinking places							
White	11,757	7,796	1,854	1,100	15.8	12.4	13.1
Black	2,935	1,045	821	323	21.9	23.6	22.3
Total	14,745	8,841	2,675	1,423	15.4	13.9	14.8

SOURCE: U.S. Department of Commerce, Bureau of the Census, *Sixteenth Census of the United States, 1940* (Washington, D.C.: GPO, 1943), vol. 3: *Population: The Labor Force: Occupation, Industry, Employment, and Income*, pp. 48–53, 94–95, 121–124.

It is noteworthy that the unemployment rate for blacks (in Table 23) is much higher in the other three industries as compared to the health care industry. The employment field with the largest percentage of its experienced workers unemployed was the domestic and personal services: 22.5 percent of these workers were idle. In the other two industries, the unemployment rates were also over 20 percent. This means that there was a huge supply of cheap labor available for the expanding hospital to draw upon.[29] Although unskilled in a formal sense, these workers were skilled in the food preparation, housecleaning, child care, and related tasks that were needed by the hospitals.

At the same time that laborers in the domestic and food service industries were becoming idle, hospitals were experiencing increasing shortages of hospital attendants and practical nurses (both licensed and unlicensed). According to labor experts of the 1940s, such hospital workers were usually under the supervision of graduate nurses, dieticians, or a non-medical supervisor. They performed housekeeping, ran errands, and assisted in feeding, bathing, and dressing patients. Also, these hospital workers often carried out tasks that were related to a patient's specific medical treatment and convalescence such as changing bandages, applying dressings to burns or wounds, helping the patient exercise an injured part of his or her body, and taking the patient on walks.[30]

Interviews with retired hospital workers also corroborate the view that black domestic laborers who had once worked for families were being absorbed by the Philadelphia hospitals. A typical experience was that of Mrs. E.S., who was employed in the dietary department of the Mt. Sinai Hospital (later Einstein) from 1937 to 1977, when she retired. Since her youth Mrs. S. had worked as a domestic for the family of a physician. In 1937, she took a higher-paying job at Mt. Sinai, the city's leading hospital for its Jewish community. Mrs. S. stated, "I was hired as a cook for the Special Diet Kitchen; you see at that time you had to cook special diets for different patients." Mrs. S. worked on the evening shift (from 4 P.M. to 12 A.M.) and was responsible for preparing and serving "nourishments" such as fruit, juices, milk, and custards to the patients. She also prepared the main evening meals each day for forty to fifty patients on restricted diets. When Mrs. S. was hired the hospital had no other black employees that she knew of nor were any black patients normally found in the wards. Through the 1940s, a few more blacks were hired as cooks, maids, and "tray-girls," or servers. All were older workers with backgrounds similar to that of Mrs. S. She recalled that the food service units at the hospital often changed, making these units more efficient and allowing more room for wards. Work life was friendly and turnover among the food service workers was infrequent. Most of the employees were usually close, "but you know death comes in and takes somebody. . . . Or either maybe they become ill, you know, and sign out. I was just fortunate to stay there from the time I started up until I quit. Forty-one years, that's a long time."[31]

It is understandable why black nurses' aides like Mrs. S. considered the newly found service jobs in the predominantly white hospitals an advance up the employment ladder. Institutional service work, as opposed to family domestic work, usually provided more stable hours, somewhat higher wages, and less subjection to personal whims. A 1940 newspaper report on the black employment situation at the University of Pennsylvania stated that in the University Hospital and Graduate Hospital there were "large numbers of [black] maids, cleaners, and other general help." The one worker quoted in the report said, "Working for the University means pleasant work, good enough pay, and a vacation every year."[32]

Yet in spite of the growth of blacks in non-professional hospital employment, racial discrimination remained a dominant force throughout the city's hospitals. During the World War II decade, employment for blacks at any level in Philadelphia's predominantly white hospitals had come only as technological and economic exigencies made it a managerial necessity or when political and social agitation for equal employment and health care opportunities made it available. One Philadelphia administrator remarked, "When I first came to the hospital as an administrator, there was not even one Negro in the place. . . . During the war I first began to hire Negro employees due to economic pressures and the lack of availability of white employees." Those blacks who did become hospital employees often had to bear cold receptions, as would the black medical professionals who would eventually gain entry into the same hospitals. Nonetheless, hospital management stood fast in protecting new black employees. The same administrator cited above remarked:

When I first began to bring Negro employees into the hospital, I had communicated this to the white employees who thereupon threatened to strike if I did this. I told them to go ahead and strike if they wanted to and said, "If you strike or quit, what I will probably do

137

is put a Negro in your job." [After that] there was absolutely no trouble.[33]

Discriminatory Treatment and "Undue Handicaps"

The racial practices that limited black professional and non-professional employment in Philadelphia's predominantly white hospitals was also symptomatic of the unequal care often received by black patients at these institutions throughout the war years. At least twelve hospitals in the city during World War II openly did not admit blacks into regular wards but instead maintained separate "colored wards." Three other Philadelphia hospitals that stated that they admitted blacks into general wards were found to be segregated upon on-site investigation by Urban Commission staff. The rationale given by hospital representatives for their separate ward policies varied from "they have more fun together," to "maternity wards are separate, all seem happier that way."[34]

Other forms of hospital and clinic discrimination against blacks prevailed during World War II. Such practices included giving black patients separate attendance hours, placing them in special sections for their examinations and treatment, and not taking black patients in turn but grouping them together so as to give them the longest waiting time. Moreover, the verbal abuse that blacks received at some hospitals was so severe that many refused to go to any hospitals, preferring instead to use "self-medication."[35]

These discriminatory practices were condemned roundly by the conscientious Urban Commission members. They found the segregated ward policies in Philadelphia hospitals "undemocratic" and reprehensible. "All of these institutions are tax free," stated the Commission in 1943, "some of them are tax-aided [and] one of them is owned and operated by one of the world's largest Christian denominations." The Commission stated further that ward segregation at this religious hospital, as well as the Woman's Medical College Hospital, an institution established as protest against sex discrimination, were "astonishing—they deny the very principles upon which they were founded and are being maintained." The resentment that the larger black community harbored against such practices was also emphasized: "It may be well for many citizens to realize that more and more Negroes all over the State and nation are increasingly objecting to any [such] types of forced segregation."[36]

Besides the racial problems that plagued black patients, there were other deficiencies in medical care resources harmful to the overall health of black Philadelphians. During the early 1940s there were insufficient facilities for controlling the high rates of venereal diseases among blacks, and maternity and child care clinics were also lacking. The serious shortage in chronic care and convalescent facilities for blacks had been debated in Philadelphia medical and political circles since the late 1920s. Yet this shortage persisted in 1942, even though the city's hospitals on a given day usually had one-third of their beds empty. Costs for long-term care were prohibitive for unemployed or working-class blacks, and the public aid received by predominantly white hospitals for treating non-paying patients was not enough to cover costly long-term treatment and custodial care for seriously ill blacks.[37]

By most measurements of health status, blacks in Philadelphia and the rest of the state were generally worse off during World War II than they had been throughout the Depression years. In 1942, the mortality, tuberculosis, and pneumonia rates, as well as incidences of child malnutrition, were all equal to or higher than those for the first few years of the 1930s.[38]

In light of such a health crisis, and with many medical facilities in the city and state flawed by discriminatory practices toward black patients, the predicament of black medical professionals was a primary concern of the Urban Commission. This research group uncovered what it termed "undue handicaps" that hampered blacks involved in medicine in three areas: medical education, hospital and clinic appointments, and operation of black hospitals. The Commission strongly criticized medical school discrimination in the state. Philadelphia was the key target of this criticism since it was the location for five of Pennsylvania's six medical schools (the University of Pittsburgh had the only other medical school in the state). In its final report issued in 1943, the Urban Commission stated, "There are some tax-aided medical schools which do not admit qualified Negro students. Secondly, of these which do admit Negroes, the number admitted is far below the Negro's ratio in the total population." In view of the fact that Pennsylvania medical schools had only a minuscule number of black matriculants, the Commission concluded that currently these institutions "cannot be regarded as a major factor in the medical education of the Negro population." In addition, the Commission pointed out that, with the exception of black-staffed hospitals, black interns and prospective nurses were openly excluded from Pennsylvania hospitals.[39]

However, the research group considered that the most damaging discrimination hampering the growth of black medical professional was in the area of hiring. There were so few hospitals with black staff members that blacks throughout the state almost never expected integrated medical services in their communities. This racial exclusion persisted despite the fact that all the institutions were either tax-free, tax-aided, or completely tax-supported. The report stated, "Negro physicians, dentists, nurses, pharmacists, medical social workers, administrators, etc. need the [employment] experience afforded by the hospitals of the State."[40]

Since the Commission recognized a strong connection between black medical personnel and the willingness of ill blacks to seek treatment, it was especially critical of restrictions in employment and affiliation placed on black physicians and nurses in Pennsylvania hospitals. "There are fewer than a dozen hospitals which permit Negro physicians to treat in-patients within their walls," the Commission reported. It acknowledged that certain tuberculosis and venereal disease clinics operated by the State Department of Health utilized some black staff members as special teams to treat black patients. Also, from time to time, the Department appointed a black physician to serve on mixed staffs at facilities treating these diseases. However, the report stated that "while this record is somewhat better, so far as clinics are concerned, there is still much to be desired."[41]

The pressure and frustration that Philadelphia's black medical professionals were experiencing between 1941 and 1943 were manifested in their formal statements submitted to the Urban Commission. Dr. W. Harry Barnes, now an officer with the Philadelphia Housing Authority, stated that for him and his fellow black doctors there was "difficulty or rather impossibility in obtaining positions on staffs of state-aided hospitals, sanatoriums, penal institutions, etc." Dr. Daniel A. Wilson, a former president of the state NMA, enunciated the needs of black physicians as follows:

(1) Representation on state, county and city boards of health.
(2) Admission to the staffs of any state or city hospital.

(3) Appointment to staffs of city institutions such as prisons, asylums, sanatoria, state hospitals for deformed children and the like.

(4) Free access to all post-graduate courses offered by medical colleges in the state.

Lastly, Wilson urged that an effective health education plan be implemented for the patients in their patient population so that these adults would in turn practice proper child care.[42]

One of the most scathing critiques came from Dr. Etheridge McKnight, a staff member at Mercy Hospital. With regard to medical education, he commented to Urban Commission officials: "It is a known fact qualified Negro students are excluded from attending white medical schools in the state of Pennsylvania," being told or advised instead to attend black medical schools elsewhere. McKnight pointed out that black citizens, like whites, were providing tax revenues for hospitals in Philadelphia and throughout Pennsylvania, yet black interns were barred from these institutions. McKnight remarked that not only were qualified black physicians forbidden from serving on the staffs of these hospitals "but are not allowed to take any part, even in the treatment of their own patients when they are sent to these hospitals." The exclusion of black dentists and nurses from these same tax-supported hospitals was also criticized. McKnight ended with an eloquent denunciation of years of encrusted discrimination in the health care establishment. His statement exemplified the frustration of most black medical professionals in Philadelphia during the war period:

We all know that the above deplorable situation does not in any way make sense. These [black] women and men who are willing to help America by training themselves to live a better life are not allowed to train in these institutions that they themselves are supporting, solely on the grounds that they are Negroes, and for no other reason. I am wondering when America will awaken. . . . The very existence of our country is now at stake, and I trust that America will awaken to the fact that she is going to need all Americans in order to maintain these same institutions from which a portion of her honest and patriotic citizens are barred.[43]

Black Hospitals Under Strain

Despite the bitterness among black medical practitioners in wartime Philadelphia, their hospitals still managed to operate effectively. Even though these institutions faced a continual battle for survival, both Mercy and Douglass hospitals relieved key problems of Philadelphia blacks in health care, medical education, and hospital employment during World War II.[44]

In 1942, Mercy Hospital, then under the directorship of Dr. Henry Minton, had a total bed capacity of 125. During that year, it treated 2,218 in-patients, 9.7 (216) of whom were white. That same year the hospital's out-patient department served 3,005 new patients, amounting to a total of 10,884 visits.[45] Mercy also still ran a fully accredited nurses' training program. In 1942, it had a total of sixty-two undergraduate nurses. Between twenty and thirty new students were admitted annually. Mercy at this time was still the only hospital in the state in which a black woman could receive nurse training. Its operations also included the Convalescent Hospital for Colored Women. This was also a sorely needed facility since black patients stood almost no chance of being admitted to most of the city's sixty-seven private nursing homes.[46]

As for Douglass Hospital, in 1942 Dr. F.D. Stubbs was its medical director. During that year, this eighty-five-bed hospital served 880 black in-patients (293 free) and had 14,908 out-patients. Its nurse training and internship programs were, however, now defunct.[47]

Perhaps the greatest impact that black hospitals had during this period on the health of Philadelphia blacks (and the smaller number of whites they served) was in the area of public health. The hospitals functioned as conduits for their professional employees to part-time clinical staff positions with city and state clinics. A few Mercy doctors continued to receive joint positions in city tuberculosis and state syphilis clinics.[48] Douglass's tuberculosis clinic, which had been helped along earlier by Lawrence Flick, and its syphilis clinic, funded by the State Department of Health, were two of the most heavily attended in the state.[49] So successful was the Douglass syphilis clinic that, in 1944, the United States Public Health Service expanded its program and facilities.[50]

The personnel of these two black hospitals were only a tiny fraction of the city's entire health care labor force, however, and could in no way be expected to serve the thousands of ill blacks in Philadelphia. The 210 combined beds for the two hospitals were only 1.5 percent of the city's estimated 13,711 total hospital beds.[51] In 1942, Mercy employed 3 administrators, 8 clerical or office workers, 50 staff physicians, 19 registered nurses, 62 undergraduate nurses, 5 dentists, 1 dietitian, 1 social worker, and 18 orderlies, kitchen helpers, and janitors. This was a personnel total of 167. As for Douglass, its employees comprised 94 workers distributed as follows: 3 administrators, 47 staff physicians, 17 graduate nurses, 3 dentists, 1 social worker, and 23 orderlies, attendants, kitchen helpers, and janitors.[52] These statistics and those of Table 23 indicate that Mercy personnel were only .8 percent, and Douglass's employees just .5 percent, of the 21,833 health care workers in Philadelphia. The professional and non-professional staffs of these two institutions combined were only about 1.2 percent of Philadelphia's total health care labor, and 16.1 percent of the black labor force in the health fields.

In 1942, in a written statement solicited by the Urban Commission, Stubbs described the services and needs of Douglass in terms that evoke the problems that beset most of the nation's black hospitals dependent on public funds. He said:

> Located centrally, in an easily accessible, congested, largely slum neighborhood, it serves an important community service but is greatly limited by its needs. These needs largely resolve themselves into financial problems which directly or indirectly affect physician equipment and the quality of all purchased services.

Because the percentage of free patients treated at Douglass was higher than that of any other state-aided institution, Stubbs believed that the hospital should receive higher annual state appropriations that would be at least commensurate with the cost for these services. "There is a very definite need," Stubbs argued, "for the Negro hospital to provide needed sympathetic care to members of our own racial group and to act as a training center for Negroes in all branches of the healing arts."[53]

Stubbs cited several specific deficiencies at the hospital, all stemming from funding or racial problems. For example, Douglass needed to expand the quarters for the syphilis and tuberculosis clinics, as well as for the hospital's other smaller clinics. (Remember that the former two clinics were among the most active in the state.) The hospital also needed money to complete and to equip a modern nurses' residence so that it could

143

reestablish its training school for nurses. The general structure and equipment of the hospital required improvement, facilities for private and semi-private care needed to be expanded, and a sanatorium needed to be built to provide more beds for tuberculosis patients. Besides these physical problems, Douglass's poor financial state forced all its employees to be underpaid.[54]

Next to providing medical and surgical treatment for needy patients, Stubbs viewed medical education as the ideal function of Douglass. He pointed out that, in order for a medical professional to become and remain proficient in treating the ill, it was essential that he or she have an ongoing connection with a hospital. As the skills of blacks in medicine grew, Stubbs believed the general health of blacks would improve. However, he remarked that "this training is not being provided in white institutions for Negro professionals and can only be secured through their own hospitals."[55]

In the area of physician education, the Douglass staff urgently needed access to training in the specialties. Although a few black physicians had been able to study special fields at other institutions, Stubbs noted black physicians needed to be able to rely on the clinical facilities of their own hospitals because they were "effectively prevented from participating in the programs of white institutions." For training its staff in the specialties, Douglass was still forced to depend on the consultantship arrangement with "an unusual group of white practitioners as consultants who [were] of outstanding caliber" and who held posts at local teaching institutions.[56]

In 1943, the Urban Commission issued their conclusions relating to urban blacks and Pennsylvania's medical establishments. Among their recommendations to the state legislature, they suggested that Philadelphia's black hospitals receive increased financial aid. The recommendation that the Commission stressed as most critical, however, pertained to full health care integration: "The major medical task of the Commonwealth [has to be] to foster those interracial measures which will lead greatly to reduce the restrictions and limitations placed upon Negro patients and members of the medical profession." The Commission urged that state-owned medical institutions add to their personnel qualified black medical professionals, as well as medical technicians and other health care employees.[57]

The Urban Commission may have brought more public attention to the health care employment problem of blacks in Philadelphia; but it did not have any immediate or lasting impact on these problems. During the remainder of the decade, the state General Assembly did not create new legislative, judicial, or appropriative changes along the lines of the Commission's recommendations that could serve to equalize health care opportunities for blacks in Pennsylvania's urban areas. Unlike similar commissions in other nearby states, after its final report of 1943 the Pennsylvania Commission was disbanded.[58]

By the end of World War II, the status of blacks in health care employment in the city was not deviating from those trends that we noted occurring in 1940 and 1942. Black women were still heavily concentrated in domestic work, even though they were disinclined to remain in this field and were striving toward more skilled, well-paying jobs. Even after having completed vocational training, many blacks were limited to domestic work; for instance, the occupational levels and wages attained by black high school students who had specialized in home economics were substantially lower than those of whites with similar training. Yet the strong tradition in the city of confining blacks to domestic service was being increasingly opposed by younger blacks who were entering the labor market. These youths disliked domestic service because it promised only low wages, long hours, much physical strain, and employers with difficult attitudes, as well as little respect from society in general.[59]

Throughout 1943, when public school counselors in Philadelphia attempted to open up alternative avenues for black graduates by means of conferences with various employers, only limited gains were made in the area of hospital employment. Since several hospitals had for the first time employed black nurses' aides and other auxiliary employees, counselors and prospective black employees hoped that more skilled hospital jobs, like dietitians and x-ray technicians, would be accessible to black graduates. However, the counselors found at the hospitals they contacted that training programs in such work was not being offered to blacks. Just like those who decades earlier had envisioned converting black domestics into trained nurses, these public school officials had hoped that black high school graduates brought into the lowest occupations in the city's hospitals would by training advance into more skilled levels. But such programs had not developed. Only one large hospital thought such opportunities would be made available, and another was considering the training of black nurses. But for the present, public school officials pointed out, "many very capable Negro girls are barred from this profession because the two Negro hospitals cannot accommodate all those who wish to train."[60]

As World War II came to a close, there had been few advances for

Philadelphia blacks in the medical, nursing, and pharmaceutical professions outside of those that they obtained at or through the two black hospitals. A major hospital did add a few black physicians to its staff; however, they were used only as clinical assistants and did not serve in the wards. Black medical professionals in predominantly white hospitals were still the exception rather than the norm. Only in 1943 did Temple University break the statewide status quo with respect to admitting blacks into its nursing school. After the approval of its board of directors and consultations by such civic figures as Rev. William Harvey, Samuel Evans, and Dr. John P. Turner, university president Robert L. Johnson put the open admission policy into affect. It promptly made headlines in the *Philadelphia Tribune.*[61]

Thus, despite the exhaustive investigation by the Urban Commission, neither the state legislature nor the Philadelphia municipal government initiated concrete steps to bring the medical education and employment of blacks up to a more equitable status. But the Commission's work did set the stage for the broad-scale efforts of black medical and lay groups who, working hand in hand with civil rights organizations, would generate the first significant steps by Philadelphia's predominantly white hospitals and medical schools toward becoming integrated.

CHAPTER VI

Black Medical Activism
After World War II

The wave of medical institutional, socio-economic, and spatial changes that had reshaped patterns of race relations in Philadelphia health life during World War II continued to gain force throughout the second half of the 1940s. In the wake of the tremendous outpouring of loyalty and service by black Americans to the domestic and foreign United States military effort, black leaders in Philadelphia medicine and their supporters viewed equal access to white medical institutions for advanced medical training and hospital affiliations as a natural right owed all earnest black physician and nurse aspirants. During this period, not only did public fact-finding on discriminatory practices in the city's medical establishment continue, but also Philadelphia blacks began to undertake specific actions to alter the stagnated situation. Black medical professionals and lay activists were striving to pressure major Philadelphia hospitals to desegregate their training programs and their staffs, as well as to strengthen existing black health institutions.

The Lingering Divide

The war did not have an immediate positive effect on the supply of Philadelphia's black medical professionals. In fact, many already scarce black professionals relocated out of Pennsylvania to serve in the military medical service.[1] The entrance of black physicians into military service was apparently a contributing factor to the decline in their number throughout the state. While the overall number of physicians in Pennsylvania from 1940 to 1948 had increased from 13,529 to 15,320, the number of black physicians had dropped from 220 to 202. The state's total ratio of physicians to populations was 1 to 765 in 1940 and 1 to 697 in 1948; but for blacks the numbers were 1 to 2,137 in 1940 and 1 to 2,487 in 1948.[2] Similarly, the supply of black dentists in the state significantly declined during the war years. In 1940, there were 131 black dentists in Pennsylvania, located primarily in Philadelphia and, to a lesser extent, Pittsburgh. By 1945, this number had been reduced by about 8.4 percent to 120. Yet medical schools in Philadelphia did not increase their enrollment of blacks during the early 1940s.[3]

On the whole, during the Second World War racial discrimination against blacks in employment and patient care in Philadelphia hospitals was not reduced. In 1945, in response to a sociological study on hospital segregation, conducted by Patricia Sullivan, only forty-seven of sixty-seven hospitals in the city replied to the survey. Only five of the hospitals stated that they had blacks on their attending staff; only six accepted black doctors on courtesy, associate, or visiting staffs; only one (Mercy Hospital) admitted blacks as interns; and only five accepted blacks for nursing training.[4]

We must consider the estimates of black participation in Philadelphia hospital life as being on the high side since they included the city's black hospitals, and administrators of other responding hospitals apparently tended to cut corners on matters relating to minorities in their institutions. Also, research methods failed to utilize on-site investigations. For example, the five hospitals reporting that they had blacks on their attending staffs could have had them at any time during the entire twentieth century, or only as "unofficial affiliates."[5] Moreover, black physicians who gained privileges to work in the predominately white hospitals through, for instance, contacts with consultants were only permitted to treat black patients, and this usually in the separate wards or basements of the hospitals.[6]

As for patient discrimination, the following conditions prevailed throughout the forty-seven hospitals: one did not admit blacks at all; two did not allow them in maternity wards; eight did admit blacks to their private rooms; and seventeen had inadequate or unequal separate facilities for the diverse illnesses of black patients seeking admission. Sullivan's study concluded that the majority of hospitals in Philadelphia were practicing other forms of racial exclusion by failing to provide adequate or equal facilities for all types of blacks needing medical treatment.[7]

In 1946, researchers of the Philadelphia Bureau of Municipal Research undertook a study of black-white relations in Philadelphia.[8] After the end of World War II, a number of violent racial outbreaks had occurred in the city. This inflamed social situation had triggered research that centered on the conditions of Philadelphia blacks in employment, housing, municipal services, recreation, and health services. The findings of the municipal study concurred with those of the Urban Commission and Sullivan's sociological study. Even well-to-do blacks, it disclosed, "no matter what emergency, . . . frequently are unable to obtain adequate medical attention."[9]

The municipal study criticized the status of blacks in the medical schools of the city. A few black medical students were matriculating at the University of Pennsylvania, but not in numbers near the proportions of the black city or state population. At Temple, the researchers found that only one black medical student had been admitted recently. Postgraduate training opportunities for blacks, with the exception of Mercy Hospital's internship program, were virtually nil.[10]

Encouragingly, the municipal study detected certain slight signs of gains for blacks in Philadelphia health care. The dental schools of both Pennsylvania and Temple were reputedly "quite fair" to black applicants; each had more than two black matriculants. In nursing, the Philadelphia General Hospital admitted its first black student nurse in more than twenty years in 1942 and, since then, had added a few others. But the study emphasized that the Mercy training school was still the only consistent avenue for preparing black nurses in the entire state; in contrast, the Philadelphia General program "did not come anywhere near meeting the need for Negro nurses."[11] The report also pointed out that there were no black faculty members at the medical schools.[12]

The color bars prevalent in the Philadelphia medical establishment in the wake of World War II angered the city's black community. After the war, the new militancy for the right to equal employment, training, and medical treatment in the nation's health institutions was fast becoming a central current in a stream of local and national black protest. In Philadelphia, one pathbreaking movement for medical equality was spearheaded by a group of leading black physicians who comprised the Health Committee of the NAACP. Stubb's appeal for more activism on the part of the local NAACP on health matters was finally being heeded.

The NAACP Health Committee

After the Second World War, the NAACP became increasingly active throughout the nation in matters pertaining to the health of blacks.[13] In addition to its National Health Committee, the Association had numerous local or branch health committees. In 1946, the Health Committee of the Philadelphia NAACP began the task of getting blacks internships and staff positions at the city's large, municipally supported Philadelphia General Hospital.[14] The key members of this Committee were all physicians: DeHaven Hinkson, the nation's first black major to head an Army hospital, Russell F. Minton, nephew of Henry M. Minton and a leading radiologist, John P. Turner, Eugene T. Hinson, and Naborne E. Bacchus. Also working along with the Committee was Charles Shorter, the executive secretary of the Philadelphia NAACP.

Early in March 1946, some of the members of the Health Committee, including DeHaven Hinkson, met with a medical official of Philadelphia General, to admit black interns, residents, and staff. Hinkson was especially outspoken, arguing that since black Philadelphians were taxpayers and since Philadelphia General was financed solely on the basis of taxes, the bar against blacks receiving appointments at the hospital should be eliminated.[15]

On March 5, the Committee met to plan strategy. After discussion of an incident involving the discouragement of a black female medical school graduate who had considered applying for an internship at the Presbyterian Hospital, the subject turned to staff segregation at Philadelphia General. To goad his colleagues on to combat, Hinkson told of one black physician who was going to Canada three days a week to study pathology because "our tax supported hospitals will not take him [and] Philadelphia, which is supposed to be the birthplace of surgery, is trailing behind."[16] The committee made plans for a follow-up meeting on this subject with Philadelphia General officials and the mayor. They also decided to concentrate on securing black internships, rather than pursuing residencies and staff positions for their older colleagues.[17]

The Committee had to overcome two interlocking barriers. One involved determining the administrative personnel or policies responsible for discriminatory practices at Philadelphia General. The other involved establishing a fair testing procedure for black internship candidates at the hospital. For some time during the initial contacts with Philadelphia General officials, the Committee experienced unnecessary delays aimed at diminishing their determination. Philadelphia General was administered under the Public Health Department, while the Department was under the control of the city's general administration. Hospital officials advised the Committee to bring their grievances to the Public Health Department, which in turn referred them to City Hall. When the Committee realized that these referrals could continue indefinitely and were merely a diversionary technique, they demanded a meeting with appropriate representatives from all three parties—namely Philadelphia General's medical director, public health officials, and the mayor.[18]

The Committee anticipated that, once it had established simultaneous talks with all the hospital and municipal authorities, the question of finding qualified black intern applicants would be raised. Therefore, once the meetings began in earnest, the Committee agreed to locate qualified black candidates. Prior to the 1946 meetings, Hinkson had known of three black physicians who had taken the test for internships at Philadelphia General, all of whom were rejected.[19] Therefore, the Committee also insisted that the entrance examination procedures and test results of their candidates be open for their review.[20]

The meeting with the mayor and hospital officials attracted a large and public interest. Reviewing the negotiations, Hinkson stated, "There was no picketing, just frank confrontation." Shortly after the meetings, Dr. Maurice C. Clifford, a black Meharry graduate (class of 1947), obtained an intern appointment at the hospital. The medical director later informed Hinkson that Clifford had become a popular figure at the hospital.[21] Clifford's appointment at Philadelphia General was both a moral and concrete victory. In Hinkson's words, blacks following in Clifford's footsteps would "learn and bring it back to our [black] managed hospitals and teach others."[22]

The city's black nurses were also concerned with equal education and employment practices. The program at the Northeastern Regional Conference of the NACGN, which took place at the headquarters of the Mercy Hospital Nurses' Home and was sponsored by the local Association of Colored Graduate Nurses of Philadelphia and Vicinity and the National Nursing Council, included topics such as "The Fair Employment Practices

Committee" and "The Integration of the Negro Student in the Mixed School."[23]

Black Lay Support Resurges

While certain Philadelphia blacks involved in medicine began to wage a war to attack obvious racial barriers existing in the predominantly white hospitals, others of the city's black community attempted to improve the black hospitals. During the early 1940s, Mercy and Douglass had plunged into the worst financial condition since their inceptions.[24] By the war's end, not only were they in a financial crisis but Douglass had also lost other forms of accreditation. At the same time, the major hospitals throughout the city were expanding to increase the range and efficiency of their services. Consequently, the controlling groups of Mercy and Douglass concluded that merging the two was the most feasible way to salvage them.

Mercy's doctors in particular were not enthusiastic about a merger with Douglass. The two hospitals had over the decades developed separate community and professional followings. However, the financial future of the two hospitals rested not only on small community donations, but on the funding policies of the state, on Philadelphia's major charitable federation called the Community Chest, and on private philanthropists. These three powerful funding groups made it clear during the war years that they would not commit any long-term support to the two hospitals if they rejected an eventual merger.[25]

In 1947 a group of lay blacks moved to put Mercy on a sounder financial and professional footing. Called the Physio-Therapy Society and formed in order to raise enough funds to equip a modern physical therapy unit in Mercy Hospital, [26] this organization was short-lived, finding that major groups of funders of Mercy and Douglass hospitals were resolute about merging the institutions so as to have one central, less costly, and more efficient black hospital for the city. The Society's ordeal illustrates how racial prejudice in Philadelphia and the rigid specialization of the medical profession made it most difficult for black lay groups to influence medical policy in the city.

The idea to establish the Society was first raised during a meeting on April 16, 1947, at the Pyramid Club. The group expressed a common interest in the study of physical medicine and in the establishment of a

152

department of physical therapy at Mercy.[27] The Society's first officers were Linton Ellis, president; John Newman, secretary; Estelle Gudze, financial secretary; and Ida T. Love, treasurer. The Society contracted with Aldophus R. Anderson, an employee of the Internal Revenue Service's Philadelphia office, to serve as the administrator of all donated monies as they were received.[28] The organization focused on physical therapy because of the importance of this medical field immediately after World War II, and as a result of the poliomyelitis epidemic, which produced a large population of severely handicapped younger people in need of physical therapy. Nationwide, treatment facilities for black children were especially limited. When physical therapy became more refined as a treatment for motor function disabilities stemming from combat injuries and polio, physicians increasingly applied it to a wider range of ailments, including strokes, fractures, nerve and back injuries, burns, and tuberculosis.[29]

Physical therapy, however, necessitated a diverse and costly array of equipment. A modern unit during the 1940s required, for instance, infrared lamps, whirlpools, electrolysis devices, and exercise apparatus. For a hospital as small and financially insecure as Mercy, the creation of such a unit was especially difficult. Moreover, due to discrimination, the training and employment of black physical therapists at the city's other hospitals was not likely.

Ida Love was in charge of the operations of the Society, whose headquarters were located at her business/home address. She was a prominent black business and vocational educator. Her successful school for beauticians had been established in 1919 and was still in operation. In addition to running her school, Love was an officer in numerous professional and welfare associations and had been a consultant with the state's Department of Public Instruction. She had aided in establishing state regulatory laws in her field, and was responsible for the hiring of blacks by the Public Instruction Department.[30]

The Physio-Therapy Society had the support of some of the doctors associated with Mercy, as well as other black physicians. On occasions, some of these doctors gave lectures on physiotherapy at the Society's meetings. At the monthly meeting of July 6, 1947, Dr. Arthur Thomas, the acting chief surgeon of Mercy, addressed the group on the great need for physiotherapy at the institution and "the magnitude and benefit the community would derive from such a department."[31] At the following meeting the hospital's medical director, Dr. John Graves, described the

153

technical aspects of physiotherapy.[32] Finally, Dr. Egbert Scott, who replaced Graves as director of the hospital, sent a statement of endorsement to the Society in November 1947 reaffirming the importance of establishing a physiotherapy department.[33]

In November of 1947, the Society began steps to obtain their objective of $5,000 for the physical therapy unit by submitting an application to the Pennsylvania State Department of Welfare to solicit funds on behalf of their non-profit effort. State law required that charitable fund drives be certified by the Department in order to protect the public from unscrupulous practices.[34] Upon receipt of any application by the Welfare Department's Community Work Bureau, an investigation of the background and legitimacy of the fund-raising organization was conducted. In the case of the Physio-Therapy Society, the Community Work Bureau's investigators correspond with a number of Philadelphia social welfare agencies and medical offices to obtain their knowledge of the Society's activities, its method of operations and personnel, necessity for its services, and community opinion of the organization. This process began on January 12, 1948, three days after the Society's application was filed, and was to last about six months. In the meantime, the Society continued to hold monthly meetings, mostly at the Pyramid Club, and to collect dues from its members.

The form letter concerning the Society sent to organizations by the Bureau was, to begin with, slightly misleading. The Society had stated in its application, under the item on purposes of its fundraising: "To equip a Department of Physio-Therapy in Mercy Hospital . . . at a minimum cost of $5,000."[35] The Bureau's letter, however, stated that the Society's purpose as set forth on the application was to "make a study of all phases of Physio-Therapy and to advance the science through research."[36] Consequently, the organizations receiving the inquiry had the impression that the Society itself intended to carry out the scientific research on physical medicine. Other initial misimpressions about the Society were probably aroused by the Bureau's failure to make clear in its letter of inquiry that the organization was in fact new. The Society had been meeting scarcely eight months before it applied for solicitation certification. This was not ample time for any welfare aid organization to build a large membership or to establish a successful track record in attracting reputable donors or supporters.

The first group of organizations that the Bureau investigators contacted

154

were the Philadelphia Health and Welfare Council, the Better Business Bureau of Philadelphia, and the Armstrong Association (Urban League) of Philadelphia.[37] These organizations all had dealings with social welfare and philanthropic business affairs, but only the Armstrong Association had worked extensively in the black communities of the city. The Health and Welfare Council responded that it had no information on the Society. The Better Business Bureau extended some information on Ida Love's business background but had no further knowledge of the group. Wayne L. Hopkins, the executive secretary of the Armstrong Association, stated that he did not have any information on the organization but was well acquainted with Ida Love and found her "highly regarded as a business woman and worker in behalf of constructive, civic movements."[38]

The next group of organizations that the solicitation investigators contacted were medical agencies and professional associations. Since even welfare organizations in the city were unable to substantiate the Society's work, it was inevitable that Philadelphia medical agencies would misunderstand the purposes of the Society and not support its application. The Hospital Council of Philadelphia replied to the investigators that it had no information about the Society.[39] The Philadelphia office of the American Hospital Association called the Society's goal of establishing a physical therapy department at Mercy a "worthy project" but expressed concern over the indication in "your [i.e., the Bureau's] letter . . . that the incorporators actually expected to practice physical therapy themselves." Since the president of the Society was not an accredited physical therapist, the Association felt it could not endorse the application.[40] The executive secretary of the Philadelphia County Medical Society also responded that a department of physical therapy would greatly improve Mercy Hospital, but he questioned the need for the group being organized to obtain the funds.[41]

When the College of Physicians of Philadelphia received the letter of inquiry, they referred it to the Committee on Public Health, Preventive Medicine, and Public Relations.[42] The Committee, a unit within the college, sought the opinion of Dr. George M. Piersol, the director of the Division of Medical Services for the Philadelphia School District. Piersol ridiculed the Society, describing them as "composed of a number of colored laymen headed by a rather aggressive individual by the name of Linton Ellis [who is] fired with a desire to establish [in Mercy Hospital] a department of physical therapy." He called the Society "perfectly unnecessary" and a "poor qualified pressure group." Of course, the Society was not a pressure group but a voluntary association seeking donations. White hospitals in the city each had several lay groups that raised funds, provided volunteers, or made large endowments. However, this director viewed the Society as a group which at best could only produce medical quackery. Piersol commented that Society members were in no sense qualified to instruct or practice physical therapy, yet "they labor under the delusion that in some way they themselves and their associates can become active in physical therapy at the Mercy Hospital," an activity he described as illegal. He closed his evaluation with this remark:

> I sympathize with their desire to further the cause of physical med-
> icine in their race and to establish such departments in their hospitals,
> but I can see no possible justification for the formation of the Phy-
> siotherapy Society which claims to be in a position to study all phases
> of physical therapy and to carry out research in that field.[43]

On the basis of this evaluation the Committee urged that the application be disapproved.[44]

Knowing that the hospital's primary funders wanted to force Mercy to merge with Douglass, the Welfare Department prolonged the investigation of the Society until the merger issue was resolved. The investigators contacted Egbert Scott, Mercy's medical director, several times to find out whether the hospital officially approved of the Society's campaign. Then he referred the matter to the Mercy board of directors.[45] Preoccupied with a strategy to resolve the merger question and with resignations and disagreements, the board was prevented from acting in unison on many matters. Thus, it never got around to defending the Society's campaign officially.[46] Finally, in March of 1948, the consolidation petition received the state's approval. The new "Mercy-Douglass" hospital now had different, presumably better, funding arrangements. The Welfare Department, therefore, rejected the Society's application and, in effect, dissolved the group.[47]

The unsupportive responses of the city's white medical professionals to the Physio-Therapy Society suggest that attitudes in Philadelphia medical and welfare establishments were not conducive to the growth of fund-raising groups managed by and for blacks. In contrast, volunteer groups and fund-raising auxiliaries were a common feature of Philadelphia's predominantly white hospitals. Furthermore, a number of these hospitals such as St. Christopher's (Catholic), Mt. Sinai (Jewish), and Presbyterian were under the control and functioned primarily in the interest of certain lay white religious or ethnic groups. But the Society's experience illustrates how hard it was for both professional and lay blacks in Philadelphia to establish long-range and successful fund-raising groups for the black hospitals within the city's politically weak and largely lower-class black community.

Black lay groups were traditionally strong social elements in the black community; the black press particularly helped to sustain Philadelphia's "black world of medicine." Lay groups had come to the aid of the two black hospitals when these institutions faced recurrent threats of bankruptcy and loss of accreditation, as well as when they were relegated to a second-class or Jim Crow status by other medical interest groups in the city. The disbanding of the Physio-Therapy Society was, however, a sign that black lay support networks for Mercy and Douglass could no longer provide the finances and political influence that would ensure significant autonomy for these struggling institutions. The two black hospitals were now totally dependent on funds provided by the city and state government. This meant that Mercy and Douglass had to have all their hospital programs approved by these two highly politicized bodies.

Gearing Up for Mercy-Douglass

The more complex medical technology, spiraling financial requirements, changing residential patterns, and a social atmosphere unfavorable to black-controlled educational and social institutions were creating great strains not only on Mercy and Douglass but on black hospitals throughout urban America.[48] Black physicians and their hospitals were being pushed to relocate in hospital sites that whites had abandoned as neighborhood race patterns changed from predominantly white to black. Rather than upgrading or building new facilities for black medical institutions that were falling behind in modern medical and funding trends, municipal policy makers and health authorities usually sought to solve the problem cheaply and quickly by urging relocation. In fact, the original site for the new Mercy-Douglass Hospital was formerly the site of the Woman's Hospital. The neighborhood surrounding that hospital had become predominantly black, and Woman's Hospital was planning to move to new quarters. Hospital officials, however, finally decided that it was more practical to close down the Douglass building and transfer all its useful equipment to Mercy.[49]

Dr. Wilbur H. Strickland became the first medical director of the new Mercy-Douglass Hospital in March of 1948. He was successful in improving the institution's personnel organization and expanding the nursing training program. Strickland believed that a hospital as small as Mercy-Douglass could not keep abreast of all the trends in modern medical science without affiliating with teaching institutions. However, none of the medical schools in the city would accept such an affiliation. Consequently, the hospital again established a type of consultantship arrangement. By March 1949, a number of leading physician-specialists, mainly from Philadelphia teaching institutions, had become members of the Mercy-Douglass Medical Advisory Council. This group monitored some of the practices of the hospital's professional staff.[50]

In 1949, Russell F. Minton replaced Strickland as the hospital's medical director and superintendent. Minton's association with Mercy dated back to 1922. His first actions were to survey both the medical and administrative operations of the hospital. He also started a public relations department, as well as a personnel department, in his words, "for centralization of all employees, both professional and non-professional." Minton restructured the medical nursing and clerical staffs to maximize performance and at the same time to reduce expenditures.[51]

The Mercy-Douglass board of directors had also been reorganized under the leadership of Philadelphia judge Herbert E. Millen. One of the ultimate aims of Minton's and Millen's policies was to have the hospital completely accredited by the American College of Surgeons and the AMA for intern and resident training.[52]

By the close of the 1940s, the nation was in the midst of a massive hospital construction program as a result of the Hill-Burton Hospital Construction Act (1946). This program provided liberal federal grants to build, remodel, and expand hospitals throughout the nation.[53] As project applications for such funds began to mount and hundreds of hospital construction projects were initiated, Mercy-Douglass administrators began to realize that perhaps they could have an entirely new hospital plant built. After all, although the merger had eliminated some of the equipment deficiencies, the site was still the congested divinity school that Mercy had occupied since 1919.[54] Moreover, the Hill-Burton Act contained a racial equity formula that provided for separate but equal, segregated facilities (similar to that of the Morrill Land-Grant College Act).[55] Thus, black hospital interest-groups could expect some of the program's funds, even if for reasons they found pernicious to racial equality.

With a new hospital plant on the horizon for Mercy-Douglass, many black medical professionals in Philadelphia began to foresee the day when a modern, black-controlled facility would at last be a feature of the city's hospital establishment. Yet, during the 1950s, the fate of a newly constructed black hospital, as well as the extent to which blacks were further integrated into the medical professions in the city, would depend largely on the effectiveness of the local and national civil rights movements. During the early 1950s, as the momentum of these movements increased, the Philadelphia medical establishment gradually began to take on a more integrated makeup.

159

PART THREE

Toward an Integrated Medical Community

The Civil Rights Movement and Medical Integration in the 1950s

T he 1940s had been a decade of growing public insight into the various forms of de facto segregation in Philadelphia's medical establishment. Yet during that period neither public inquests, black activism, nor the institutional modernization that occurred in the city's hospitals had been strong enough to reduce this discrimination significantly. Blacks were still substantially under represented in the medical professions and in medical school admissions. However, during the 1950s, social and political claims by blacks for equality reached into Philadelphia health institutions. Gradually, the status of black medical professionals in the city was increasingly equalized. New linkages emerged between the city's white and black medical professionals and their respective institutions, and these trends encouraged previously white institutions to absorb black medical trainees and personnel. Integration accelerated the demise of Philadelphia's black medical subworld.

As in previous decades, during the 1950s there was a sizable growth in the number of low-income blacks coming from the South to settle in Philadelphia. In 1950, some 381,649 non-white persons were residing in Philadelphia—18.3 percent of the population. Five years later, the non-white population was estimated to be between 450,779 and 456,806 persons, of whom blacks were the overwhelming majority (about 98 percent).[1]

In the early 1950s, liberal sectors of the city's political, business, and social welfare communities became disturbed over the immense range of socio-economic problems associated with this minority population. Although by this time tuberculosis death rates had dwindled to negligible numbers for both blacks and whites, "new" public alarm had arisen over crises in housing, education, employment, public health services, social welfare, and urban rehabilitation.[2] At the same time, fueled in 1954 by controversy over the Supreme Court decision in the *Brown v. Board of Education*, historic civil rights campaigns were being waged in other regions of the country. Movements for voting rights, equal public education, and fair employment opportunities were gaining momentum.[3]

In such a local and national context, four significant developments took shape in Philadelphia during the opening years of the 1950s and contributed to eroding racial barriers in the city's medical institutions. First, the persons involved with the movement to improve Mercy-Douglass Hospital became pivotal in forcing before both the public and medical authorities the issues of advanced medical education and health service needs for blacks. Second, outside (i.e., non-medical) interest groups—namely the city's branches of national civil rights and fair employment organizations—continued their anti-discriminatory activities. The agitation of the Philadelphia NAACP, begun in the late 1940s, continued through the 1950s, and they were joined by similar organizations, such as the Philadelphia Commission on Human Relations, the American Civil Liberties Union (ACLU), and the Urban League. Third, by the mid-1950s, a new willingness emerged among the city's predominantly white hospitals and medical schools to integrate their professional staffs and training programs, especially as shortages of interns and residents began to develop. Fourth, the changing occupational and financing structure of the city's hospital establishment generated increased employment of blacks in the lower-level hospital occupations. This disproportionate presence of black technical and non-professional health care employees, who witnessed patterns of differential treatment for black patients, also tended to intensify the actions of local civil rights organizations.

The Mercy-Douglass Issue

If there was one subject that captured the collective focus and expectations of Philadelphia black physicians and their supporters in the early 1950s it was the fate of Mercy-Douglass Hospital. The black doctors felt caught between two conditions that were compounding their professional isolation. One was the increasing specialization in the medical professions, which necessitated longer spans of post-medical school training as well as ongoing affiliations or courtesy privileges with hospital specialty departments for patient referrals. The other condition was the general tendency of the large, white medical institutions not to seek blacks for training and hirings within their professional staffs. Thus, local black medical leaders placed the utmost importance on upgrading and expanding Mercy-Douglass to become a model of a well-rounded interracial medical center with strengths in specialty training for its physicians.

The twelve-month period between April 1949 and April 1950 was particularly crucial in the movement for having a new building constructed for Mercy-Douglass Hospital. It was this immediate issue that forced the leading figures in the city's black medical community to decide whether their priorities should be placed on trying to maintain a black-controlled institution or to depend fully on gaining opportunities within the city's predominantly white hospitals.

The consensus favored the former objective. Training and employment openings for black medical professionals in the city's predominantly white institutions were still sparse. Since this discrimination seemed unlikely to change without painstaking, potentially fruitless protest, these mostly older, pragmatic black professionals opted to improve their traditional hospital. Echoing Nathan Mossell's anti-segregationist hospital policy of World War I era and Virginia Alexander's 1930s concept of an interracial medical center, Russell Minton and the hospital's other leaders in 1950 sought to create a genuinely integrated institution that would serve the entire city. They anticipated that this institution would, in the long run, generate a larger and steady supply of black and white physician-specialists and nurses, who would, in turn, work in connection with the hospital in elevating the health status of medically needy blacks citywide.

This was the argument employed by the Mercy-Douglass leadership as they negotiated with Governor James H. Duff and state legislators for appropriations for the new building. They candidly criticized the steep racial barriers prevalent in the Philadelphia and statewide medical establishments. In the months immediately preceding the spring legislative session of 1950, Judge Herbert E. Millen, the president of the Mercy-Douglass board of directors, constantly communicated with Duff on behalf of the hospital's administrators and medical staff.[4] Judge Millen and other

Mercy-Douglass officials also prepared two reports that they circulated to Duff and state legislators. The Mercy-Douglass officials hoped that the briefs would enhance the chances for passage of the appropriation bill for their new building. This legislation was to come to vote in April of 1950 and then be placed before the governor for his signature.

In one of their reports on the proposed new construction, the Mercy-Douglass officials stated that they envisioned a hospital where black doctors could intern, acquire residencies, and staff appointments "which are denied to them in Pennsylvania at the present time." They pointed out that of the 386 internships available throughout the state in 1949 only three had been filled by blacks. Furthermore, they stressed that just eight blacks could be found among Pennsylvania's 592 residents, and staff appointments were not a possibility for these residents.[5]

The Mercy-Douglass leaders also believed that, as a consequence of the small supply of black medical professionals, the overall health of blacks in the region was well below average. Lacking black physicians who could continually retrain and benefit from hospital affiliations, black citizens were not receiving the medical care that their numbers and health problems required. The officials of Mercy-Douglass were careful to indicate that the new enlarged hospital would be conducted on an "interracial basis." This policy would apply to staff, administrators, residents, interns, technicians, other employees, and patients. They believed that Mercy-Douglass "would be setting an example of all groups of persons working together in the medical field and allied sciences."[6]

A second, more lengthy report on the need for the new Mercy-Douglass building was compiled by Wilbur Strickland, the medical director, and Kermit J. Hall, the business manager. They too emphasized that the new hospital would be fully integrated. Pointing out that in metropolitan Philadelphia "there are more than 250 Negro doctors and dentists who are denied hospital privileges, except in one or two token instances," they stressed that the new Mercy-Douglass Hospital would have no differential practices on the basis of race in the trusteeships, medical staff, non-professional employees, or patient treatment. Moreover, to remedy the shortage of private hospital beds for blacks at least 60 percent of the hospital's 250 beds would be for in-patient health care. The hospital would, in short, "operate on a full scale interracial policy."[7]

When the construction appropriation was approved in late April of 1950,[8] Millen and the Mercy-Douglass administrators prepared for a new

166

day in black medical professionalism in the city. While they were generally optimistic about the hospital's fate, they still had to face complexities. The city's medical community began to divide along three schools of opinion. One predominantly white group favored the abolition of the black hospital completely and presumed that black doctors, nurses, and technical staff would one day find places in the city's predominantly white hospitals.[9] The second group, a core of black professionals, supported making Mercy-Douglass a distinct and separate facility for blacks supported either by the municipality or by the Commonwealth. The example that they cited for such an arrangement was the successful Homer G. Phillips Hospital in St. Louis.

Those in charge of Mercy-Douglass and its new building campaign, however, chose to maintain a third position, the same one they had espoused when lobbying for the construction funds: to keep the hospital under its traditional black control, but, at the same time, to integrate it at all levels, creating an institution "for the practice of American medicine in which all groups, nationalities and races will work side by side."[10]

Mercy-Douglass officials also intended that their institution stress postgraduate medical training programs. Consequently, they placed a high priority on gaining affiliations with the city's medical schools. The hospital's medical advisory committee, which had been assembled in 1949 during the new building campaign, consisted of the following professionals: Dr. Burgess Gordon, Jefferson Hospital; Dr. I. S. Ravdin, University of Pennsylvania; Dr. William P. Belke, Episcopal Hospital; Dr. Joseph L. Johnson, dean, Howard University, Washington, D.C.; Dr. Joseph Stokes Jr., Children's Hospital; Dr. P. F. Lucchesi, medical director, Philadelphia General Hospital; Dr. W. Edward Chamberlain, Temple University; Dr. William G. Leaman, Woman's Medical College; Dr. Michael J. Bent, dean, Meharry Medical College, Nashville, Tenn.; Dr. Paul C. Swenson, Jefferson Hospital; Dr. Robin C. Buerki, University of Pennsylvania; and Dr. Lloyd B. Greene, Pennsylvania Hospital.[11] The presence of Johnson and Bent of the nation's two black medical schools is notable, for it underscored the importance attached by the national medical community to the hospital's growth, especially since Mercy-Douglass promised to provide increasing numbers of sorely needed internships and residencies for blacks.[12]

Even though Mercy-Douglass officials had fallen short of their goal of obtaining a strong affiliation with one of the local medical schools, they pushed forward with the committee's support in strengthening its various

167

specialty internship and residency programs. "Within the next two or three years," Dr. Minton remarked at a dinner in 1950 honoring the hospital's departing residents, "the efficiency of our intern and resident training will be second to none."[13]

At the end of the 1950 operating year, for the first time in the history of Mercy and Douglass, the merged hospital had a surplus in its operational funds. Minton attributed this fiscal success to higher daily occupancy rates, greater administrative efficiency, and increased donations from the general public. Some fifty-four organizations, eleven churches, and sixty individuals donated monies and supplies (such as food and linen). The most prominent givers included the Wayne Fellowship Guild, an interracial civic group; the Cotillion Society; the hospital's Women's Auxiliary; and the Links.[14]

In addition, by 1951 the advisory committee had been instrumental in arranging special affiliations for Mercy-Douglass residents with Children's Hospital in pediatric training, Temple and Jefferson hospitals for radiology, and the University of Pennsylvania in surgery.[15] With the new nine-story, 250-bed structure for Mercy-Douglass scheduled to be completed in 1954, the hospital's leaders pressed forward with a new optimism.[16] Heralding these events, Minton stated that a "renaissance in Negro Medicine" was unfolding in Philadelphia.[17]

While the Mercy-Douglass Hospital leaders worked at reorganizing for the changeover in facilities, some local medical institutions removed racial barriers that limited professional opportunities for blacks. In July 1950, Dr. Edward Sewell became assistant physician at the Children's Hospital, the first black physician to receive an appointment at that hospital. A 1947 graduate of the University of Pennsylvania Medical School, Sewell had been permitted to work as a special student at Children's for six months in 1947, but then completed his internship at Harlem Hospital. In 1948, he became the first black resident at Children's. Sewell considered his staff appointment important for two reasons. First, later on in his career, he was planning to train other black pediatricians. Second, Children's Hospital was a key resource for medical services for black children in the city. "The hospital treats more than 4,000 children a month," he stated, and "of the children confined to beds in the hospital, the ratio is 40 percent Negro [and] the outpatient ratio is 60 percent."[18]

In that same year, Dr. William C. Foster, an instructor in psychology, was the only practicing black member of the teaching staff at Hahnemann

Hospital. Foster, along with two of his colleagues (Horst A. Agerty and Ronald M. Bernadin), did an extensive study of lead poisoning in the black community. Examining children both at the hospital and in their homes, they found that this ailment afflicted black children at a ratio of eight to three in comparison to whites.[19]

But despite these gains, widespread racial inequities in medical hiring and hospitalization persisted throughout the city. In general, prior to 1950, legal actions and government directives to integrate medical facilities were only sporadic.[20] However, in Philadelphia, as in other nearby regions, the early 1950s marked the turning point when discrimination in hospitals and other medical institutions would come under greater public scrutiny.[21]

Civil Rights Organizations and Initiatives Against Hospital Discrimination

Civil rights groups in Philadelphia were stirred into action in particular by discriminatory incidents at Presbyterian Hospital. During October 1952, several blacks complained of the harsh treatment black patients received at this hospital. Charles Shorter, still the executive director of the Philadelphia N A A C P, received a letter from Alphonso A. Woods, a black man, about his bad experiences at Presbyterian. Writing from his ward bed at Philadelphia General, Woods wrote in part:

Dear Sir:
Indeed it gives me a very great pleasure to inform you of myself. I am the young man that called you . . . stating the fact that I was being discharged from Presbyterian Hospital and I was still sick. . . . I came here in a cab. I almost passed out vomiting blood and having bloody stools just as I had when I left the hospital. I told the doctor at the Presbyterian Hospital that I was too sick to be discharged. I have been here since then a very sick man.
It is a shame for them to treat a person like that. I am leaving it up to you because I informed you of this inhuman act.
I remain sincerely
Alphonso A. Woods[22]

169

In October, Ralph White and Rev. George Ellison, a black minister, also complained to the NAACP about the treatment White had received at this hospital several months earlier.[23] And on November 7, 1952, one of the officers of the Methodist Church Board of Lay Activities for the Philadelphia District, Alphonso W. Shockley, wrote Shorter that Mrs. Sadie Dickerson, a former YWCA Interracial Branch president, wanted to know "why the Philadelphia Branch NAACP does not do something about the deplorable conditions (Racially) at the Presbyterian Hospital?"[24]

On November 12, 1952, Shorter referred the Presbyterian Hospital matter to Dr. Carleton C. Richards, the chairman of the Philadelphia NAACP's newly initiated Branch Health Committee.[25] Also on this committee were Drs. Hinkson and Bacchus, both of whom had fought a few years earlier along with Shorter for integrated internships at Philadelphia General, as well as Drs. Daniel B. Taylor, chief of medical affairs at Mercy-Douglass, Edward E. Holloway, chief of internal medicine at Mercy-Douglass, and Daniel A. Wilson, a surgeon.[26]

The NAACP's branch health committees operated under the rubric of its National Health Committee. This national body included representatives of all the health professions, as well as lay health experts. The local committees carried out the Association's anti-discrimination activities aimed at hospitals, government health programs, and other medical services.[27] The branch health committees were not formally operative until April 1953. Thus, although the Philadelphia NAACP pursued the legal aspects of these incidents (apparently by supporting civil suits by the patients), Richards and the Association's health committee did not collectively review the Presbyterian Hospital issues until its first meeting on April 16 of that year. Also considered at this meeting was another discrimination controversy involving the Jefferson Medical College and another black man, Alfred Heath.[28] Shortly after the meeting, Dr. W. Montague Cobb, the chairman of the National Health Committee, was apprised of the hospital discrimination problems existing in Philadelphia. He advised Richards to send him a summary of the specific problems so that he could present them before the Association's national convention at St. Louis in June.[29]

While the Philadelphia NAACP was involved in patient maltreatment cases, other civil rights developments were occurring in the city affecting hospital and medical school discrimination. Beginning in 1951, the Democratic Party administration of Philadelphia became especially active in hiring blacks for municipal jobs. After World War II, black wards were voting heavily for the Democratic party. Thus, in 1951, when the administration established a new city charter, it contained several provisions assuring equal rights for all citizens in the entire range of municipal government and services.[30]

Clearly spelled out within these provisions was the responsibility of the board of trustees of Philadelphia General Hospital to enforce non-discriminatory policies in the hospital's operations and personnel procedures for its more than 2,000 employees.[31] In 1952 and early 1953, the city's five medical schools and one graduate medical school were jointly laying groundwork for closer, full-scale affiliations with this hospital.[32] Yet, in view of the new city charter, the board of Philadelphia General insisted that the schools agree to build equal opportunity conditions into their affiliation plan. In addition to the new charter, this action had no doubt been influenced by the activities a few years earlier of Shorter, Russell Minton, and other black physicians who had challenged the all-white intern tradition at Philadelphia General.

The official affiliation proposal by the committee of deans from the six medical schools was completed on March 23, 1953. The Philadelphia General board of trustees required that the following comprehensive anti-discrimination section be inserted:

> In any relationship with any of the Medical Schools of the area, it should be clear that the several Medical Schools involved must demonstrate in their procedures and practices in the selection and upgrading of the staffs of the schools involved, that there are no discriminatory practices against people because of race, color, religion or national origin that will now or hereafter affect the employment, upgrading or conditions of work of any qualified man or woman in the various professional or non-professional activities of the Philadelphia General Hospital.[33]

The board also invited assistance from the Philadelphia Commission on Human Relations on this matter. This too indicated the seriousness of the board's intentions to have its affiliated medical institutions implement a fully equal placement policy.

The city's Commission on Human Relations served as the local office of the federal Fair Employment Practices Commission. Primarily under the control of the mayor, the Commission had considerable legal leverage.[34]

Agreeing to the request for assistance, the Commission reviewed the affiliation plan of the medical schools in order to make certain that interns, residents, and staff would be fairly appointed. The Commission did this at a meeting with representatives from its own Health and Welfare Committee, the Philadelphia NAACP Medical Committee (Dr. Daniel Taylor), the Philadelphia Health and Welfare Council, the Philadelphia Fellowship Commission, Philadelphia General's executive director (Dr. August H. Groeschel), and two black medical consultants (Drs. Arthur H. Thomas and Helen O. Dickens).[35]

Besides the episode concerning the affiliation plan, other developments suggested that the new liberal political climate was opening employment and training opportunities for blacks at Philadelphia General during the early 1950s. Its nursing school now graduated a small, yet regular number of blacks. In 1953, there were among its eighty-nine nursing school graduates three black women. Given the virtually total bar against black students in the state's white nursing schools through World War II, this was an important advance.[36] This huge hospital, which had over 1,000 beds, also employed a substantial number of black non-professional employees as municipal employment became increasingly available to the city's blacks.[37]

During 1954, racial practices in Philadelphia hospitals and medical schools were once again being investigated by outside anti-discrimination groups. Not only were racial problems of individual hospitals being questioned by the city's several civil rights and fair employment agencies, but also that year an important citywide issue arose concerning employment of black medical professionals. The organization that pursued this problem was the Philadelphia chapter of the American Civil Liberties Union.

Since the new Mercy-Douglass Hospital was being constructed on the original site and involved destroying parts of the old complex, the hospital was forced to close indefinitely beginning April 1, 1954. This action greatly disturbed many in the Philadelphia black community because they feared their hospital was in jeopardy.[38] In anticipation of the unemployment that this measure would force on the hospital's staff, the Mercy-Douglass administration asked a number of the city's predominantly white hospitals to take on its unemployed personnel temporarily. Prior to the request by Mercy-Douglass, many of these hospitals had complained publicly of professional personnel shortages. The pressure to move forward on integrating professional staff was now incumbent on the city's white hospitals.[39] Most of these hospitals did not honor Mercy-Douglass's request. However,

172

a few of the white hospitals did make temporary commitments to use Mercy-Douglass employees. For example, Philadelphia General and the Episcopal Hospital agreed to take the junior and senior classes of Mercy-Douglas's nursing school.[40]

At the same time that Mercy-Douglass personnel were pursuing these jobs—jobs never before attained by blacks at most Philadelphia hospitals— more complaints of abuse of black patients were being filed with the ACLU office. These grievances were examined by the ACLU's Committee on Equality, an interracial group of representatives from other civil rights organizations and ACLU staff.[41]

The numerous discrimination complaints and the Mercy-Douglass staff displacement situation served to indicate to the ACLU a larger racial problem in the city's hospitals. Consequently, in June 1954, the ACLU conducted a citywide survey in all areas of hospital activities. The survey was originally aimed at uncovering racially motivated malpractice that might merit legal action. Due to the particularly wide range of racial issues under question, however, it was enlarged to cover general employment and admission practices with respect to blacks.[42]

Several hospitals did not cooperate with the ACLU in its study. Even so, when the results were in, discriminatory practices against both black medical practitioners and black patients were found to be widespread. The forty-one hospitals that responded to the survey employed a total of 5,035 physicians, only 29 (.6 percent) of whom were blacks. Among these hospitals' 733 residents, only 14 (1.9 percent) were blacks; and there were merely three blacks among their 322 interns. Of the 2,505 graduate nurses employed at the hospitals surveyed there were 155 blacks (6.2 percent). Mercy-Douglass Hospital employed the bulk of these black medical professionals with the exception of the black nurses. Thus, black medical professionals were severely underrepresented in Philadelphia's predominantly white hospitals. Moreover, black and white in-patients of several of the hospitals were frequently separated.[43]

Although neither the NAACP nor the ACLU undertook large-scale class action suits against hospitals in the city for racial discrimination, their investigative activities had an important collective impact. Since hospital administrators feared the legal clout of these organizations, these investigations put the hospitals on the defensive with respect to their racial policies. Between 1953 and 1956, the number of predominantly white hospitals employing or educating black doctors and nurses seems to have

173

reached a historic high. Evidently, more white hospitals, as well as medical and nursing schools, were taking in a few blacks for the first time ever. For instance, while there were only about one dozen black residents in the city in 1956, they were distributed throughout nine hospitals.[44]

The gains that blacks made were small in the higher or skilled levels of non-professional employment, such as x-ray technicians, dietitians, and physical therapists. Yet these improvements were valuable symbolic victories in the eyes of the city's liberals. For instance, in 1953, the Armstrong Association (Urban League) of Philadelphia successfully arranged the hiring of a black assistant dietitian by Presbyterian Hospital. The Association had located and referred this candidate and considered its actions one of the year's most noteworthy achievements in the area of employment.[45] The ACLU also expressed limited optimism. While it had uncovered widescale racial discrimination in the city's medical establishment between 1954 and 1956, the ACLU still held that medical opportunities for blacks had developed.[46]

At the city's medical schools, there were more blacks attending in the 1955–1956 academic year than at any other time since World War I. Hahnemann Medical School had no black students in 1938, but had five in 1955. Jefferson also had no blacks in 1938, but two in 1955. Black enrollment over the same period also increased at the University of Pennsylvania Medical School from one to three, at Temple University Medical School from one to five, and at Woman's Medical College from one to four.[47] Such increases were minute compared to each institution's total enrollment. But a new, small group of black matriculants was also appearing at other white medical schools nationwide, many of which previous to the civil rights period of the 1950s had discriminatory admission policies, and, nationally, the total number of black medical students educated at predominantly white as opposed to black medical schools increased significantly from 21.2 percent in 1950 to 29.1 percent in 1955.[48]

A similar trend was evident in the attendance of blacks in the city and state nursing schools. A greater number of these institutions had taken their first few black candidates during the early 1950s than during any other time in their history. The average number of black students at each of Philadelphia's eleven nursing schools in 1954 was six. This meant that each of the three classes for these institutions (i.e., first-year, second-year, and third-year students) had one or two blacks admitted among them.[49]

The New Supply of Black Physicians

As mentioned earlier, the gains that blacks had made during the early and mid-1950s in professional employment throughout Philadelphia's predominantly white hospitals, as well as in admissions to the city's medical and nursing schools, were considered of great moral and future significance. Blacks and whites both in and outside of the Philadelphia medical professions anticipated wider and more equitable opportunities for blacks in the city's medical establishment.[50] However, the decline and stagnation in Philadelphia's supply of black medical professionals that ocurred in the 1930s and 1940s had been great, while the population of the city's black community had soared over these years. Thus, at bottom, the accomplishments for blacks in Philadelphia medicine occurring roughly between 1950 and 1958 were of small consequence in reversing earlier trends. This fact is pointed out by a more detailed profile of the actual quantity of black medical professionals and students in the city.

Data on Philadelphia's black physicians for 1956—the year integration gains in the city during the 1950s apparently peaked—reveal that the overall historic shortage was not being reduced but was intensifying. In 1956, there were 142 black physicians in the city. This comprised only 4 percent of the city's 3,576 physicians and was a drop of 25 from the 167 recorded in 1950.[51] Philadelphia ranked fifth in the number of black doctors when compared with thirteen other large American cities, after New York (305), Chicago (226), Washington (224), and Detroit (160).[52]

Philadelphia's ratio of black physicians to black population was one of the worst among the nation's major cities. This ratio is a crude measure of the physicians who flowed out of or, once trained, back into the city's black community. According to Table 24, Philadelphia ranked eleventh among fourteen major cities in the number of black physicians available to the local black population. The city's 1956 ratio of one black physician to every 3,211 blacks was worse than the 1950 level, which was about 1 to 2,285.[53] In fact, the 1956 ratio was the worst the city had experienced in any previous period of the twentieth century.

Not only was the number of Philadelphia black physicians exceedingly small, but their ages and types of practices also indicated that they were a stagnant sector in the city's physician community. In 1956, thirty-three,

TABLE 24
Physician/Population Ratios in Selected Cities, by Race, 1956

City	White*	Black†	Rank†
Nashville	1:279	1:1,235	1
Washington	1:294	1:1,674	2
Kansas City	1:699	1:1,694	3
St. Louis	1:419	1:2,012	4
Los Angeles	1:656	1:2,104	5
Boston	1:355	1:2,108	6
Detroit	1:755	1:2,111	7
Indianapolis	1:486	1:2,571	8
New York	1:480	1:2,754	9
Chicago	1:587	1:3,123	10
Philadelphia	1:496	1:3,211	11
Gary	1:11,018	1:3,587	12
Atlanta	1:469	1:4,530	13
New Orleans	1:446	1:6,429	14

*Ratio of white physicians to white population.
†Ratio of black physicians to black population.
SOURCE: Dietrich C. Reitzes, *Negroes and Medicine* (Cambridge, Mass.: Harvard University Press, 1958), p. 389.

or 23.2 percent, of the city's black physicians were under forty years of age; thirty-six, or 25.3 percent, were between the ages of forty and forty-nine; thirty-two, or 22.5 percent, were between fifty and fifty-nine; and forty-one, or 28.9 percent, were over sixty. Thus, more than three-quarters of Philadelphia's black doctors were over forty years old, and more than half were over fifty. Although black physicians in Philadelphia were significantly older than white physicians in 1938 as well, the proportions were not as extreme: 60 percent of the black physicians in the city were below the age of fifty in 1938 as compared to 48.6 percent in 1956.[54] Not only was a growing body of newly trained black physicians not emerging in the city, the tradition in which the black hospitals and lay community had to rely upon only a certain core group of older black physicians year after year was increasing.

176

The majority of the city's black physicians had specialized fields of practice. Consequently, since there was such a minute number of black physicians in Philadelphia, the number of black GP's available to the wider community in 1956 was much worse than the 1 to 3,211 ratio figure indicated. Of the 142 black physicians, only sixty-six, or 46.5 percent, were general practitioners. This placed Philadelphia last among the fourteen cities in percentage of GP's among its total number of black physicians.[55]

This high percentage of specialists among Philadelphia's black physicians in 1956 could be interpreted as an indication that they were as a whole a professionally advanced group. Yet a closer assessment of the relative size and age of the specialist group does not confirm this view. Only seventeen of the seventy-six black specialists were board-certified. This number represents only 1.2 percent of the total number of board-certified specialists in the city (1,392). The average percentage of black certified specialists in the thirteen other cities was 1.5 percent. Moreover, Philadelphia's black certified specialists comprised only 12 percent of the city's black physicians—far below the percentage of such specialists in the city's white physician population; the 1,375 white board-certified physicians made up 48 percent of all the white physicians in Philadelphia.[56]

The age distribution of the black board-certified specialists demonstrate further that the city's black physician supply was essentially static and considerably aged. Only one in every four of Philadelphia's black certified specialists was under the age of forty. Indeed, the city had the lowest percentage of black specialists under age forty of the nation's other thirteen major cities.[57] If in 1956 Philadelphia's black specialists had been on the whole a younger group, this would indicate a more rapid integration of blacks into the most modern, specialized levels of medicine. But, as it stood, specialization was coming to black physicians only after two or perhaps three decades of preparation for certification.

A comparison of the black and white enrollments at the city's medical schools, as well as the educational origins of Philadelphia's black doctors during 1956, also indicates that a substantially large group of new black physicians was not being trained.[58] Although black student enrollment was up at Philadelphia's five medical schools in comparison to earlier decades, these students still comprised a minute proportion of the student bodies. Only nineteen, or 0.8 percent, of a total of 2,246 medical students in the city were black. Hahnemann's five black students were only 1.25

percent of its total enrollment of 399; Temple's five blacks were only 1.02 percent of its 488 students; Woman's Medical College's four blacks were only 2.2 percent of its 182 students; Pennsylvania's three blacks were only 0.6 percent of its 500 students; and Jefferson's two blacks were only 0.3 percent of its 677 students. Compared to the percentages of black enrollment at forty-three other predominantly white medical schools in the nation, Pennsylvania and Jefferson ranked near the bottom while the other three Philadelphia medical schools ranked about the middle range.[59] The small proportion of black students in the city's medical schools actually dropped in the closing years of the decade. At the Woman's Medical College, for instance, six blacks had graduated between the years of 1952 and 1956, yet only three did so in the subsequent four years.[60]

Since the physicians graduating from Philadelphia medical schools tended to form the great majority of the physicians for the city, small black enrollments precluded the development of a larger local supply of black physicians. Moreover, the tendency for the nation's black medical schools to provide the bulk of Philadelphia's black physicians also seemed to be growing through the mid-1950s.[61] Of the 167 black physicians in Philadelphia in 1950, 109 were products of the two black medical schools (Howard and Meharry), and 58 were graduates of predominantly white schools.[62] In 1956, the number of black physicians graduating from black medical schools stood at 107, while those from predominantly white schools had dropped to 35. Thus, while 65.3 percent of the city's black physicians of 1950 were black medical school graduates, this number increased to 75.4 percent in 1956.[63]

The lack of larger numbers of black graduates from Philadelphia medical schools left the city's hospitals with very few black candidates to draw upon for internship or residency positions. Like other Northern hospitals, Philadelphia's hospitals were exhibiting a rapidly growing admission rate for black patients, yet, in contrast, there was a negligible number of black residents and other professional staff at these same hospitals.[64] Moreover, Philadelphia's predominantly white hospitals tended to offer affiliations to those black physicians who had completed residency training at predominantly white hospitals. Since most of the city and nation's black physicians had to depend on black hospitals for residencies, only a few black physicians gained residencies in the city's predominantly white hospitals. In 1956, of the twenty black doctors with residency training completed at white hospitals, sixteen (or 80 percent) attained affiliations at predominantly

178

white hospitals. By contrast, ten of thirty-one black doctors (or 32 percent) with residency backgrounds at black hospitals had affiliations at predominantly white hospitals.[65]

Blacks in the Allied Health Occupations: Growth and Friction

The status of blacks in professional positions in Philadelphia's medical establishment was, then, changing profoundly throughout the 1950s, even though quantitatively the growth was limited. However, blacks were being absorbed much more rapidly into the technical and non-professional health occupations. The expansion of America's hospitals begun in the 1930s had become even more rapid in the 1950s. The personnel shortages of hospitals had become so great during this decade that these institutions absorbed the largest quantities of black allied health workers in their history.

The personnel demands of hospitals picked up tremendous momentum during the 1950s, as the number of middle-class Americans receiving medical treatment within the hospital expanded.[66] The volume of annual admissions in the nation's hospitals, for instance, was substantially higher in 1957 than in 1951—22,993,000 and 18,783,000 for these two years respectively. Over the same period, beds used for long-term (i.e., months of in-patient care) and short-term hospital services increased nationwide from 62,766 to 77,608 for the former and from 1,521,959 to 1,558,691 for the latter.[67] This increase in both long-term and short-term forms of hospitalization necessitated more technical and non-professional hospital personnel. Furthermore, the nature of medical treatment in the 1950s required more medical instruments, medications, and laboratory tests, as well as greater use of operation, maternity, and bed quarters.[68] In addition to care for the patients, these rooms and equipment had to be rapidly and repeatedly sterilized to avoid the spread of infections among patients and personnel.[69]

With the multiplication of personnel and equipment needs during the 1950s, hospitals employed an even larger number of and more specialized employees. Short-term hospitals, in particular, were characterized by rapid patient turnover and thus placed greatest burdens on x-ray, laboratory, nurse support, dietary, maintenance, and clerical personnel. Whereas in

1946 the average non-profit, short-term hospital used about 156 medical workers for every 100 patients, in 1958 the same number of patients required 213 workers. The greater financial resources allocated by the state to Philadelphia hospitals during the 1950s is a measure of the expanded personnel and operations of these institutions. On the average, about 60–70 percent of hospital finances in the late 1950s went to cover payroll expenses.[70]

Not only were Philadelphia's hospitals enlarging services for the middle-income population, but they were also under pressure to treat the substantial numbers of the poor. Most sizable among the city's working poor were the black newcomers from the South. Unable to afford expensive private, fee-for-service care, they invariably sought care in the hospital clinics and emergency rooms.[71] By the late 1950s, a general economic crisis was gripping Philadelphia hospitals. According to an official report released in 1959 by the Philadelphia Community Policy Committee on Health and Hospital Services, many hospitals were overrun by needy persons brought in "at death's door by reason of strokes, heart attacks, automobile accidents, fires, or other catastrophes." Since the poverty-stricken usually experienced the worst illnesses, they were draining these hospitals of much of their resources. The Committee warned the public that "constantly rising costs of personnel, equipment, and supplies, coupled with increasing demands for hospital services, are steadily worsening the hospitals' financial problems."[72]

Under economic, social, and health care pressures such as these, blacks were increasingly hired by Philadelphia's hospitals for jobs throughout the entire range of technical and non-professional services. These employees included licensed practical nurses (LPN's), nurses' aides, orderlies, attendants, and dietary workers. Blacks were also attaining employment, although less frequently, as registered nurses, a "lower" professional job, as well as x-ray technicians and dietitians, skilled non-professional jobs.

The trend that first emerged in the late 1930s and 1940s in which former domestic workers frequently became hospital employees grew throughout the 1950s. A typical experience was that of Mrs. V. T., a black woman who came to Philadelphia from Columbia, South Carolina, during the 1930s in search of work. Mrs. T. became a domestic worker for a family in an upper-class section of the West Oak Lane area of the city. During World War II, she took intermittent jobs in factories, but domestic service remained her primary field of employment. In the early 1950s, Mrs. T.

180

managed to attend the Philadelphia School for Practical Nurses, a private vocational school, although at this time the school catered in general to white suburban students. After receiving her LPN training in 1954, Mrs. T. worked at the Jeanes, Methodist, and Frankford hospitals, all located in Philadelphia, for about a year each. She finally found stable employment in 1956 at Temple University Hospital, where she would work for the next twenty-two years until her retirement. Even during the early 1950s, Mrs. T. recollected, blacks were highly concentrated in her job area and in other non-professional jobs at the hospitals where she had worked.[73]

By the end of the 1950s, a virtual flood of blacks into hospital employment had occurred throughout Philadelphia. The general pattern that this influx took was a continuation of the one observed during the 1940s: the higher the intellectual specialization, prestige, and earnings of a particular health care occupation, the lower the proportion of new black employees. The strengthening of this pattern was clearly manifested in the proportional changes of blacks as compared to whites in the key health care occupations from 1950 to 1960.

The health care occupations as listed in Table 25 are ranked from the highest professional (doctor or surgeon) to the lowest unskilled (attendant) occupations. Between 1950 and 1960, there were either declines or only slight growths in the percentages of blacks in the professional or skilled occupations. By contrast, black health care laborers had by 1960 become the greater portion of lower-level health care workers, while whites were entering these non-professional fields at a decreasing pace. For example, in 1960 blacks comprised about 52 percent of the city's hospital attendants and 45 percent of its practical nurses. The large proportion of black hospital employees in the lowest-paying, less prestigious, and most physically demanding jobs indicates the disadvantaged background of most black applicants for hospital employment. The labor pool from which hospital administrators drew the non-professional employees were, as we have observed, largely the Southern-born blacks who settled in Philadelphia without skills and whose work experiences were limited to the domestic or personal services fields.

The increased massing of blacks in the lowest levels of hospital employment also reveals the discrimination and lack of mobility that these black workers faced once in hospital work. Local civil rights groups and some of these employees themselves became aggravated over prejudicial hiring, training, work assignment, promotion and dismissal practices, which

TABLE 25
Philadelphia Health Care Employment, by Race, 1950 and 1960

	1950		1960	
Position	White (%)	Black (%)*	White (%)	Black (%)
Physician	97.39	2.61	97.55	2.45
Dentist	96.25	3.75	96.06	3.94
Pharmacist	97.35	2.65	96.95	3.05
Professional nurse	95.26	4.74	88.66	11.34
Student Nurse†	98.68	1.32	97.71	2.29
Medical/Dental Technician	93.48	6.52	85.88	14.12
Dietician/Nutritionist	86.55	13.45	68.13	31.87
Practical Nurse‡	78.15	21.85	54.84	45.16
Hospital Attendant	61.84	38.16	48.09	51.91

†Upper-class nursing students employed in hospitals as part of their nurses' training.
‡Includes a minute proportion of midwives (less than 1 percent).
*Includes a minute proportion (about 1 percent) of other nonwhites.
SOURCES: U.S. Department of Commerce, Bureau of the Census, *Seventeenth Census of the United States: 1950* (Washington, D.C.: GPO, 1952), vol. 2: *Characteristics of the Population,* pt. 38: *Pennsylvania,* pp. 397–399, and *Eighteenth Census of the United States: 1960* (Washington, D.C.: GPO, 1962), *Pennsylvania,* pt. 40, pp. 749–751.

they found widely prevalent throughout the city's hospitals. Between 1955 and 1959, formal complaints against hospitals for racial discrimination in their employment policies were continuously received by the Philadelphia Human Relations Commission. One of the Commission's primary duties was to investigate racial discrimination in employment at such establishments as real estate offices, educational institutions, manufacturing plants, and labor organizations. From 1955 to 1959, the Commission pursued nine cases alleging unlawful discrimination in employment on the part of hospitals.[74] This was small percentage (about 3 percent annually) of the Commission's total employment discrimination caseload for this five-year period. But, it should be remembered that at this time discrimination in hospitals was still a relatively new field for investigators of civil rights and labor agencies. Unfair racial practices at hospitals were quite difficult and expensive for outside lay parties to investigate effectively.

Several factors tended to make investigations of discrimination in hospital employee relations cumbersome. The physician's traditional, almost absolute authority within the medical setting over subordinate personnel such as nurses, LPN's, aides, and technicians could rarely be challenged or even complained about by these personnel without fear of reprimand or dismissal by hospital authorities.[75] Second, the researchers of the Human Relations Commission pointed out that it was difficult for lay investigators to find legal infractions in apparently racially prejudiced decisions or behavior of hospital administrators. When queried about alleged discrimination these administrators invariably described their actions as being in line with the medical standards set by their institution's medical staff and licensing bodies.[76] Since agencies like the Commission that monitored civil rights did not have medical or hospital administration experts on their staffs, it was not often possible to refute these defenses.[77] Lastly, the general public tended to ascribe more autonomy and self-regulation to the medical profession and hospitals than other professions or service establishments, such as those related to government, business, or education. Since they presumed that the medical profession required special expertise, Americans usually depended on the internal sanction power of those within the medical profession to protect the public's interest, be they the interests of hospital personnel or patients.[78] The murky waters that the Human Relations Commission sank into when investigating discrimination in hospital employment frequently caused them to categorize any complaints relating to hospital employment as "cases of discrimination not covered by law."[79]

The Commission repeatedly pointed out that, because of their limited administrative and investigative resources, they pursued but a fraction of the valid complaints of racial discrimination against blacks that they received or were aware existed.[80] And many incidents were never reported at all. At one university hospital in the city, for example, a black LPN with a number of years of experience was given verbal directives by a supervising nurse on treatment to be administered to patients (e.g., washings or rest periods). However, later a white physician would criticize the LPN in a racially derogatory manner for carrying out the directives, claiming that they had never been originally given. This situation caused the LPN severe mental anguish and yet she never complained for fear of losing her job. At the same hospital a young black attendant was fired after being seen chewing a piece of toast while leaving a room to push a food cart down a corridor. One of the hospital's regulations prohibited employees from eating during rounds (i.e., when servicing patients in a particular section), but since the attendant was a young, not necessarily experienced worker, black employees felt that an initial reprimand would have been more appropriate and that the firing had been motivated by racial prejudice.[81]

The work conditions and assignments of black allied health employees were at times unequal, yet frequently undetected by the Human Relations Commission. Mrs. V. T. recalled that, when she went to work at Jeanes Hospital as an LPN in the 1950s, she discovered her fellow black employees had to eat in a separate cafeteria: "When I [first] went down to the dining room there . . . I was shocked! I didn't know they had segregated dining rooms. . . . I had never seen that. They had a dining room for the blacks and a dining room for the whites. From then on I didn't go back there [to eat] anymore." At this same institution, black employees usually had to perform the hardest work. Mrs. T. recollected that "there wasn't too many black workers there and those that were there were doing the hardest work; the RN's [registered nurses] sat behind the desks and pushed pills." Since the hospital had hired very few male orderlies, such tasks as the lifting of disabled patients and the adjusting of heavy beds were handled by one or two female LPN's.[82]

These kinds of complaints continued throughout the 1950s as civil rights activism concurrently increased. By 1959, the State Advisory Committee for Pennsylvania of the United States Commission on Civil Rights found that degrees of discrimination varied for individual medical institutions, but it particulary singled out the unfair practices toward black physicians, such as not allowing them equal access to hospital employment or use of facilities. The Committee criticized such practices especially since all Pennsylvania hospitals, even those labeled "private," received substantial state funds.[83]

Overall, the most significant developments of the 1950s in Philadelphia's medical establishment were a new willingness to admit blacks into local medical schools and an unprecedented integration of their numbers into both professional and non-professional health care employment throughout the city. But, although this had been a decade in which barriers of traditional segregation in Philadelphia medicine were jarred open, many conditions preventing a more equal assimilation of blacks still prevailed. The rate of admissions of blacks into Philadelphia medical schools crested in

1956 and trailed off to less than one percent by the 1959–1960 academic year. Since discrimination in medical school admissions was at this time known to have affected certain white ethnic groups, some welfare groups felt that blacks had suffered only the same degree of discrimination as had such white minority groups.[84] After investigation, however, medical school enrollments of Jewish and Italian American students were found to be much higher than those of blacks. In 1959, Jewish American students comprised about 19 percent of the students at Philadelphia's five medical schools, and Italian Americans represented 8 percent.[85]

The traditional barriers in the professional fields that kept blacks from receiving internships, residencies, and hospital staff appointments did not drop all at once. Instead, one by one individual facilities had opened their doors to one or two blacks. More of such openings had occurred in the 1950s, particularly around 1956, than in any previous period in the city's medical history. Prior to 1950, with the exception of Philadelphia General, not one white hospital in the city had admitted a black intern or resident. However, between 1950 and 1958, fourteen white hospitals in the city admitted their first black resident.[86]

Despite these victories, however, black physicians of Philadelphia at the close of the 1950s were a disparate and thinly spread group of mostly aging specialists. Of the black physicians and professionals who had led the challenge against discrimination in the city's medical profession or sustained the black hospitals and medical associations, a number had either retired or passed away. F.D. Stubbs died in 1947 at the age of forty-one and Virginia Alexander two years later at forty-nine. Judge Millen died in 1956, John P. Turner died in 1958, and DeHaven Hinkson retired in 1958.

The young black physicians coming to Philadelphia in the late 1950s opted for the new training and employment positions opening up at the far more prestigious and sturdier white medical institutions. As the older generation of black medical professionals became decimated, so did the usefulness and vitality of the Philadelphia Academy of Medicine and the Jackson Dental Society. The strong sense of community and self-reliance characteristic of the city's black medical professionals prior to the end of World War II had all but disappeared. Now the lone hope of the black medical professionals in the city who felt black-controlled medical institutions were both necessary and possible, centered on the new Mercy-

Douglass Hospital. And Mercy-Douglass—no longer the only avenue for internships for blacks, still groping for an affiliation with a city medical school, and lacking the strong voices of physicians like Mossell, the Mintons, and J. P. Turner—faced another critical period in 1959.[87]

While the gains that blacks had made in the medical professions and educational institutions generally attracted more attention from Philadelphia's civil rights agencies, press, and liberal politicians,[88] the most momentous change in race relations within the health care establishment was the massive growth of blacks in the ranks of technical and non-professional health care employment. Although in the 1950s there had been a tapering off in the integration of blacks into the city's professional health care fields, the opposite was true of the technical and non-professional health care occupations. With integration now at hand on all fronts in the medical profession and allied health occupations, both the city's traditional black medical community as well as the larger medical establishment faced an unprecedented period of self-criticism and changes in race relations.

186

CHAPTER VIII

The Integration of Philadelphia Medicine

During the Eisenhower and Kennedy years, as civil rights protests rippled across the country, the issue of equality for blacks became a priority for the nation's politicians, the Supreme Court, and the mass media.[1] Three local developments that grew out of this nationwide momentum toward integration finally brought an end to Philadelphia's racially dualistic medical community. First, the cohesiveness of the black medical professional community based around Mercy-Douglass Hospital and their medical associations eroded. Second, the integration of a diverse range of black physicians and other medical professionals, technicians and allied health employees into predominantly white-staffed hospitals in the city accelerated to an unprecedented level. Third, local and federal government agencies became increasingly forceful in the movement against racial discrimination in medical training programs and hospital employment. The Hill-Burton Hospital Construction Act of 1946 had triggered a flood of government funds into privately controlled hospitals, clinics, and medical schools for construction and reimbursement for services. The growing dependence of these health centers on such funds made these institutions "public" in the eyes of the federal judiciary and of agencies charged with administering employee rights and health and welfare expenditures. Hence, a proliferation of governmental standards, investigative bodies, and judicial remedies whittled away at barriers that had traditionally impeded the free flow of black medical personnel and patients into the hospitals of Philadelphia and similar cities.[2] As these

187

developments both within and outside of Philadelphia's black and white medical communities took hold in the late 1950s and early 1960s, a new integrated medical community came into being.

The Failure of the Black Medical Renaissance

Although Philadelphia's black leaders in medicine had in the early 1950s envisioned a renaissance for black medicine in the city centered at Mercy-Douglass Hospital, several developments undermined their hopes. Chief among these obstacles was an inability to upgrade its educational resources to a level of quality that would attract an affiliation with a local medical school. Also, the hospital was hindered by burgeoning local and national competition for candidates for postgraduate programs, as well as a financial crisis that intensified after its new building opened in 1956.

The staff at Mercy-Douglass was still of high quality: in 1957, its ninety physicians included fifteen black doctors and five white doctors who were diplomats of American boards.[3] But the institution was still not competitive with other area hospitals. In the mid-1950s, Mercy-Douglass officials decided that the medical advisory committee composed of educators from a variety of Philadelphia hospitals and medical schools was inadequate for the hospital's daily operations and educational program. As a result, Mercy-Douglass officials began negotiating for a formal affiliation with the University of Pennsylvania Medical School because of its close proximity. During the negotiations, the hospitals leader stated their institution's fundamental goals for future development:

(1) Professional development of the Negro physician;
(2) Professional interracial contact between white and black medical professionals;
(3) A training facility for our nurses;
(4) A training facility at the post-graduate level for our Negro medical graduates;
(5) To enhance medical service to the needy sick.

As a result of the negotiations, Mercy-Douglass did get assurance of support by the medical school, but not a formal tie between the boards or administrative heads of the institutions. The resolution between the medical school and the hospital that was finalized during the 1954–1955 academic year emphasized instead that both parties "recognized that there was to be no organic affiliation, but a close association extremely helpful to Mercy-Douglass." An advisory group of faculty and administrators from the medical school was established that would periodically make suggestions to the Mercy-Douglass board on ways to improve the hospital's intern-resident program. In addition, interns, residents, and staff of Mercy-Douglass could attend staff and teaching conferences at the medical school.[4]

Russell Minton interpreted this advisory relationship with cautious enthusiasm. "So, 60 years after Dr. Mossell, the first Negro graduate of the University of Pennsylvania Medical School, put into being our institution . . . to provide [an interracial and technically superior] hospital . . . we today stand at a threshold where we will be tested to see whether or not we can perpetuate these philosophies." He stated that medicine was an "ever and rapidly advancing practice" whose "problems are more complex and demanding today than 60 years ago." For Minton, chief among these new problems was the competition to achieve higher levels of scientific expertise in hospital and medical affairs.[5]

To Minton's dismay, the failure of Mercy-Douglass to gain teaching hospital status under the auspices of one of the local medical schools seriously hurt the attractiveness of the hospital to internship and residency candidates. With a shortage of physician-trainees intensifying both locally and nationwide in the late 1950s, Mercy-Douglass officials made attempts to broaden their institution's visibility to black medical school graduates but most often lost out to the more widely recognized postgraduate programs at Philadelphia General and the non-profit teaching hospitals in the city.[6] For example, in 1958 three graduates of black medical schools selected internships in Philadelphia. James Williams (Howard) chose an internship at Philadelphia General, and John L. Agnew (Meharry) selected Albert Einstein Medical Center-Northern Division; only Lionel Wardlaw (Howard) picked Mercy-Douglass. Despite the brisk competition for black interns and residents, the hospital still tried to meet the educational needs of physicians of color by welcoming greater numbers of Asian and African medical school graduates. In 1963, Minton referred to his corps of interns as the hospital's own "League of Nations" since it included young doctors from Afghanistan, Thailand, the Philippines, British Guiana, China, Turkey, and Greece.[7]

Besides the stiff competition facing its postgraduate program, the hospital had to manage an economic crisis that was deepening with every passing year. At the Imhotep National Conference on Hospital Integration organized by the NMA, the NAACP, and the National Urban League,[8] Russell Minton explained the complexity of the problems facing black hospitals. "It is sometimes asked", he observed, "Why is there a segregated hospital in a northern city? The answer is the same as for other cities. It is because the Negro physician has been denied the privileges and opportunities afforded in other hospitals and he was hungry for training and learning." Minton and his colleagues considered the few black physicians recently brought into the city's predominantly white hospitals as isolated gestures, "rather than [signs of] any real spirit of integration":

> There are 100 hospitals in the Philadelphia area. Five of these . . . are teaching institutions. Only two of the teaching hospitals have Negroes on their staffs. By being on the staff, I mean a full staff member with all the privileges of staff membership. Among the rest of the hospitals, nine have Negroes on their staffs, but only as courtesy, in the out-patient departments.

But, though black physicians needed Mercy-Douglass, black patients did not. "We know that the majority of Negroes go to white hospitals in Philadelphia," Minton remarked. The dilemma, then, was: "Why do you need a new [Negro] hospital when 95 percent of Negro patients who need hospitalization are in white hospitals?" Minton believed that while Mercy-Douglass provided excellent opportunities for black physicians and nurses to become staff heads and clinical leaders, as well as to oversee the entire treatment of long-term hospitalized patients, the black patient community at large seemed unaware of these benefits.[9]

John Procope also spoke about this problem at Mercy-Douglass: black patients were opting for treatment at other hopitals and, thereby, causing the hospital to fall short of the minimal patient population needed to sustain its clinical, nursing, and financial resources. An administrator with many years of experience heading other black hospitals around the country prior to coming to Mercy-Douglass, Procope stated that he found "Philadelphia, although in the northern orbit, has the mores of a southern town." Because many in the black public evinced a subservient attitude on medical matters, "many of the institutions which welcome the [Negro] patient with open arms," Procope commented, "brush away the Negro physician from whom he comes."[10]

Within a few years of the 1957 Imhotep Conference, Mercy-Douglass was in dire financial straits. The expensive large physical plant of the hospital had compounded the problem of the declining inflow of patients. The new structure required much greater operating capital in comparison to the old Mercy-Douglass site. Requiring an annual budget of over $2 million, and with community gifts amounting to only about $20,000 per year, the hospital was virtually dependent on city and state appropriations and on fees from paying patrons.[11] Like the several other non-profit hospitals in the city caught in economic difficulties in 1959, Mercy-Douglass became ensnared in cycle of insolvency. Because the bulk of its patients were poor, Mercy-Douglass frequently expended a great deal of physician time, hospital personnel, and medications for which it was never paid.[12] The state of Pennsylvania provided only a ten-dollar maximum compensatory payment to the hospital for each day of care it provided to an indigent patient, while the hospital actually incurred a daily average of twenty-six dollars' worth of expenses for that care. By 1963, the hospital's yearly deficit was $150,000 and the number of its allied health employees and nurses were reduced. While Mercy-Douglass did survive the rest of the 1960s and was able to provide some superlative community health programs, it closed as a hospital enterprise by the early 1970s.[13]

Another reason why a cohesive black medical community failed to re-emerge was the decline of the Philadelphia Academy of Medicine and a concommitant increase in black membership in the Philadelphia County Medical Society during the 1950s. As we noted earlier, the Academy had functioned as a closely knit local branch of the NMA. However, physicians in the city were required by most hospitals in Philadelphia to be a member of the County Society in order to gain affiliations, and after 1950 this body openly admitted blacks. Thus, while many black physicians kept their membership in the NMA and attended the Association's annual conventions, overall paid membership declined during the fifties, as did the involvement of Philadelphia black donors as officers in the Association.[14] On the other hand, by 1962 over one-half of the city's black physicians were members of the County Society.[15]

191

A final weight against a renascent black medical community was the improving situation for black nursing students in the city. The academic, financial, and personnel problems at Mercy-Douglass, on the one hand, and the acceptance of black students by previously all-white nursing schools, on the other, resulted in the closing of Mercy-Douglass's School of Nursing in 1961.[16] This school was one of the fifteen black nursing schools that had shut down since the early 1950s.[17] Like the Mercy-Douglass nursing program, these other recently closed black nursing schools had suffered from declining enrollments. The drop was due largely to the newly integrated admissions policies of previously all-white schools and hospital nursing program, which were experiencing severe nursing shortages while simultaneously growing financially and serving greater numbers of patients.[18]

Since the Mercy-Douglass nursing school and the other declining black nursing schools were part of hospitals that were themselves institutionally frail, authorities on nursing education saw no purpose in encouraging the patching up of such programs when they could concentrate on strengthening larger, more prestigious nurse training institutions. As one former officer of the American Nurses Association, herself a Negro, stated in 1964: "I firmly believe that there is no need for all-Negro schools of nursing today. Most of the all-Negro schools are weak, and weak schools perpetuate an injustice to the student, the patient and the community."[19]

Black Medical Professionals and the New Integrated Hospital

The forces of integration were not only weakening Philadelphia's traditionally all-black medical and nursing institutions, but also broadening the distribution and career attainments of local black physicians. The quantitative supply of black doctors did not grow significantly from 1950 to the mid-1960s. But certain patterns in their hospital affiliations and specialties indicated that black doctors were by now dispersed throughout a diverse spectrum of hospital and health facilities to an extent never before reached in Philadelphia medical history. Between 1950 and 1960, the total number of black physicians in Philadelphia went from 177 (including ten women) to 193 (five women). This was 2.6 percent of the 6,809 total physicians (531 women) in the city area in 1950 and 2.4 percent of the total 7,907 (661 women) in 1960.[20] Yet, when one considers that these figures were for a metropolitan region that included Philadelphia and four other southeastern Pennsylvania counties, as well as three New Jersey counties, this overall gain of sixteen black physicians was negligible. Moreover, the number of black doctors practicing in Philadelphia proper in 1955 was 145 compared to 142 in 1956. This also indicated that the long-term results of the integration of medical schools and postgraduate physician training education that occurred in the 1950s was not wide enough to increase the general supply of black physicians in Philadelphia in proportion to the city's greatly expanded black population.[21]

However, in the area of hospital affiliations, there was a definite gain for black physicians in comparison to prior decades. During 1965, some 75 percent of black physicians had hospital affiliations. Almost all white physicians in the city (97 percent) held hospital affiliations, and , further, most of the affiliated black physicians held their primary connection with Mercy-Douglass. Nonetheless, many of the black doctors with affiliations had joint or triple affiliations with predominantly white hospitals in the city, a substantial improvement over the pre-1950s period, when affiliations for black physicians outside of Douglass and Mercy Hospitals virtually never occurred.[22]

A significant gap remained between black and white specialists, yet black physicians had sifted into a range of specialties that was far wider than opportunities available before the fifties. Of the 145 black doctors practicing in Philadelphia in 1965, approximately 50 percent were in specialty practice and about 45 percent in general practice, compared to 84 and 16 percent, respectively, for the city's white physicians. However, despite this general disparity between white and black physicians in the specialty fields, black specialists in the early 1960s had made considerable progress over previous decades. In 1925, black physicians in Philadelphia practiced in only three specialties while whites were in over one dozen, and in 1938 blacks were in only seven specialties. By 1965, blacks were represented in fifteen (compared to twenty-three for whites).[23]

Progress for blacks in other medical professions in Philadelphia generally is also considerable when measured against previous periods. From 1950 to 1960, the number of black dentists in metropolitan Philadelphia increased from 84 to 97. This slight addition was still about four times greater than the growth rate of white dentists, which went only from 2,246 to 2,318 during the 1950–1960 decade. Similarly, the black pharmacist group in the Philadelphia area expanded somewhat, from 70 in 1950 to 76 in 1960, at a time when the number of white pharmacists dropped from 2,579 to 2,492.[24]

The greatest gains for Philadelphia blacks in medical fields during the 1950s and 1960s came in nursing, technical, and paraprofessional occupations. By 1960, there were 1,670 black nurses in the city compared to 533 ten years earlier. This tripling in the number of black nurses brought their proportion of the city's entire nursing force up more than twofold— from 4.7 percent of the total 11,252 in 1950 to 10.2 percent of 16,401 in 1960.[25] The rate at which blacks were entering the technical and non-professional hospital occupations continued to remain high in comparison to those blacks advancing into the professional health fields. For instance, the proportion of blacks employed as medical and dental technicians, dietitians, LPN's, and hospital attendants increased sharply from 1960 to 1965. Over this six-year period the supply of black technicians grew 29 percent, black dietitians 5 percent, black LPN's 17 percent, and black hospital attendants 34 percent.[26]

Civil Rights and the New Push for Integration in Medicine

With black medical professionals and allied health workers becoming dispersed throughout the spectrum of hospital employment in Philadelphia, and the traditional black medical institutions no longer available to serve the city's ever-expanding black population, Philadelphia's health institutions became prime targets for both governmental and popular civil rights agitation. Local civil rights agencies were increasingly called upon by individual black health care employees seeking to overcome the unequal practices they encountered at various hospitals. During these years, the Philadelphia office of the Commission on Human Relations was pivotal in investigating complaints from blacks who either were working or sought employment at medical institiutions. Most of the cases were initiated by technicians, nurses, or assistants. In 1961, the Commission pursued two cases of alleged unlawful discrimination in employment by local medical facilities, five in 1962, and six in 1963.[27] One case in 1963 involved the refusal by a teaching hospital to hire a black dental assistant even though the applicant had apparently met all the necessary qualifications.[28] Another case was initiated that same year by a black biochemist who was terminated from employment allegedly for racial reasons by the city's Department of Public Health.[29] In 1964, the Commission supported a black nurse in overcoming racial discrimination from her supervisors at another teaching hospital, where this nurse and other workers recounted incidents of racial prejudice going back to 1960.[30] Also in 1964, a black EEG (electroencephalogram) technician pursued a hiring discrimination case against a woman's hospital,[31] and early the following year, a black man filed a complaint against still another teaching hospital after he had been denied a promotion to an x-ray technician position.[32]

To be sure, in most of its cases between 1960 and 1964, the Human Relations Commission took a moderate stance. It usually established that racial discrimination had not been the sole motive by the accused hospital and did not exercise any subpoena powers.[33] Nonetheless, the Commission did have a strong symbolic influence on Philadelphia's body politic and black public as a whole. Its activities served as "writing on the wall" to hospital administrations throughout the city. An investigation of a case by the Commission normally lasted five months and sometimes involved on-site visits and wide-scale reviews of a particular hospital's personnel practices. Such an investigation at a time when the black community's frustration with employment discrimination in the city was at a fever pitch served indirectly to pressure hospital administrators to guard against any blatant racial imbalances in their employment practices.[34]

Two other sources for pressure on Philadelphia hospitals emerged in 1964 that, in turn, forced the Commission to take a more aggressive stance against hospital employment discrimination. One such source was the intense unrest among blacks throughout the city in 1964. That year, Philadelphia became the scene of one of the most devastating race riots of the decade. During the summer, a three-day disturbance in one of the city's major black ghettos resulted in several hundred arrests and civilian injuries, as well as several scores of injured policemen.[35]

The widespread dissatisfaction among the city's black poor over police brutality and impoverished conditions spilled over into the issue of mistreatment of blacks by some hospitals located in black neighborhoods. Throughout the summer of 1964, a local university hospital was the target of complaints from community groups angry over inadequate service in the emergency room, out-patient clinics, and wards of the hospital.[36] One day that summer, black workers at the hospital also walked off their jobs in protest over the unjust firing of a black woman maintenance worker.[37]

The inability of blacks living in Philadelphia to get adequate medical care was a burning issue among black leaders. Cecil B. Moore, a prominent black lawyer and president of the Philadelphia NAACP, was particularly incensed over this issue. When asked by the *Bulletin* researchers to explain why the black infant gets fatal illnesses at more than twice the rate of white infants, Moore replied: "Add up all of the things that are wrong—rats in the house, overcrowding, no health education, unemployment, no visits to the doctor—and that's your problem."[38]

At the same time that serious racial disorders were breaking out in Philadelphia and other cities like New York, the federal government was becoming a central agent in removing racial barriers in Philadelphia medicine. Through new legislation, it was widening its control and surveillance over racial inequities throughout the nation's urban and Southern hospitals and health facilities. Most notably the Civil Rights Act of 1964 contained strong measures prohibiting discrimination in, for instance, public accommodations and public education. The measures that had the greatest impact on black employment in Philadelphia hospitals were Titles III, VI, and VIII, which effectively eliminated the "separate but equal" policy of the Hill-Burton program.[39] The first two sections required that programs receiving federal financial assistance, such as public building projects or job-training programs, could not discriminate against anyone involved because of race or national origin without engendering lawsuits by the U.S. Attorney General and/or stoppage of funds. Title VII, the section on "equal employment opportunity," forbade employers from practicing discrimination in the hiring, promotion, or termination of employees. It also established the Equal Employment Opportunity Commission (EEOC), which was empowered to investigate cases of racial discrimination and assist complainants in federal lawsuits.[40]

Thus, while officials of the Philadelphia Human Relations Commission were witnessing local racial outbreaks, they were also being contacted by the EEOC to cooperate in stepping up anti-discrimination activities in employment and public institutions throughout the city.[41] Ironically, the chairperson of the city's Human Relations Commission was at this time Sadie T. Mossell-Alexander, who as a young social scientist had conducted the important tuberculosis study among Philadelphia blacks during the

1920s.[42] Now a veteran lawyer and widely respected civic leader, Mossell-Alexander was intent upon directing the Commission to pursue all complaints of racial inequality in the city's hospitals, as well as to expose discriminatory patterns throughout the institutions.[43]

During July 1963, in one of its first official acts, the EEOC initiated an industry-wide investigation of patterns of discrimination in employment. On December 21, 1965, Mossell-Alexander and the black Philadelphia congressman Robert N. C. Nix Sr. announced that a full-scale inquiry into employment discrimination within Philadelphia hospitals was being launched by the city's Human Relations Commission in cooperation with the EEOC. They stressed that hospitals had been selected because, like any other large industry in the city, the institutions represented a vital dimension of the overall local economic and public life. Philadelphia's hospitals had an annual payroll of $75,000,000 involving 20,000 employees. Moreover, at least thirty-seven of the city's hospitals held large government contracts. Violations of fair employment laws at these institutions could thus lead to grounds for local and or federal government agencies to reduce or cancel such contracts.[44]

Nix pointed out that it had become clear to the Human Relations Commission and EEOC officials that their former dependence on individual complaints had not proved to be an effective deterrent to racial discrimination in employment at hospitals and other large industries. "The processes of discrimination have become more subtle," he stated, "and in many instances undetectable by the persons most affected." Furthermore, they had discovered that many blacks and other minority people who knew they were being discriminated against frequently would not file a complaint with the Human Relations Commission because they believed that they would, in the end, not get any return for their time and effort. Nix and Mossell-Alexander emphasized that now the EEOC and Human Relations Commission would seek new data from which the EEOC could formulate tighter federal controls on hospital employment practices. Mossell-Alexander described the hospital project as "part of our unrelenting action to bring about true equality for all citizens of Philadelphia without distinctions based on their race, color, religion or national origin."[45]

The EEOC investigation conducted in 1965 and 1966 found that the status of practicing black physicians in Philadelphia was limited by racial discrimination. Practices on the part of hospital department heads, medical committees, governing boards, and influential funding resources were de-

197

nying black doctors opportunities for residents and staff privileges "primarily on the basis of race." The study found that blacks comprised only 2.7 percent of the city's 5,405 physicians and, even more disturbing, only 1.1 percent of all staff physician positions.[46] Throughout 1965 and early 1966, no fewer than eighteen Philadelphia hospitals had been approached by the Human Relations Commission about complaints over personnel discrimination. In addition, four hospitals in the city had been called to task for similar reasons by either the Congress of Racial Equality (CORE), the NAACP, the Urban League, or a black neighborhood group.[47]

The 1965 EEOC investigation signaled the end of the initial stage in the integration of Philadelphia medical life. The aggressive advocacy throughout the duration of the 1960s and 1970s toward inclusion of qualified blacks and other minorities in Philadelphia medical institutions by both government and citizens' groups, as well as by progressive hospital and medical school administrators, was in marked contrast to the early decades of the twentieth century. The century had begun with racially separate medical communities only weakly linked by a common, albeit selfish, interest in stemming epidemics in the black and white communities. However, as the century wore on, the small number of medical activists, like Mossell, Henry Minton, Landis, and Virginia Alexander, who challenged the racial division in the city's medical life, were joined by politicians, government agencies, and civil rights groups. The city's twentieth-century philanthropic and neighborhood-based health care institutions, themselves reflecting the racial barriers of larger urban social life, had given way to government regulation and third-party financing of health services, as well as the new mass hospital. These modern hospitals, like their industrial counterparts in manufacturing, welcomed labor regardless of color even though they opened only certain occupations to blacks.

Throughout the first four decades of the twentieth century, the experience of blacks in the medical institutions of Philadelphia was determined more by the general racial patterns carved deeply into the social, residential, and economic institutions of the city than by developments from within the formal medical establishment. Neither black lay populations nor black medical practitioners were allowed a substantial role in the major medical institutions of the city. Indeed, the city's leaders in medicine and public health strove to bend their institutions to reflect the racial segregation common to the neighborhood and work life of the larger city. By the 1920s and 1930s, when the phrase "disease knows no color line" became a common slogan for public health authorities and black health activists, the city's public health and medical leaders became preoccupied with containing the diseases that were striking down most rapidly the black poor. True, the ethnic character of the city's essential medical institutions—its hospitals, medical schools, and professional associations—was not changed. However, one important branch of this medical network, namely community health centers and out-patient clinics sponsored by philanthropic black self-help and liberal public health elements of the city, were designed to foster the transfer of medical expertise and resources from the dominant medical providers to health programs that serviced the city's black communities.

After the Depression and throughout the decade of World Was II the traditional isolation of black health care institutions and medical professionals became dysfunctional to the mainstream medical institutions of Philadelphia. These institutions had to provide health care to a new urban community, largely black and with a multitude of middle-income families drawn to hospitals for their health needs. Major changes ensued in medical care policy and technology, including great expansion of hospitals, an upsurge in third-party medical coverage, and liberalized, integrated admissions policy. These changes in the structure of the hospital sliced into the racial caste system that had been so dominant in both the medical and social life of the city in previous decades. As important in this overthrow of the dual health system were the increasingly aggressive elements of the city and state political communities, black health activists, and civil rights organizations—all of which publicly attacked racial discrimination in city health affairs.

By the late 1950s and early 1960s, Philadelphia medical institutions themselves had joined the struggle against racial discrimination in medical training and health care institutions. Philadelphia branches of major civil rights and civil liberties organizations served as the chief protagonists in this drive for integration of Philadelphia's medical system. But now many hospital administrators, medical school officials, and local public service leaders closed ranks with this civil rights movement and actively pushed for more black medical trainees and personnel as well as for removing discriminatory health care practices.

This post-World War II initiative to integrate Philadelphia medical life marked only the beginning of a fundamental breakdown of a racially divided health care structure. After 1965, unlike any previous period in the twentieth century, the federal government and civil rights groups attacked inequality in all aspects of Philadelphia's health care establishment.[48] Federal civil rights agencies, usually stimulated by local agitation both from within and outside of health institutions, would aggressively monitor and, if necessary, intervene in hospitals and medical educational institutions that they found practicing racially unfair employment or admission policies. In addition to the forceful regulatory role of the federal government, the unionization movement among hospital employees in Philadelphia and other cities was to become one of the most effective weapons against discrimination and inadequate working conditions in health care facilities. Indeed, by the 1980s the hospital workers union would become the most powerful organized labor organization in the city. Finally, the women's health movement would contribute to dismantling discrimination in the health care sector by hacking away at gender barriers in medical care provision and employment. This wider involvement by the federal government, civil rights organizations, unions, and women's health groups promised to eliminate all vestiges of segregation and uneven integration that had plagued Philadelphia's medical establishment for over six decades.

Appendixes

Appendixes

Methodological Note on Physician's Survey

The data for the survey of Philadelphia physicians was based on information provided on all licensed American physicians by the American Medical Association in its *American Medical Directory*.[1] This comprehensive directory was published by the AMA every three or four years beginning in 1919. The information on the physicians entered in the *American Medical Directory* is quite diverse. The typical entry includes the physician's race, date of birth, medical school attended, date graduated, internship, current hospital affiliation, specialty, medical military connection, membership status in the AMA, and address. Black physicians were signified (through the 1938–1940 edition) with the symbol "C" for "colored" next to their names. The chief shortcoming of these directories is that they did not include information about affiliations with black hospitals.

The information on eminent black physicians in Philadelphia was compiled from the *Who's Who in Colored America* for the years 1925 and 1938. These volumes provided much more information on its entrants than the *American Medical Directory*. In most cases, besides the information provided by the *American Medical Directory*, *Who's Who* gives the physician's place of undergraduate education, military rank, membership in black medical professional associations, membership in black social clubs, and political and religious affiliation.

Specifically, the profile of the Philadelphia physicians was derived from analyzing three sets of data. First, the information on all the black physicians entered in the 1925, 1929, and 1938 editions of the *American Medical*

Directory was compiled. For these three years, respectively, there were 72, 98, and 109 black physicians listed. White physicians were, of course, much greater in number for these three years. According to the *American Medical Directory* there were 3,430 white physicians in Philadelphia in 1925, 3,714 in 1929, and 4,112 in 1938.

Therefore, for the second set of data, large random samples were taken from these three groups of white doctors. For the 1925 and 1929 groups, five hundred physicians were used, or roughly every seventh entry from each directory. For the white physicians of 1938, a larger sample was taken—600, or roughly every sixth entry.

Third, all the Philadelphia physicians listed in the *Who's Who in Colored America* for the 1925/1927 edition and the 1938/1940 edition were analyzed. As mentioned earlier, there were twenty-nine outstanding black doctors practicing in Philadelphia in 1925–1927 and thirty in 1938–1940 according to these volumes. This group formed the city's "eminent black physicians" for the interwar period.

Second Annual Mercy Hospital Clinical Lectures

(February 26 to March 2, 1934)

The following is the list of speakers at the 1934 Mercy Hospital clinical lectures. The list is taken from Mercy Hospital, *Biennial Report, 1933/1934* (Philadelphia: The Hospital, 1934), pp. 21–22.

PATHOLOGY. J. D. Aronson, M.D. Assistant Professor of Pathology, Henry Phipps Institute. "Laboratory Methods in the Diagnosis of Tuberculosis."

PEDIATRICS. E. L. Bauer, M.D. Professor of Diseases of Children, Jefferson Medical College. "Diagnosis and Treatment of Gastro-Intestinal Diseases in Children."

SURGERY. Hubley R. Owen, M.D. Professor of Clinical Surgery, Woman's Medical College. "Treatment of Fractures of Long Bones."

NEUROLOGY. George Wilson, M.D. Professor of Clinical Neurology, University of Pennsylvania Medical School. "The Diagnosis and Treatment of Neurosyphilis."

GYNECOLOGY. Brooke M. Anspach, M.D. Professor of Gynecology,

Jefferson Medical College. "Functional Disturbances Underlying Amenorrhea, Sterility and Uterine Bleeding."

MEDICINE. John A. Kolmer, M.D. Professor of Medicine, Temple University School of Medicine. "Diagnosis and Treatment of Amoebic Dysentery."

RADIOLOGY. G.E. Pfahler, M.D. Professor of Radiology, University of Pennsylvania Graduate School of Medicine. "The Treatment of Carcinoma of the Uterus by Irradiation."

OBSTETRICS. Edmund B. Piper, M.D. Professor of Obstetrics, University of Pennsylvania Medical School. "Treatment of Some Obstetrical Complications."

DENTISTRY. James R. Cameron, D.D.S. Professor of Oral Surgery, Temple University School of Dentistry. "Osteomyelitis of the Upper and Lower Jaw."

BRONCHOSCOPY. Louis H. Clerf, M.D. Professor of Bronchoscopy and Esophagoscopy, Jefferson Medical College. "Bronchoscopy in the Diagnosis of Pulmonary Diseases."

Notes and
Index

Notes

Abbreviations

AWMC—Archives of Woman's Medical College, Philadelphia

CP-BMRA—City of Philadelphia, Bureau of Municipal Research and Archives, Philadelphia

CTTU—Collection of Templana, Special Collection, Paley Library, Temple University, Philadelphia

GEB—General Education Board Records, RAC

HHMA—Hahnemann Medical College, History of Medicine Archives, Philadelphia

JNMA—Journal of the National Medical Association

JRFA-FU—Julius Rosenwald Fund Archives, Special Collections, Fisk University, Nashville

JRP—Julius Rosenwald Papers, Special Collections, University of Chicago Library, Chicago

PCPS—Philadelphia College of Physicians and Surgeons Library, Philadelphia

PSA—Pennsylvania State Archives, Harrisburg, Pa.

PSMDPA—Pennsylvania State Medical, Dental, and Pharmaceutical Association

RAC—Rockefeller Archive Center, Pocantico Hills, North Tarrytown, N.Y.

RFA—Rockefeller Foundation Archives, Pocantico Hills, North Tarrytown, N.Y.

TUUA—Temple University Urban Archives, Philadelphia

Introduction

1. R. S. Hanft, L. S. Fishman, and W. J. Evans, *Blacks and the Health Professions in the 80's: A National Crisis and a Time for Action* (Washington, D.C.: Association of Minority Health Professions Schools, 1983); L. W. Sullivan, "Preface," in *ibid.*, p. vi. Another study that echoes this sentiment is L. W. Sullivan, "The Status of Blacks in Medicine: Philosophical and Ethical Dilemmas for the 1980s," *New England Journal of Medicine* 309 (Sept. 29, 1983): 807–808.

2. Abraham Flexner, *The Flexner Report on Medical Education in the United States and Canada,* 1910 (Report to the Carnegie Foundation for the Advancement of Teaching, Bulletin No. 4; New York: The Foundation, 1910), pp. 180–181.

The Flexner Report was instrumental in closing five of the seven black medical colleges in America at the time. Predicting that "the practice of the Negro doctor will be limited to his own race," the report recommended further funds for Howard and Meharry but described the other five schools as "feeble, ill-equipped institutions" that were "wasting small sums annually and sending out undisciplined men, whose lack of medical training is covered up by the imposing M.D. degree." Black patients, according to the report, were the victims of these doctors, since blacks were "more easily 'taken in' " than whites. The report also contended that, because blacks were incorrigibly given to uncleanliness, their overall health outlook was bleak (*ibid.*, pp. 180–181). Policies growing out of the Flexner Report and Abraham Flexner's own influence among funders and policymakers of medical education carried over into the early 1920s and 1930s, perpetuating scarce, substandard education for black medical students. See Herbert M. Morais, *The History of the Negro in Medicine* (New York: Publishers Co., 1968), pp. 60–66, 89–90; Darlene C. Hine, "The Pursuit of Professional Equality: Meharry Medical College, 1921–1938, a Case Study," in *New Perspectives on Black Educational History*, ed. Vincent P. Franklin and James D. Anderson (Boston: G. K. Hall, 1978), pp. 173–192; Hal Strelnick and Richard Younge, "Affirmative Action in Medicine," in *Reforming Medicine: Lessons from the Last Twenty-Five Years*, ed. Victor W. Sidel and Ruth Sidel (New York: Pantheon Books, 1984), pp. 150–175; James Summerville, *Educating Black Doctors: A History of Meharry Medical College* (University: University of Alabama Press, 1983), pp. 51–54.

3. For a synopsis of the nineteenth- and early twentieth-century roots of this transformation in American hospital care, see Morris J. Vogel, "The Transformation of the American Hospital, 1850–1920," in *Health Care in America: Essays in Social History*, ed. Susan Reverby and David Rosner (Philadelphia: Temple

University Press, 1979), pp. 105–116. For a review of the subsequent literature, see Morris J. Vogel, *The Invention of the Modern Hospital: Boston, 1870–1930* (Chicago: University of Chicago Press, 1980); David K. Rosner, *A Once Charitable Enterprise: Hospitals and Health Care in Brooklyn and New York, 1885–1915* (Cambridge, Eng.: Cambridge University Press, 1982); and Paul Starr, *The Social Transformation of American Medicine* (New York: Basic Books, 1982).

4. Stanley Wohl, *The Medical Industrial Complex* (New York: Harmony Books, 1984), p. 79; James Z. Appel, "Health Care Delivery," in American Assembly, Columbia University, *The Health of Americans*, ed. Boisfeuillet Jones (Englewood Cliffs, N.J.: Prentice-Hall, 1970), p. 143; and James L. Goddard, "Health Protection," in American Assembly, *Health of Americans*, p. 124. For background, see Temple Burling, Edith M. Lentz, and Robert N. Wilson, *The Give and Take in Hospitals: A Study of Human Relations in Hospitals* (New York: Putnam's Sons, 1956), pp. 6–7, and Virginia H. Walker, *Nursing and Ritualistic Practice* (New York: Macmillan, 1967), pp. 8–9, 174–179.

5. See, for instance, Rosemary Stevens, *American Medicine and the Public Interest* (New Haven, Conn.: Yale University Press, 1973); George Rosen, *A History of Public Health* (New York: Schumann, 1958); George Rosen, *From Medical Police to Sound Medicine: Essays on the History of Health Care* (New York: Science History Publications, 1974); George Rosen, *Preventive Medicine in the United States, 1900–1975: Trends and Interpretations* (New York: Prodist, 1977); Vogel, *Invention of the Modern Hospital*; Rosner, *A Once Charitable Enterprise*; Starr, *Social Transformation of American Medicine*.

6. Charles Prudhomme and David F. Musto, "Historical Perspectives on Mental Health and Racisms in the United States," in *Racism and Mental Health*, ed. Charles V. Willie et al. (Pittsburgh: University of Pittsburgh Press, 1973), pp. 54–55; Stevens, *American Medicine and the Public Interest*, p. xiii; Hine, "Pursuit of Professional Equality," p. 190; Ronald L. Numbers, "The History of American Medicine," in *The Promise of American History: Progress and Prospects*, ed. Stanley I. Kutler and Stanley N. Katz (Baltimore: Johns Hopkins University Press, 1982), p. 255. The most important, though now dated, study outlining the black experience in American medicine remains Morais's *History of the Negro in Medicine*.

7. U.S. Department of Labor, Bureau of Labor Statistics, *Health Manpower, 1966–1975: A Study of Requirements and Supply* (Report No. 323; Washington, D.C.: GPO, June 1967); U.S. Department of Commerce, Bureau of the Census, *Statistical Abstract of the United States, 1975* (Washington, D.C.: GPO, 1975), p. 69; U.S. Department of Commerce, Bureau of the Census, *Nineteenth Census of the United States, 1970* (Washington, D.C.: GPO, 1973), *Pennsylvania*, sec. 2, table 171, pp. 971–972, table 181, p. 1286, table 185, p. 1313.

8. The phrase "two worlds of race" comes from John Hope Franklin's article "The Two Worlds of Race: A Historical View" in *The Negro American*, eds. Talcott

211

Parsons and Kenneth B. Clark (Boston: Beacon Press, 1966), pp. 47–68. Franklin adopted the duality theme from the studies of W. E. B. Du Bois, who described the collective psychology of black Americans as a peculiar "double-consciousness . . . of measuring one's soul by the tape of a world that looks on in amused contempt and pity, . . . an American, a Negro; two souls, two thoughts, two warring ideals in one dark body" (*The Souls of Black Folk* [orig. pub. 1903; rpt. New York: CBS, 1961], pp. 16–17). Du Bois later maintained that the "two world" caste arrangement in American life also governed the health care sector. See Du Bois, *Dusk of Dawn: An Essay Toward an Autobiography of a Race Concept* (orig. pub. 1940; rpt. New York: Schocken Books, 1968), pp. 173–220.

9. The racial division in American medical life before World War II was so severe that Du Bois wrote in 1940: "I am certain that for many generations American Negroes in the United States have got to accept separate medical institutions" (quoted in Gunnar Myrdal, *An American Dilemma: The Negro Problem and Modern Democracy* [orig. pub. 1944; 2 vols.; rpt. New York: Pantheon Books, 1962], p. 796).

Chapter I

1. Nathan F. Mossell, "An Address on Hospital Efficiency," in Frederick Douglass Memorial Hospital and Training School, *Eighteenth, Nineteenth, Twentieth Annual Report of the Board of Managers, Ending November 1st, 1916* (Philadelphia: [The Hospital], 1916), pp. 12–15, esp. pp. 12, 14.

2. *Ibid.*, p. 14.

3. Erwin H. Ackerknecht, *A Short History of Medicine* (Baltimore: Johns Hopkins University Press, 1982), p. 219; Brooke Hindle, *The Pursuit of Science in Revolutionary America, 1735–1789* (Chapel Hill: University of North Carolina Press, 1956); George H. Daniels, *Science in American Society: A Social History* (New York: Alfred A. Knopf, 1971); Richard H. Shryock, *Medicine and Society in America, 1660–1860* (New York: New York University Press, 1960); Carl Binge, *Revolutionary Doctor: Benjamin Rush, 1746–1813* (New York: W. W. Norton, 1966).

4. Allen F. Davis, "Introduction," in *The Peoples of Philadelphia: A History of Ethnic Groups and Lower-Class Life, 1790–1940*, ed. Allen F. Davis and Mark H. Haller (Philadelphia: Temple University Press, 1973), p. 6.

5. John F. Sutherland, "Housing the Poor in the City of Homes: Philadelphia at the Turn of the Century," in *Peoples of Philadelphia*, ed. Davis and Haller, p. 180.

6. W. E. B. Du Bois, *The Philadelphia Negro: A Social Study* (orig. pub. 1899; rpt. New York: Schocken Books, 1971), pp. 47, 58; John T. Emlen, "The Movement for the Betterment of the Negro in Philadelphia" (orig. pub. 1913), in *Black*

Politics in Philadelphia, ed. Miriam Ershkowitz and Joseph Zikmund (New York: Basic Books, 1973), pp. 40–43.

7. The proximity of residence and workplace for the majority of the Philadelphia working class during the late nineteenth and early twentieth centuries, as well as the inability of many of these workers to pay for expensive public transportation, is documented in Theodore Hershberg et al., "The 'Journey-to-Work': An Empirical Investigation of Work, Residence, and Transportation, Philadelphia, 1850 and 1880," in *Philadelphia: Work, Space, Family, and Group Experience in the Nineteenth Century*, ed. Theodore Hershberg (New York: Oxford University Press, 1981), pp. 128–173; Margaret S. Marsh, "The Impact of the Market Street 'El' on Northern West Philadelphia: Environmental Change and Social Transformation, 1900–1930," in *The Divided Metropolis: Social and Spatial Dimensions of Philadelphia, 1800–1975*, ed. William W. Cutler III and Howard Gillette Jr. (Westport, Conn.: Greenwood Press, 1980), pp. 169–170. On welfare and health conditions, see Du Bois, *Philadelphia Negro*, p. 145; Cecile P. Frey, "The House of Refuge for Colored Children," *Journal of Negro History* 66 (Spring 1981): 10–25. On segregation in public schools and neighborhood life in early twentieth-century Philadelphia, see Vincent P. Franklin, *The Education of Black Philadelphia* (Philadelphia: University of Pennsylvania Press, 1978), chaps. 1–2; Judy J. Mohraz, *The Separate Problem: Case Studies of Black Education in the North, 1900–1930* (Westport, Conn.: Greenwood Press, 1979), pp. xiv, xv, 8, 9–10, 86–93.

8. Du Bois, *Philadelphia Negro*, pp. 21–22; Theodore Hershberg, "Free Blacks in Antebellum Philadelphia," in *Peoples of Philadelphia*, ed. Davis and Haller, pp. 120–122.

9. Hershberg, "Free Blacks," p. 122.

10. Du Bois, *Philadelphia Negro*, pp. 115–118, 222.

11. Similar ethnic and class divisions developed in other northeastern cities like New York and Boston in the late nineteenth century. On ethnic hospitals in early twentieth-century Boston, see Morris J. Vogel, *The Invention of the Modern Hospital: Boston, 1870–1930* (Chicago: University of Chicago Press, 1980), pp. 125–132, and Selig Greenberg, *The Quality of Mercy* (New York: Atheneum, 1971), pp. 54–58. For New York, see David K. Rosner, *A Once Charitable Enterprise: Hospitals and Health Care in Brooklyn and New York, 1885–1915* (Cambridge, Eng.: Cambridge University Press, 1982), pp. 1–3, 19, 21, 24, 90–91. National trends are described in Paul Starr's *The Social Transformation of American Medicine* (New York: Basic Books, 1982), pp. 171, 173–176.

12. On Lankenau, see interview with Dr. Joseph Ritter, former chief of pediatrics at Philadelphia General Hospital, Philadelphia, July 8, 1977; Albert G. Miller, *History of the German Hospital of Philadelphia and Its Ex-Resident Physicians* (Philadelphia: J. B. Lippincott, 1906), pp. 17 ff. On health care for the Jewish community, see Haven Emerson et al., *Philadelphia Hospital and Health Survey*,

1929 (Philadelphia: Philadelphia Chamber of Commerce, 1929), pp. 705–706, 712–713; Henry N. Wessell, *History of the Jewish Hospital Association of Philadelphia* (Philadelphia: Board of Officers of the Jewish Hospital Association, 1915); Edwin Wolf II, "The German-Jewish Influence in Philadelphia's Jewish Charities," in *Jewish Life in Philadelphia, 1830–1940*, ed. Murray Friedman (Philadelphia: ISHI Publications, 1983), p. 141. On the Catholic hospitals, see *Philadelphia Public Ledger*, July 9, 1917, Jan. 31, 1919, and June 30, 1919; between 1917 and 1919 Philadelphia Italian-Americans established an Italian-American hospital near 65th and Vine streets. On Chestnut Hill and Philadelphia General, see Emerson et al., *Philadelphia Hospital and Health Survey, 1929*, pp. 686–688. According to Philadelphia General's monthly patient census for June 1917–June 1920, blacks constituted (in annual succession) 18.4 percent, 21.6 percent, and 22.8 percent of its admissions (City of Philadelphia, Bureau of Charities, " 'Statistical Reports'— Philadelphia General Hospital," June 1917–Dec. 1922, CP-BMRA). Also see Charles E. Rosenberg, "From Almhouse to Hospital: The Shaping of Philadelphia General Hospital," *Milbank Memorial Fund Quarterly/Health and Society* 60 (Winter 1982): 108–154, esp. pp. 121–122, 126, 146.

13. By the 1920s, eight of metropolitan Philadelphia's fifty-eight hospitals were under church auspices—five Roman Catholic, one Presbyterian, one Episcopalian, and one Methodist Episcopalian (Emerson et al., *Philadelphia Hospital and Health Survey, 1929*, p. 527). Also see Philip Taylor, *The Distant Magnet: European Immigration to the U.S.A.* (New York: Harper & Row, 1971), p. 225. Church hospitals, commonly classed as part of the nation's non-government, non-profit "voluntary" hospitals, have had a significant role in the history of American hospitals. See James A. Hamilton, *Patterns of Hospitals Ownership and Control* (Minneapolis: University of Minnesota Press, 1961), p. 89.

On Episcopal Hospital, see Emerson et al., *Philadelphia Hospital and Health Survey, 1929*, pp. 693–694. A study conducted around 1920 recorded that of thirty-two Philadelphia maternity hospitals five refused to admit unmarried mothers and five would take them only in cases of emergency. Among other city health and welfare agencies under religious control, twelve of twenty discriminated against such mothers and their children. The researcher concluded that "the amount of discrimination [toward unwed mothers] was four and one-half times greater than it would have been if judged by the standard of the non-sectarian institutions" (Carol Aronovici, unpublished study of illegitimacy in Philadelphia cited in Ruth Reed, *Negro Illegitimacy in New York City* [Columbia University Studies in History, Economics, and Public Law, No. 277; New York: Columbia University Press, 1926], pp. 23–24).

14. Midian O. Bousfield, "An Account of Physicians of Color in the United States," *Bulletin of the History of Medicine* 17 (Jan. 1945): 61–69; Herbert M. Morais, *The History of the Negro in Medicine* (New York: Publishers Co., 1968),

pp. 21–38; John Duffy, *The Healers: A History of American Medicine* (Urbana: University of Illinois Press, 1979), pp. 285–286; James L. Curtis, *Blacks, Medical Schools, and Society* (Ann Arbor: University of Michigan Press, 1971), pp. 9–13. On the lack of statistics for physicians generally in the pre-Civil War decades, see U.S. Department of Commerce, Bureau of the Census, *Historical Statistics of the United States: Colonial Times to 1957* (Washington, D.C.: GPO, 1962), p. 34. Individual blacks who attended Philadelphia medical schools or performed medical procedures in the city before the Civil War are mentioned in Bousfield, "Account of Physicians of Color," pp. 61–69; Curtis, *Blacks, Medical Schools, and Society*, p. 10; Raymond Pace Alexander's appraisal of the Negro in Philadelphia, in Herman L. Collins, *Philadelphia: A Story of Progress*, vol. 2 (New York: Lewis Historical Publishers Co., 1941), p. 388; Winthrop Neilson and Frances Neilson, *Verdict for the Doctor: The Life of Benjamin Rush* (New York: Hastings House, 1958), pp. 80–81, 141–143.

15. Eugene P. Foley, "The Negro Businessman: In Search of a Tradition," in *The Negro American*, ed. Talcott Parsons and Kenneth B. Clark (Boston: Beacon Press, 1966), pp. 555–592, quote on p. 565. See also Theodore Hershberg, "Free Blacks in Antebellum Philadelphia: A Study of Ex-Slaves, Freeborn, and Socioeconomic Decline," in *Philadelphia*, ed. Hershberg, pp. 376–385.

16. Du Bois, *Philadelphia Negro*, p. 113.

17. Bousfield, "Account of Physicians of Color," pp. 70–73; Morais, *History of the Negro in Medicine*, p. 59; Duffy, *The Healers*, pp. 287–288; James Summerville, *Educating Black Doctors: A History of Meharry Medical College* (University: University of Alabama Press, 1983), p. 37; Morais, *History of the Negro in Medicine*, pp. 82, 85. On the general black hospital movement in the North, see William Giffin, "The Mercy Hospital Controversy Among Cleveland's Afro-American Civic Leaders, 1927," *Journal of Negro History* 61 (Oct. 1976): 328–329.

18. Morais, *History of the Negro in Medicine*, p. 80; "National Officers, Executive Committee, and General Committee, December, 1910," in Warren D. St. James, *NAACP: Triumphs of a Pressure Group* (orig. pub. 1958; rpt. Smithtown, N.Y.: Exposition Press, 1980), app. E, pp. 249–250; "The First Board of Directors," in St. James, *NAACP*, app. F, p. 251; Federal Writer's Project, Works Progress Administration, Commonwealth of Pennsylvania, *Philadelphia: A Guide to the Nation's Birthplace* (Philadelphia: William Penn Association, 1937), p. 107.

19. Morais, *History of the Negro in Medicine*, p. 81; John P. Turner, "Review of the Medical Profession of Philadelphia," *The Colored Directory: A Handbook of the Religious, Social, Political, Professional, Business, and Other Activities of the Negroes of Philadelphia* (Philadelphia: Philadelphia Colored Directory Co., 1910), p. 68. In 1912, the largest public hospital in the city, Philadelphia General Hospital, served an average of 1,619 in-patients per day, admitted 15,855, and treated a

total of 17,550. The same year, the oldest and largest private hospital in Phila-delphia, the Pennsylvania Hospital, treated 24,836 out-patients (City of Philadel-phia, Department of Public Health and Charities, *Annual Report of Philadelphia General Hospital, 1912* [Philadelphia: The City, 1912]; *Annual Report of the Penn-sylvania Hospital, 1912* [Philadelphia: The Hospital, 1912]).

20. Edward S. Cooper, "The Mercy-Douglass Hospital: Historical Perspec-tive," *JNMA* 53 (1961): 4.

21. In 1927 only 71 of 111 (or 60 percent) of black medical school graduates served internships; 68 of these internships were at black hospitals, two of which were not accredited for certifiable internships. Through 1930, according to Dr. Midian O. Bousfield, a pre-1950 authority on black medical education and con-sultant to the Julius Rosenwald Fund, "the shortage of approved internships worked a great hardship on colored graduates." During the 1920s and early 1930s, each year more than thirty of the usually one hundred black graduates of medical schools could not locate internships and "there were no residencies at all" (Bous-field, "Account of Physicians of Color," p. 78). Biographical information on Bous-field is found in Morais, *History of the Negro in Medicine*, pp. 102, 125, and 129. By the mid-1930s, when more black hospitals were built or expanded, most notably Provident Hospital in Chicago and Homer G. Phillips Hospital in St. Louis, the number of internships for blacks topped one hundred annually. Because of the Depression, however, the number of black graduates of medical schools had fallen to 91 in 1932–1933 and 73 in 1935–1936, when black hospitals were offering 120 internships (Numa P. G. Adams, "Sources of Supply of Negro Health Personnel, Section A: Physicians," *Journal of Negro Education* 6 [July 1937]: 472–474).

22. On the Republican political machine that controlled Pennsylvania's General Assembly and state affairs from 1900 through the Depression, see John L. Shorer, "The Emergence of a Two-Party System in Republican Philadelphia, 1924–1936," *Journal of American History* 60 (March 1974): 985–1002; Lloyd M. Abernethy, "Progressivism, 1905–1919," in *Philadelphia: A 300-Year History*, ed. Russell F. Weigley (New York: W. W. Norton, 1982), pp. 524–565; and Arthur P. Dudden, "The City Embraces 'Normalcy,' 1919–1929," in *Philadelphia*, ed. Weigley, pp. 567–600. On the influence of Dr. Mossell and other black progressivist figures in Philadelphia like state assemblymen Harry Bass and John C. Asbury, see Dennis Clark, "Urban Blacks and Irishmen: Brothers in Prejudice," in *Black Politics in Philadelphia*, ed. Ershkowitz and Zikmund, p. 23, and J. T. Salter, "The End of Vare," *Political Science Quarterly* 50 (June 1935): 229. The loyalty of the majority of black voters in Philadelphia to the Republican machine is also covered in "Along the Color Line," *The Crisis* 3 (Dec. 1911): 53.

23. Turner, "Review of the Medical Profession," pp. 68–69; "Report of the Treasurer," in Frederick Douglass Memorial Hospital and Training School, *Twenty-*

Fifth Annual Report—June 1, 1916 to November 30, 1920, Philadelphia Afro-American Historical and Cultural Museum, Miscellaneous Archive Material, Philadelphia, p. 77; Emerson et al., *Philadelphia Hospital and Health Survey, 1929*, pp. 627–628.

24. William Halloch Johnson, dean of Lincoln University, "Exhibit of the Work of the Graduates of Lincoln University Pennsylvania, Who Have Entered the Medical Profession," March 27, 1920, mimeo., pp. 9–10, GEB, ser. 1, ser. 4, box 665, folder 6903. In his report, Johnson stressed the respect and leadership achieved by black physicians in the Philadelphia black community. On the lack of black practitioners, see Nathan Sinai and A. B. Mills, *A Survey of the Medical Facilities of the City of Philadelphia, 1929: Being in Part a Digest of the "Philadelphia Hospital and Health Survey, 1929"* (Publications of the Committee on the Costs of Medical Care, No. 9; Chicago: University of Chicago Press, 1931), p. 27; Starr, *Social Transformation of American Medicine*, pp. 125–126.

It is not likely that more than 10 to 15 percent of the nation's physicians practiced in hospitals in the 1910s. In 1929, about the time that exact figures began to be recorded, over 83 percent of American physicians were still in private practice (Committee on the Cost of Medical Care, *Medical Care for the American People* [Chicago: University of Chicago Press, 1932], p. 4). Another estimate made in 1927 reported that only 5 percent of the nation's ambulatory cases were cared for in institutions. In addition, the incapacitated hospitalized cases amounted to another 12 percent of the nation's medical patients. Thus, about 83 percent of American medical care was applied either in the physician's office or at the patient's bedside in the home (Michael M. Davis, *Clinics, Hospitals, and Health Centers* [New York: Harper, 1927], p. 6).

25. Superior resources for both basic medical education and specialty training were available in Philadelphia, but distribution of these medical professionals to the city's medically needy was chronically inadequate; see Sinai and Mills, *Survey of the Medical Facilities of the City of Philadelphia*, pp. 260–263.

26. For the impact of progressivist social reform ideals on the health and civic activists working in the black urban slums, see Garrett Power, "Apartheid Baltimore Style: The Residential Segregation Ordinances of 1910–1913," *Maryland Law Review* 42 (1982): 290–294; Jesse T. Moore Jr., "Resolving Urban Racial Problems: The New York Urban League, 1919–1959," *Afro-Americans in New York Life and History* 4 (Jan. 1980): 27–28, 30; and Peter Gottlieb, "Pittsburgh Urban League and the Black Migrants, 1918–1930," *Blacks in Pennsylvania History: Research and Educational Perspectives*, ed. David McBride (Harrisburg: Pennsylvania Historical and Museum Commission, 1983), pp. 65–66. On this social welfare movement in the black community generally before 1925, see Robert L. Allen, *Reluctant Reformers* (Washington, D.C.: Howard University Press, 1983), and John

H. Franklin, *From Slavery to Freedom* (New York: Alfred A. Knopf, 1974), pp. 330–332.

27. "The Douglass Hospital," *The Crisis* 3 (Jan. 1912): 120.

28. *Philadelphia Public Ledger*, April 3, 1916, June 29, 1919, Oct. 11, 1919, and Oct. 12, 1919; note by Sears, Roebuck magnate Julius Rosenwald in "Subject Index Notebooks," April 26, 1913, JRP, box LII, folder 12. In his note, Rosenwald commends the *Public Ledger* for running "favorable" and "militant" editorials in behalf of blacks. The *Ledger* also frequently invited national liberal figures such as Rosenwald to write guest editorials on racial problems in Philadelphia and elsewhere. Its support for funding for Douglass Hospital was commended in *The Crisis* 3 (Feb. 1912): 140.

29. For Jefferson, see *Philadelphia Inquirer*, Oct. 21, 1924. By 1963, Jefferson was America's largest medical school with 20,370 graduates (Edward L. Bauer, *Doctors Made in America* [Philadelphia: J. B. Lippincott, 1963], p. ix). For Medico-Chirurgical, see Bauer, *Doctors Made in America*, p. 180; Federal Writers' Project, *Philadelphia*, p. 302. Since each medical school's approach to admitting black applicants was a matter of internal decision-making unique to each school, it is not possible to explain exactly why Temple and Pennsylvania had the highest number of black medical students. Probably admission officials at these two institutions felt comfortable drawing upon their own university's black undergraduates; the city's other medical schools, of course, had no such affiliated undergraduate colleges. While information on the undergraduate background of Philadelphia black medical students is extremely skimpy, at least two black University of Pennsylvania and two Temple graduates were admitted to their colleges' respective medical schools: A. Robert Burton (M.D., 1917) and M. Russell Nelson (M.D., 1920) of the University of Pennsylvania and Wilbur L. Archer (M.D., 1925) and Charles A. Scott (M.D., 1925) from Temple University (University of Pennsylvania Medical College, *The Scope, 1917*, p. 136, and *The Scope, 1920*, p. 118, Van Pelt Library, University of Pennsylvania; Temple University Medical College, *The Skull, 1925*, pp. 38, 58, CTTU).

30. Thomas Yenser, ed., *Who's Who in Colored America: A Biographical Dictionary of Notable Living Persons of African Descent in America, 1930–1932* (4th ed.; Brooklyn, N.Y.: Thomas Yenser, 1933), p. 189; *Philadelphia Tribune*, June 23, 1917, and June 24, 1919; "The Far Horizon," *The Crisis* 34 (Aug. 1927): 202, 214. By 1910, certain blacks, like the editors of the *Journal of the National Medical Association*, considered the status of black medical students in Philadelphia to be improving relative to the rest of the state (W.A., "Notes," *JNMA* 1 [1909]: 249; *JNMA* 2 [1910]: 202).

31. U.S. Department of the Interior, Office of Education, *Negro Education: A Study of the Private and Higher Schools for Colored People in the United States*, dir. Thomas Jesse Jones (Bulletin 1916, No. 38; Washington, D.C.: GPO, 1917), vol.

1, p. 68. Leonard Medical School was a part of Shaw University in North Carolina.

32. Abraham Flexner, "Negro Medical Students, 1919–1920," GEB, box 22, folder 7221 (unpublished survey, 3 pp.).

33. Gerald E. Markowitz and David Rosner, "Doctors in Crisis: Medical Education and Medical Reform During the Progressive Era, 1895–1915," in *Health Care in America: Essays in Social History*, ed. Susan Reverby and David Rosner (Philadelphia: Temple University Press, 1979), p. 195; Elton Rayack, *Professional Power and American Medicine: The Economics of the American Medical Association* (Cleveland: World Publishing Co., 1967), pp. 68–69, 76; Morais, *History of the Negro in Medicine*, pp. 89–90. In addition, the number of newly trained doctors fell sharply from 5,700 graduates in 1900 to 2,300 graduates in 1910 (John Z. Bowers, "Changes in the Supply and Characteristics of American Doctors in the Twentieth Century," *Medical History and Medical Care: A Symposium of Perspectives*, ed. Gordon McLachlan and Thomas McKeown [London: Oxford University Press, 1971], p. 21).

34. Carter G. Woodson, *The Mis-Education of the Negro* (Washington, D.C.: Associated Publishers, 1933), pp. 74–82; W. Montague Cobb, *Progress and Portents for the Negro in Medicine* (New York: National Association for the Advancement of Colored People, 1948), p. 22; Allison B. Henderson and Lionel F. Swan, "Negro Physicians in Michigan," *JNMA* 61 (1969): 450. A detailed description of long-standing roadblocks facing black medical students in need of clinical training facilities of American hospitals is given by W. S. Carter of the Rockefeller Foundation in "Medical Education for Negroes," remarks made at the Association of American Medical Colleges in Indianapolis, Oct. 30–31, 1928, RFA, record group 2, General Correspondence (1928), folder 7, pp. 5–6.

Besides the general presumption that blacks might not be able to handle higher education (see Buell G. Gallagher, *American Caste and the Negro College* [New York: Columbia University Press, 1938], esp. pp. 176–179, also p. 48), which was clearly disproved by the success of black students in Philadelphia medical schools, there were more realistic presumptions. Medical educators assumed, correctly, that their black graduates would not be allowed to intern at white hospitals in the city and around the country. If the internship barrier was overcome, by interning at Mercy, Douglass, or another black institution, hospital affiliations were not available for blacks at any of Philadelphia's large or small white hospitals. Finally, because of lack of such hospital affiliations, once in practice, black doctors could not expect to provide ongoing care to their more seriously ill patients.

35. J. H. Musser, comp., *Thirty Years After: Alumni of the University of Pennsylvania Medical Department Class of 1908* (New Orleans: Wetzel, 1938), p. 54; "Deaths," *Journal of the American Medical Association* 150 (1952): 1500; "Meharry, Hartshorn, and Walden," *The Crisis* 26 (July 1923): 123; Summerville, *Educating Black Doctors*, p. 79; John J. Mullowney, *America Gives a Chance* (Tampa, Fla.:

Tribune Press, 1940), p. 164, cited in Summerville, *Educating Black Doctors*, p. 79. For a detailed description of Mullowney's paternalistic views on the medical educability of blacks, see Darlene C. Hine, "The Pursuit of Professional Equality: Meharry Medical College, 1921–1938, a Case Study," in *New Perspectives on Black Educational History*, ed. Vincent P. Franklin and James D. Anderson (Boston: G. K. Hall, 1978), pp. 179–180, 183–185, 189–190.

36. Jefferson Medical College, *The Neurone, 1912*, p. 100, Scott Memorial Library, Thomas Jefferson University; Johnson, "Exhibit of the Work of the Graduates," p. 10; University of Pennsylvania Medical College, *The Scope, 1919* p. 136, Van Pelt Library, University of Pennsylvania. "Anthracosis," when etymologized, means coal or charcoal. Earlier in the decade, the negligible status of black students at this campus dissuaded the Alpha Phi Alpha fraternity, the nation's oldest and most prestigious black fraternity, from attempting to establish a chapter there (Charles H. Wesley, *A History of Alpha Phi Alpha: A Development in College Life* [orig. pub. 1929; rev. ed., Chicago: Foundation Publishers, 1961], p. 121).

37. Carter, "Medical Education for Negroes," p. 5; interview with Dr. Wilbur H. Strickland, former medical director at Douglass and senior staff member at Mercy-Douglass hospitals, Philadelphia, June 16, 1986. For a detailed description of the transfer policy and its effects on black medical students in New York, see Aubre de L. Maynard's autobiography, *Surgeons to the Poor: The Harlem Hospital Story* (New York: Appleton-Century-Crofts, 1978), pp. 33–35.

38. William Leroy Berry, for example, was the only black student enrolled in Jefferson Medical College in 1918 and 1919. He satisfactorily completed his work in the bacteriology department but failed in the anatomy and chemistry departments, was required to attend summer school, and evidently never graduated (Dean R. V. Patterson to Abraham Flexner, July 14, 1919, GEB, box 22, folder 7221). Dr. William Pepper, dean of the University of Pennsylvania Medical School, throughout his tenure was concerned that his school's black students succeed. But, when queried by Abraham Flexner in 1919 about the number and status of blacks at the university, Dr. Pepper replied that of his school's three black enrollees "two . . . have conditions [that is, unsatisfactory grades] and [since] the reexaminations are held in September, we cannot tell until that time what class they will be in next year" (William Pepper to Abraham Flexner, July 23, 1919, and Pepper to Flexner, Oct. 29, 1919, GEB, box 22, folder 7221).

39. *Philadelphia Tribune*, Feb. 22, 1919; W. Montague Cobb, "Nathan Francis Mossell, M.D., 1856–1946," *JNMA* 46 (1954): 125–126; *Philadelphia Tribune*, Feb. 22, 1919. Mossell himself had graduated from the University of Pennsylvania Medical School and had experienced prejudice there first hand. When he started at the school, he was told that he had to sit behind a screen. When he refused, he was sent into the amphitheater, where only students but no faculty appeared. The students began to yell, "Put the nigger out" (Cobb, "Nathan Francis Mossell,"

p. 122).

40. *Philadelphia Tribune*, Feb. 22, 1919, May 5, 1917, April 21, 1917, and May 19, 1917; Morais, *History of the Negro in Medicine*, p. 81; *Philadelphia Public Ledger*, Feb. 20, 1919.

41. *Philadelphia Tribune*, March 17, 1917, March 24, 1917, and June 28, 1919.

42. *Ibid.*, April 7, 1917, and June 16, 1917; Cooper, "Mercy-Douglass Hospital," p. 1; *Philadelphia Public Ledger*, February 20, 1919, July 12, 1919, October 11, 1919, Oct. 12, 1919, Oct. 15, 1919, and Oct. 18, 1919.

43. Douglass Memorial Hospital, *Twenty-Fifth Annual Report*, pp. 76–77, 112

44. "The Horizon," *The Crisis* 20 (July 1920): 145.

45. Roberta West, *History of Nursing in Pennsylvania* (n.p.: Pennsylvania State Nurses Association, 1932?), p. 33; U.S. Office of Education, *Negro Education: A Study of the . . . Schools for Colored People in the U.S.*, p. 176; Vern Bullough and Bonnie Bullough, *The Care of the Sick: The Emergence of Modern Nursing* (New York: Prodist, 1978), pp. 132–134; Susan Reverby, "The Search for the Hospital Yardstick: Nursing and the Rationalization of Hospital Work," in *Health Care in America*, ed. Reverby and Rosner, pp. 206–225; Barbara Melosh, *The Physician's Hand: Work Culture and Conflict in American Nursing* (Philadelphia: Temple University Press, 1982); Rosenberg, "From Almshouse to Hospital," pp. 143–145.

46. Mossell, "Address on Hospital Efficiency," p. 13; Emil Frankel, *State-Aided Hospitals in Pennsylvania: A Survey of Hospital Finances, Resources, Extent of Services, and the Nursing Situation* (Pennsylvania Department of Public Welfare, Bulletin No. 25; Harrisburg: The Department, 1925), p. 80; West, *History of Nursing in Pennsylvania*, p. 33.

47. *Philadelphia Public Ledger*, June 26, 1915; Jones, *Negro Education*, p. 176; Kelly Miller and Joseph R. Gay, *Progress and Achievements of Colored People* (Washington, D.C.: Austin Jenkins, 1917), p. 326.

The comments by William C. Bolivar, a prominent black banker, scholar, and bibliophile, at the 1913 Mercy nursing school commencement exemplify the widely held view that black nurses, more than their white counterparts, should strive for charitable and studious professional ideals. Bolivar emphasized that the nurses' "calling means a predilection for the work, not a mere vehicle for the fattening of the wallet." He also told the graduating nurses that "there is hardly an alliance in our twentieth century movement equal to that of [our] Doctor or Nurse" (W. C. Bolivar, "Address Delivered to the Graduating Class of Nurses from Mercy Hospital, Class of 1913," Henry Slaughter Collection, Atlanta University Center). On Bolivar's career as a community leader, see James G. Spady, "The Afro-American Historical Society: The Nucleus of Black Bibliophiles," *Negro History Bulletin* (June/July 1974): 254–257, esp. p. 256.

48. Douglass Memorial Hospital, *Twenty-Fifth Annual Report*, p. 36.

49. "Along the Color Line," *The Crisis* 34 (July 1927): 161–162.

50. Woman's Medical College, "Negro Graduates . . .," mimeo., Jan. 27, 1948, and "Black Graduates," mimeo., c. 1972, Medical College of Pennsylvania Collection, AWMC.

51. Isabella T. Smart, "Report on Internships for Women," *Women's Medical Journal* 27 (March 1917): 59.

52. Isabella Vandervall, "Some Problems of the Colored Woman Physician," *Women's Medical Journal* 27 (July 1917): 156–158; see also Emma W. Gillmore, "A Call to Arms," *Women's Medical Journal* 27 (Aug. 1917): 183–184. In its 1915 annual review of young blacks who were graduating from leading white and black colleges and graduate schools, the editors of the NAACP's *The Crisis* stated the Isabella Vandervall's achievement deserved a special mention. "Dr. Vandervall graduated at the head of her class . . . and was the youngest student and the only colored one in her class of ten. [Moreover] she maintained an average of 97.8% during her course" ("Our Future Leaders," *The Crisis* 10 [July 1915]: 142). Vandervall had received praise from *The Crisis* years earlier when she won the medical college's top freshman prize (fifty dollars) for academic achievement, as well as two awards (twenty-five dollars and a gold watch) for leading her junior class in both academic average and a major exam grade ("The Year in Colored Colleges," *The Crisis* 4 [July 1912]: 134, and "Colleges and Their Graduates in 1914," *The Crisis* 8 [July 1914]: 138).

53. Gillmore, "A Call to Arms," pp. 183–184.

54. Henry Phipps Institute, *Sixteenth Report* (Philadelphia: The Institute, 1923), p. 1; letter from Martha Tracy, dean of the Woman's Medical College of Pennsylvania, to Charles J. Hatfield, Jan. 25, 1924, in "Lillian A. Moore-Clark," Deceased Alumni File, AWMC. See also H. Work, U.S. secretary of the interior, to Dean Tracy, Jan. 23, 1924, in Medical College of Pennsylvania Collection, AWMC.

55. W. E. B. Du Bois, "Opinion: The Woman's Medical College," *The Crisis* 26 (Aug. 1923): 154, which reprints the March 2, 1923, letter from Tracy to Moore; Tracy to Hatfield, Jan. 25, 1924.

56. For a general overview, see Mary H. Walsh, *"Doctors Wanted, No Women Need Apply": Sexual Barriers in the Medical Profession, 1935–1975* (New Haven, Conn.: Yale University Press, 1977), and Virginia G. Drachman, *Hospital with a Heart: Women Doctors and the Paradox of Separatism at the New England Hospital, 1862–1964* (Ithaca, N.Y.: Cornell University Press, 1984).

57. Mary H. Walsh, "The Rediscovery of the Need for a Feminist Medical Education," *Harvard Educational Review* 49 (Nov. 1979): 417–466. The historical and comparative complexities involved in black and white women's immobility in the medical professions have yet to be adequately studied. Walsh's studies, while most valuable as overviews to the position of black women, include only passing general references (*"Doctors Wanted,"* pp. 31, 32, 192–194, 218; "Rediscovery,"

pp. 451, 455, 462–463). For example, documenting the experience of a black graduate of Bellevue Hospital Medical College in the 1920s who was insulted and refused assistance in initiating practice by her black male colleagues in New York City, Walsh states that black women physicians, "once in the profession, . . . suffered from discrimination by black male physicians as well as white society" ("Rediscovery," p. 451). But Walsh cites no further incidents or data to corroborate her general statement. My research indicates that, through the 1920s, black Philadelphia hospitals provided internships for black women physicians when no local white male or female hospitals would accept them and black women were admitted into and supervised the nursing schools at the city's black hospitals although they were barred absolutely by white local and state nursing schools.

This discrepancy between individual incidents in New York and Philadelphia suggests that a range of factors will need to be analyzed in future studies of the impact of sex discrimination on white and black women entering the medical professions. These factors, such as the family status of women, ethnicity and race, the numbers and ages of children, spouses' educational and economic status, and newness to the city, have been illuminated in Susan J. Kleinberg's "The Systematic Study of Urban Women," in *Class, Sex, and the Woman Worker*, ed. Milton Cantor and Bruce Laurie (Westport, Conn.: Greenwood Press, 1977), pp. 28–29. Other factors relating to the medical profession not mentioned by Kleinberg include quantitative and interregional comparisons of medical school, internships, and specialty training experiences of women from both races, the types of peer and professional contacts black and white women had with each other as well as with men in the profession, and the extent to which racial and economic factors influenced black men's discrimination toward their female counterparts. For an examination of similar types of factors for black women college graduates of the early 1950s in general, see Jeannie L. Noble's *The Negro Woman's College Education* (New York: Columbia University Teachers College Bureau of Publications, 1956).

58. *Philadelphia Public Ledger*, Jan. 10, 1919, and July 13, 1919; Temple University Medical College, *The Skull, 1925*, CTTU. Among the female medical institutions that provided internships in Philadelphia were the West Philadelphia Hospital for Women, the Women's Homeopathic Association of Pennsylvania, and Woman's Southern Hospital (Smart, "Report on Internships for Women," p. 59).

59. *Philadelphia Public Ledger*, May 19, 1919, and April 3, 1918.

60. On women physicians in Philadelphia during World War I, see *Public Ledger*, June 1, 1917, July 7, 1917, March 24, 1918, Sept. 19, 1918, and Nov. 11, 1918. Women's activism and advances in the health field during the war years in other parts of the nation are discussed in Richard H. Shryock, *History of Nursing: An Interpretation of the Social and Medical Factors Involved* (Philadelphia: W. B. Saunders, 1959), p. 309; Walsh, *"Doctors Wanted,"* pp. 207, 209–211, 218–219, 221–222, 226–227; W. A., "The American Women's Hospitals: A Half-Century

of Service," *Journal of the American Medical Women's Association* 22 (Aug. 1967): 548; Estelle Fraade, "American Women's Hospital Service: 48 Years of Continuing Service," *Journal of the American Medical Women's Association* 20 (April 1965): 341.

61. Morais, *History of the Negro in Medicine*, p. 112. Once again black community reformers attempted to alleviate this condition through self-help measures. In June of 1918, the Crispus Attucks Circle for War Relief commenced a campaign to raise one million dollars for an all-black hospital in Philadelphia "to purchase, equip, and maintain a hospital and convalescent home where invalided Negro soldiers may be cared for by physicians and nurses of their own race."

62. Henry L. Phillips, president, Mercy Hospital board of directors, to Edwin R. Embree, president, Julius Rosenwald Fund, May 7, 1928, JRFA-FU.

63. Douglass Memorial Hospital, *Twenty-Fifth Annual Report*, pp. 97, 112, quote on p. 112. A list of these religious and social organizations and auxiliaries appears in Appendix A. These groups represented black neighborhoods near Douglass Hospital as well as black communities in outlying areas such as Jenkintown, Devon, and Darby.

64. Patrick O'Connell, "Abstract of Address Delivered at the Twenty-Fifth Anniversary of the Frederick Douglass Memorial Hospital," in *ibid.*, pp. 27, 28.

65. *Philadelphia Tribune*, Aug. 25, 1917, and Sept. 1, 1917. This same newspaper account reveals that the lynching incidents that had forced the Association to change the meeting location had left a cloud of dismay over the convention. The keynote address delivered by the NMA's president Dr. D. W. Byrd did not dwell strictly on medical scientific subjects. "The address was strong and rigorous," the report reads, "touching many phases of the race problem and health conditions of our people."

66. Turner, "Review of the Medical Profession of Philadelphia," p. 69; Woodson, *The Negro Professional Man and the Community* (Washington, D.C.: Association for the Study of Negro Life and History, 1934), pp. 118–119. Blacks could only join the AMA through local medical associations. Because these chapters were overwhelmingly segregated, the national body of the AMA received very few blacks as members prior to its great desegregation controversy of the 1960s. For a description of this controversy, see Morais, *History of the Negro in Medicine*, chap. 9.

67. Between 1912 and 1924 these were Walter Hackett Scudder, M.D., Shaw University, 1906 (registered in 1912); David Wilbert Postles, M.D., Howard University, 1895 (reg. 1912); John Sherman Carter, M.D., Howard University, 1909 (reg. 1918); and Abel Erastus West, M.D., Leonard Medical College, 1908 (reg. 1924). Registries were directories maintained by state and country medical societies, as well as state legislatures, in order to identify fully licensed, reputable doctors. For more information on the value of registries, see Richard H. Shryock,

Medical Licensing in America, 1650–1965 (Baltimore: Johns Hopkins University Press, 1967), pp. 48–49.

68. The primary function of the County Society's publication, *The Weekly Roster of the Medical Organizations of Philadelphia*, was to make regular announcements pertaining to candidacies, balloting, membership approvals, and so on.

69. Woodson, *Negro Professional Man*, p. 119.

70. Philadelphia County Medical Society, *Weekly Roster* 8, no. 25 (Jan. 11, 1913): 4, and no. 32 (April 12, 1913): 7; W. Montague Cobb, "John Patrick Turner, M.D., 1885–1958," *JNMA* 51 (1959): 160–161.

71. Turner, "Review of the Medical Profession of Philadelphia," p. 69; Monroe N. Work, ed., *Negro Year Book: An Encyclopedia of the Negro, 1921–1922* (Tuskegee Institute, Ala.: Negro Year Book Publishing Co., 1922), p. 370; Philadelphia County Medical Society, *Weekly Roster* 8, no. 23 (Dec. 28, 1912): 4.

72. J. Max Barber, "The Philadelphia Negro Dentist," *The Crisis* 7 (Feb. 1914): 179. Clifton I. Dummett and Lois D. Dummett, *Charles Edwin Bentley: A Model for All Times* (St. Paul, Minn.: North Central Publishing Co., 1982), p. 194.

73. Barber, "Philadelphia Negro Dentist," p. 179. On Barber's career as an editor and influential "race man," see "A Plucky Man," *The Crisis* 5 (Nov. 1912): 16; and "Away from Accommodation: Radical Editors and Protest Journalism, 1900–1910," *Journal of Negro History* 62 (Oct. 1977): 325–338.

74. Mabel K. Staupers, *No Time for Prejudice: A Study of the Integration of Negroes in Nursing in the United States* (New York: Macmillan, 1961), p. 10; Mary E. Carnegie, *The Path We Tread: Blacks in Nursing, 1854–1984* (Philadelphia: J. B. Lippincott, 1986), pp. 19, 149–152, 236.

Chapter II

1. U.S. Department of Commerce, Bureau of the Census, *Negro Population in the United States, 1790–1915* (Washington, D.C.: GPO, 1918), pp. 68, 350–351; Monroe Lerner and Odin W. Anderson, *Health Progress in the United States, 1900–1960* (Chicago: University of Chicago Press, 1963), pp. 15–17, 126–127; Commission on Chronic Illness, *Chronic Illness in the City: The Baltimore Study* (Cambridge, Mass.: Harvard University Press, 1957), p. 84.

2. Bureau of the Census, *Negro Population, 1790–1915*, p. 330.

3. W. E. B. Du Bois, *The Philadelphia Negro: A Social Study* (University of Pennsylvania, Series in Political Economy and Public Law, No. 14; Philadelphia: University of Pennsylvania, 1899), pp. 140–141.

4. John T. Emlen, "The Movement for the Betterment of the Negro in Philadelphia," *Annals of the American Academy of Political and Social Science* 49 (Sept.

1913): 88–89.

5. Barbara Klaczynska, "Why Women Work: A Comparison of Various Groups—Philadelphia, 1910–1930," *Labor History* 17 (1976): 81. On the replacement of white native and immigrant women by black southern migrants in the industrial workforce of the large northern cities during the early twentieth century, see David M. Katzman, *Seven Days a Week: Women and Domestic Service in Industrializing America* (New York: Oxford University Press, 1978), chap. 7. The disproportionate concentration of blacks in domestic service nationwide during the 1910s and 1920s is discussed by William H. Harris in *The Harder We Run: Black Workers Since the Civil War* (New York: Oxford University Press, 1982), pp. 64–65.

6. During the early decades of the twentieth century, when domestics were common in upper-class households, general practice physicians treated medical illness primarily in the home. See Michael M. Davis, *Clinics, Hospitals, and Health Centers* (New York: Harper, 1927), pp. 3–4. Additional insights are provided by the British public health scholar Abel-Smith, who states: "Illness creates dependency—the sick need not only medical treatment, but personal service" (Brian Abel-Smith, *A History of the Nursing Profession in Great Britain* [London: Heinemann, 1960], p. 1).

7. For instance, in 1910, the National Medical Association noted a public statement of a certain, apparently prestigious, medical council that "the Negro servant will spread tuberculosis among her employers, and thereby become a menace to the white race" (editorial, *JNMA* 2 [1910]: 132). Some years earlier, the Phipps Institute published a staff member's statement on the inordinately high prevalence of tuberculosis among black people. Blacks were a severe threat to the health of whites because "they constitute the servant class of our community and are in intimate association with other people." Henry Phipps Institute, *Second Annual Report, 1904–1905* (Philadelphia: The Institute, 1906), p. 14. See also Elizabeth R. Haynes, "Negroes in Domestic Service in the United States," *Journal of Negro History* 8 (Oct. 1923): 384–433; George Rosen, *Preventive Medicine in the United States, 1900–1975: Trends and Interpretations* (New York: Prodist, 1977), pp. 25–27; "Tuberculosis and the Negro," *JNMA* 7 (1919): 137–138; Frank A. Craig, "A Study of the Housing and Social Conditions in Selected Districts of Philadelphia," in Henry Phipps Institute, *Eleventh Report* (Philadelphia: The Institute, 1915).

8. Esther L. G. Price, *Pennsylvania Pioneers Against Tuberculosis* (New York: National Tuberculosis Association, 1952), pp. 163–164. The occupational data began to appear in 1905 and 1906 (Henry Phipps Institute, *First Annual Report, 1903–1904* [Philadelphia: The Institute, 1905], pp. 14–17, and *Second Annual Report, 1904–1905*, pp. 18–19).

9. Philadelphia Department of Public Health and Charities, *Annual Reports*

of the Bureau of Health, 1915 (Philadelphia: The City, 1915), pp. 534–538.

10. Whittier Center, *Annual Report, 1915* (Philadelphia: The Center, 1915), p. 5. The official name of this center was the Whittier Center for the Study and Practical Solution of Negro City Problems.

11. Henry R. M. Landis, "The Clinic for Negroes at the Henry Phipps Institute," *Transactions of the National Tuberculosis Association* 17 (1921): 433.

12. Nathan F. Mossell, "An Address on Hospital Efficiency," in Frederick Douglass Memorial Hospital and Training School, *Eighteenth, Nineteenth, Twentieth Annual Report of the Board of Managers, Ending November 1st, 1916* (Philadelphia: The Hospital, 1916), pp. 13, 14. On the rising militancy in urban black communities in the 1910s, see August Meier and Elliot Rudwick, *From Plantation to Ghetto* (New York: Hill & Wang, 1970), pp. 220–222, and Robert L. Allen, *Reluctant Reformers* (Washington, D.C.: Howard University Press, 1983), pp. 270–272.

13. *Philadelphia Public Ledger*, April 3, 1916.

14. One 1913 social study on trained black nurses and the cities stated that "reports show that Negro women are employed in large numbers as maids or housekeepers . . . but rarely as yet are learned professions open to them." The study urged that a means be sought for black women to escape domestic work. "One such vista," according to the study, "is the vocation of trained nurse. For this work nature had endowed the Negro women, and race experience laid sound foundations" (Robert McMurdy, "Negro Women as Trained Nurses: Experiment of a Chicago Hospital," *Survey* 31 [Nov. 8, 1913]: 159–160).

15. John Duffy, *A History of Public Health in New York City, 1866–1966* (New York: Russell Sage Foundation, 1974), pp. 539–544; James H. Jones, *Bad Blood: The Tuskegee Syphilis Experiment* (New York: Free Press, 1981), pp. 21–22; David Rosner, "Health Care for the 'Truly Needy': Nineteenth-Century Origins of the Concept," *Milbank Memorial Fund Quarterly/Health and Society* 60 (Summer 1982): 355–385; Robert H. Bremner, *From the Depths: The Discovery of Poverty in the United States* (New York: New York University Press, 1956), pp. 129–130; George Rosen, "The First Neighborhood Health Center Movement: Its Rise and Fall," in *Sickness and Health in America: Readings in the History of Medicine and Public Health*, ed. Judith W. Leavitt and Ronald L. Numbers (Madison: University of Wisconsin Press, 1978), p. 186. On early twentieth-century developments in public health and medical practice that stemmed from a growing awareness of the influence that social context had on ill patients, see, for instance, James Reed, "Doctors, Birth Control, and Social Values, 1830–1970," in *The Therapeutic Revolution: Essays in the Social History of American Medicine*, ed. Morris J. Vogel and Charles E. Rosenberg (Philadelphia: University of Pennsylvania Press, 1979), pp. 116–123 and 120 n. 1; Jones, *Bad Blood*, pp. 30–34; and Lloyd C. Taylor Jr., *The Medical Profession and Social Reform, 1885–1945* (New York: St. Martin's Press, 1974),

pp. 24–26, 51–61.

16. Morris J. Vogel, "Machine Politics and Medical Care: The City Hospital at the Turn of the Century," in *Therapeutic Revolution*, ed. Vogel and Rosenberg; Rosner, "Health Care for the 'Truly Needy' "; George Rosen, "Historical Trends and Future Prospects in Public Health," in *Medical History and Medical Care: A Symposium of Perspectives*, ed. Gordon McLachlan and Thomas McKeown (London: Oxford University Press, 1971), p. 68; Jones, *Bad Blood*, p. 34.

17. Rosen, "The First Neighborhood Health Center Movement," pp. 185–199; Rosemary Stevens, *American Medicine and the Public Interest* (New Haven, Conn.: Yale University Press, 1973), p. 74. Separate black health centers or small hospitals did emerge throughout the nation in the twenties. But they were initiated mainly in southern, usually rural regions. In these states well-founded, larger black hospitals were non-existent. Furthermore, impoverished black communities were denied any form of public services by local and state government (Adah B. Thoms, *Pathfinders: A History of the Progress of Colored Graduate Nurses* [New York: A. B. Thoms, 1929], pp. 167–195; Council on Medical Education and Hospitals of the American Medical Association, "Investigation of Negro Hospitals," *Journal of the American Medical Association* 92 [April 1929]: 1375–1376).

18. George S. Counts, *The Social Foundations of American Education* (New York: Charles Scribner's Sons, 1934), p. 218; Thomas N. Bonner, *Medicine in Chicago, 1850–1950: A Chapter in the Development of a City* (Madison, Wisc.: American History Research Center, 1957), p. 84; Christopher Jencks and David Riesman, *The Academic Revolution* (Garden City, N.Y.: Anchor Books, 1969); Jones, *Bad Blood*, pp. 30–60.

19. Waldemar A. Nielsen, *The Big Foundations* (New York: Columbia University Press, 1972), p. 49; E. Richard Brown, "He Who Pays the Piper: Foundations, the Medical Profession, and Medical Education," in *Health Care in America: Essays in Social History*, ed. Susan Reverby and David Rosner (Philadelphia: Temple University Press, 1979), pp. 132–154; Allan Chase, *The Legacy of Malthus* (Urbana: University of Illinois Press, 1980), pp. 198–200; Stevens, *American Medicine and the Public Interest*, pp. 44–54.

20. *Philadelphia Public Ledger*, July 15, 1919; Taylor, *Medical Profession and Social Reform*, p. 34; *New York Times*, January 10, 1903, Feb. 28, 1905, and April 2, 1905. The industrial and philanthropic activities of Henry Phipps are detailed in Stanton Belfour, "The Philanthropic Tradition in Pittsburgh," *Western Pennsylvania Historical Magazine* 37 (Summer 1954): 101, 105, and "Henry Phipps," *Dictionary of American Biography*, ed. Dumas Malone, vol. 14 (New York: Charles Scribner's Sons, 1953), pp. 550–551. Phipps had followed the anti-tuberculosis work of Dr. William Osler for several years, ever since Osler had treated one of Phipps's children. It is possible that Phipps gained an interest in endowing a tuberculosis research center as a result of these contacts (Harvey Cushing, *The*

Life of Sir William Osler [2 vols.; London: Clarendon Press, 1925], vol. 1, pp. 609 n. 1, 616, vol. 2, pp. 106, 136, and Taylor, *Medical Profession and Social Reform*, p. 34).

21. S. Adolphus Knopf, *A History of the National Tuberculosis Association: The Anti-Tuberculosis Movement in the United States* (New York: National Tuberculosis Association, 1922), p. 16; Taylor, *Medical Profession and Social Reform*, p. 34; Esmond R. Long, "Report of the Henry Phipps Institute of the University of Pennsylvania for the Period 1933–1937," in Henry Phipps Institute, *Twenty-Seventh Report* (Philadelphia: The Institute, 1937), pp. 5–7; *Philadelphia Public Ledger*, July 15, 1919; "The Henry Phipps Institute," Henry Phipps Institute, *Twentieth Report* (Philadelphia: The Institute, 1928), p. 10.

22. Charles J. Hatfield, "Henry Robert Murray Landis, 1872–1937," Phipps Institute, *Twenty-Seventh Report*, pp. 1–4; D. J. McCarthy, "Memoir of Henry Robert Murray Landis, M.D.," *Transactions and Studies of the College of Physicians of Philadelphia* 6 (1938): 254–256. For a succinct history of Philadelphia General Hospital, see Charles E. Rosenberg, "From Almshouse to Hospital: The Shaping of Philadelphia General Hospital," *Milbank Memorial Fund Quarterly/Health and Society* 60 (Winter 1982): 108–154.

23. Fox, "Social Policy and City Politics: Tuberculosis Reporting in New York, 1889–1900," in *Sickness and Health in America*, ed. Leavitt and Numbers, p. 418; Hatfield, "Henry Robert Murray Landis," p. 2. For the general acceptance of bacterial etiology and epidemiology in early twentieth-century public health circles, see Lawrence F. Schmeckebier, *The Public Health Service: Changing Views in Massachusetts, 1842–1936* (Cambridge, Mass.: Harvard University Press, 1972), pp. 103–112, and Rosen, "Historical Trends and Future Prospects," pp. 67–68.

24. Price, *Pennsylvania Pioneers*, pp. 163–164; Lawrence F. Flick, "The Work of the First Year," Phipps Institute, *First Annual Report*, pp. 12–13; and Lawrence F. Flick, "The Work of the Year," Phipps Institute, *Second Annual Report*, p. 3.

25. Millberry, "Medical and Dental Expansion After 1900," typescript in "The Negro in Philadelphia, 1938–39, 1941," Records of the Works Progress Administration Pennsylvania History Survey, Ethnic Survey, 1938–1941, record group 41, PSA, p. 5. The information on Lewis in Millberry's article is based on interviews conducted with Lewis, Bernard J. Newman, and Algernon B. Jackson in 1939.

26. See, for example, F. L. Hoffman, *Race Traits and Tendencies of the American Negro* (New York: American Economic Association, 1896); J. B. Rogers, "Comparison of Gross Tuberculosis Lesions in Whites and Negroes as Based on 150 Autopsies," *American Review of Tuberculosis* 4 (1920): 669–675; William T. Howard, *Public Health Administration and the Natural History of Disease in Baltimore, Maryland, 1797–1920* (Washington, D.C.: Carnegie Institution of Washington, 1924), esp. pp. 507–562; W. G. Smillie and D. L. Augustine, "Vital Capacity of the Negro Race," *Journal of the American Medical Association* 87 (1926): 2055–

2058; and M. Pinner and J. A. Kasper, "Pathological Peculiarities of Tuberculosis in the American Negro," *American Review of Tuberculosis* 28 (1932): 463–491. On social Darwinism, see Daniel J. Kevles, *In the Name of Eugenics: Genetics and the Use of Human Heredity* (New York: Alfred A. Knopf, 1985), pp. 20, 70–72, 90–91. See also Thomas F. Gossett, *Race: The History of an Idea in America* (New York: Schocken Books, 1968), pp. 144–175.

27. J. M. Taylor, "Remarks on the Health of the Colored People," *JNMA* 7 (1915): 162. In their rebuttal, the *JNMA* editors made it clear that Taylor was to be respected for bringing his thoughts before the black public, but that his ideas should be "food for thought" and inspiration for black medical professionals to work to refute. They pointed out that Afro-Americans were not becoming extinct but, indeed, were prospering despite social, economic, and environmental oppression. To Taylor's remarks that the "white and black races will not fuse [because] they are too totally unlike in characteristics and confirmation" and that unless "these colored people in a body realize these facts and adopt their forms of life . . . they will disappear," the editors replied: "The races . . . have been intermingling for the past 250 years . . . and the advice to the colored people to realize these facts seems to us a little far-fetched; for it is a fact well known in the South . . . that it is not the colored people who are responsible for the racial fusion, and that whatever mixing of bloods there may have been in almost every instance has come from the side of whites. . . . Hence it [Taylor's advice] would be more properly rendered to the members of the white race as a whole" ("Editorial: On Dr. Taylor of Philadelphia," *JNMA* 7 [1915]: 206–208).

28. White House Conference on Child Health and Protection, *The Home and the Child: Report of the Subcommittee on Housing and Home Management* (orig. pub. 1931; rpt. New York: Arno Press and New York Times, 1972), p. xi; Millberry, "Medical and Dental Expansion," p. 5. Newman was also connected with the Whittier Center between 1910 and 1920.

29. Millberry, "Medical and Dental Expansion," p. 5. Evidently no copy of the Lewis study has survived. After completing his work with the Phipps Institute, Lewis remained on the staff of Douglass Hospital through 1948. He also headed a black tuberculosis clinic for the city of Philadelphia in 1938, and during the 1950s he served on the board or as a prominent member of several local medical and social welfare organizations, including the Berean School, the Philadelphia Housing Association, and Mercy-Douglass Hospital (which was established by the merger and modernization of Douglass and Mercy hospitals). See G. James Fleming and Christian E. Burkel, eds., *Who's Who in Colored America: An Illustrated Biographical Directory of Notable Living Persons of African Descent in the United States* (7th ed.; Yonkers-on-Hudson, N.Y.: Christian E. Burkel and Associates, 1950), p. 338.

On the Phillips study, see Rosen, "First Neighborhood Health Center Movement," pp. 189–190. Phillips's philosophy of public health reform and his development of "demonstration districts" in Milwaukee is detailed in Judith W. Leavitt, *The Healthiest City: Milwaukee and the Politics of Health Reform* (Princeton, N.J.: Princeton University Press, 1982), pp. 214–239. The Phillips approach, which became known as the "social unit" idea, emphasized a two-pronged method of assessing the public health needs of a particular city section. First, the section was divided into "blocks" of approximately five hundred people, which were then surveyed and monitored door to door by neighborhood and social welfare workers. These workers, in turn, reported the general health needs of block residents to neighborhood health centers and sent needy individuals to these centers for treatment (Rosen, "First Neighborhood Health Center Movement," pp. 190–191).

30. Lewis's inquiry about black susceptibility to tuberculosis was by no means a new issue. Indeed, the debate within the American medical community over whether blacks were racially susceptible to tuberculosis stretches back to before the Civil War. For a review of this debate, see Todd L. Savitt, *Medicine and Slavery: The Disease and Health Care of Blacks in Antebellum Virginia* (Urbana: University of Illinois Press, 1978), pp. 41–45, 52, 142–45. For a fresh and incisive study of the international context of the slavery debate, see Kenneth F. Kiple and Virginia H. King, *Another Dimension to the Black Diaspora: Diet, Disease, and Racism* (Cambridge, Eng.: Cambridge University Press, 1981), pp. 7–8, 139–146.

Current medical thought concerning the susceptibility of blacks to tuberculosis nearly ignores the idea of an inherent predisposition to the disease among blacks. Indeed, over the past four decades, the issue of racial-genetic susceptibility has become increasingly obsolete in American medicine due to the emergence of effective immunization and chemotherapy for treatment of tuberculosis, as well as the immunity acquired by many Americans as a result of previous exposure. For instance, writing in 1968, William A. Soderman and William A. Soderman Jr., two leading pathologists, stated that racial-genetic factors were "of some importance in the development of tuberculosis," and that blacks were more susceptible than whites. However, the Sodermans cautioned, "hereditary constitutional characteristics, age and sex are factors influencing the course of tuberculosis in the individual; yet the role of these parameters in causing fluctuation in the level of resistance to infection is not understood." According to the Sodermans, even African natives (who were, presumably, highly susceptible to tuberculosis), once mildly infected, readily acquired a resistance similar to that of whites (William A. Soderman and William A. Soderman Jr., *Pathologic Physiology: Mechanisms of Disease* [Philadelphia: W. B. Saunders, 1968], pp. 54, 556). See also Byung H. Park and Robert A. Good, *Principles of Modern Immunobiology: Basic and Clinical* (Philadelphia: Lea & Febiger, 1974), pp. 546–547, and Harvey B. Simon, "Mycobacteria," *Scientific American Medicine Index* 5 (1980): 1201–1202, 1212.

By 1980, eminent medical clinicians such as Harvey B. Simon held that the overwhelming majority of tuberculosis patients in the United States developed the disease as a consequence of the reactivation of the old disease, which "by present standards had almost always been inadequately treated." Simon does not mention black susceptibility. Instead, he states that, given the disparity in treatment resources, tuberculosis in the United States, "not surprisingly," tends to cluster in certain sociological as opposed to racial groups and "is most common among males, the economically disadvantaged, and inner-city residents." Other social and hospitalized groups who experience a disproportionately high incidence of tuberculosis, according to Simon, are "immigrants, alcoholics, drug-dependent individuals, and patients with gastrectomies, neoplasia, uremia, or debilitating disease" (Simon, "Mycobacteria," p. 1). Simon's etiological summation has been reaffirmed in the updated 1984 *Scientific American Medicine Index.*

31. In the mid-1940s, streptomycin was discovered, followed by isoniazid in the early 1950s. These so-called "wonder drugs" provided safe means for healing tuberculosis and made prior treatment approaches—such as isolation and "collapse therapy"—obsolete. See Harold J. Simon, "Microbial Resistance in Tuberculosis," in *Rational Therapy and Control of Tuberculosis: A Symposium,* ed. Joseph E. Johnson (Gainesville: University of Florida Press, 1970), pp. 29–30; S. H. Ferebee, "Controlled Chemoprophylaxis Trails in Tuberculosis: A General Review," in *Advances in Tuberculosis Research,* vol. 17, ed. George Carnetti (Basel and New York: S. K. Kanard, 1970), pp. 19, 98; Robert Taylor, *Saranac: America's Magic Mountain* (Boston: Houghton Mifflin, 1986), pp. 275–278.

32. A valuable overview of the anti-tuberculosis campaigns among black Americans during the first half of the twentieth century is found in Marion M. Torchia, "The Tuberculosis Movement and the Race Question, 1890–1950," *Bulletin of the History of Medicine* 49 (Summer 1975): 152–168. Torchia identifies three dominant phases of anti-tuberculosis work in America during these six decades: the sanitarium movement, government-sponsored public health programs, and voluntary campaigns of the anti-tuberculosis societies. According to Torchia, the sanitarium movement was most influential before 1920, and the other two programs assumed central roles during the 1930s, as the federal social welfare policies of the New Deal era unfolded. Although Torchia describes voluntary self-help movements among black communities under the leadership of Booker T. Washington and the Negro Health Week Movement stretching back to 1907, Torchia overlooks the Phipps Institute and its influence on other anti-tuberculosis work throughout the nation and the contributions that black medical professionals made to the Institute's research and treatment efforts.

33. Landis, "Clinic for Negroes," p. 429; Whittier Center, *Annual Report, 1920* (Philadelphia: The Center, 1920), p. 4.

34. Whittier Center, *Annual Report, 1914* (Philadelphia: The Center, 1914), pp. 4–5.

35. Mabel K. Staupers, *No Time for Prejudice: A Study of the Integration of Negroes in Nursing in the United States* (New York: Macmillan, 1961), pp. 7–8; Rosen, "First Neighborhood Health Center Movement," p. 187; Duffy, *History of Public Health in New York City*, pp. 188, 274; Whittier Center, *Annual Report, 1914*, p. 5.

36. Landis, "Clinic for Negroes," pp. 429, p. 431; Whittier Center, *Annual Report, 1915* (Philadelphia: The Center, 1915), pp. 4–5; *The Story of the Whittier Center, 1924* (Philadelphia: The Center, 1924), p. 10.

37. Landis, "Clinic for Negroes," p. 430. As in other states with large urban black populations, in Pennsylvania blacks were generally excluded from state-operated sanitaria. Thus, the Pennsylvania legislature supported the employment of black medical personnel at Phipps because it expected that the Institute's services for blacks would both offer an immediate treatment resource for this overlooked (and growing) minority and improve preventive services to curtail the longstanding high tuberculosis and smallpox rate among blacks. See Torchia, "Tuberculosis Movement and the Race Question," p. 155; Henry M. Minton, "Negro Physicians and Public Health Work in Pennsylvania," *Opportunity: Journal of Negro Life* 2 (1924): 74.

38. Clement Richardson, ed., *The National Cyclopedia of the Colored Race* (Montgomery, Ala.: National Publishing, 1919), p. 282; Whittier Center, *Annual Report, 1914*, p. 1, and Whittier Center, *Annual Report, 1916* (Philadelphia: The Center, 1916), p. 2; Richardson, ed., *National Cyclopedia of the Colored Race*, p. 282; Edward Trust, *Trust's Professional Directory of Philadelphia, Camden, and Atlantic City and Nearby Towns, 1916–1917* (5th ed.; Philadelphia: Trust, 1917), p. 265; Thomas R. Peyton, *Quest for Dignity: An Autobiography of a Negro Doctor* (Los Angeles: Warren F. Lewis, 1950), p. 13 (Dr. Peyton was an intern at Mercy in the early 1920s and studied under Dr. Minton); "Henry McKee Minton, 1870–1946," *JNMA* 47 (1955): 285–286.

39. H. A. Pattison, "General Discussion of Some of the More Essential Problems Concerned in the Prevention and Control of Tuberculosis," in U.S. Public Health Service, *Municipal Health Department Practice for the Year 1923* (Public Health Bulletin No. 164; Washington, D.C.: GPO, 1926), pp. 195–202; Leavitt, *Healthiest City*, p. 243; F. B. Smith, *The People's Health, 1830–1910* (New York: Holmes & Meier, 1979), p. 287; George I. Lythcott et al., "Infectious Diseases," in *Textbook of Black-Related Diseases*, ed. Richard A. Williams (New York: McGraw-Hill, 1975), p. 166; Walsh McDermott, "Evaluating the Physician and His Technology," in *Doing Better and Feeling Worse*, ed. John H. Knowles (New York: W. W. Norton, 1979), p. 143. For a technical description of such a diagnosis, see Lythcott et al., "Infectious Diseases," p. 166.

40. Henry McKee Minton, "A List of Some of the Projects Completed by Me During My Superintendency of Mercy Hospital (ca. 1939), JRFA-FU, p. 1; Landis,

"Clinic for Negroes," p. 429.

41. Whittier Center, *Annual Report, 1915*, pp. 5–6.

42. Fannie Eshleman, "The Negro Nurse in a Tuberculosis Program," *Public Health Nursing*, July 19, 1935, reprinted in Henry Phipps Institute, *Twenty-Sixth Report* (Philadelphia: The Institute, 1935), p. 2; Trust, *Professional Directory, 1916–1917*, p. 250; Edward Trust, *Trust's Professional Dictionary, 1918–1919* (6th ed.; Philadelphia: Trust, 1919), p. 200.

43. Landis, "Clinic for Negroes," pp. 430–431; Millberry, "Black Medical and Dental Expansion," p. 7.

44. *Philadelphia Public Ledger*, July 15, 1919, Oct. 15, 1919, and April 11, 1920; "The Henry Phipps Institute . . . Advisory Council," in Henry Phipps Institute, *Sixteenth Report* (Philadelphia: The Institute, 1923), p. 2.

45. *Story of the Whittier Center*, pp. 10–11.

46. *Ibid.*, p. 8; Richardson, ed., *National Cyclopedia of the Colored Race*, p. 282.

47. Sadie T. Mossell, *A Study of the Negro Tuberculosis Problem in Philadelphia* (Philadelphia: Whittier Center and Henry Phipps Institute, 1923), pp. 18–19. In later decades, Mossell became a lawyer and civic leader in Philadelphia.

48. The three other clinics did not keep organized records on the race of their patients.

49. Mossell, *Study of the Negro Tuberculosis Problem*, pp. 19–20.

50. *Ibid.*, pp. 18–20.

51. "Background Material of Dr. H. R. M. Landis' 'Study of the Negro Tuberculosis Problem in Philadelphia, in 1921,' " Biographical Archive Section, Philadelphia College of Physicians and Surgeons, cage z8c-9; "Discussion on Paper ['Clinic for Negroes'] by Dr. Landis," *Transactions of the National Tuberculosis Association* 17 (1921): 434–435. Also see "Phipps Institute Looks After the Health of the Negro," *Nation's Health* 5 (1923): 364. Stuart Galishoff makes passing mention of Newark's Negro clinic in *Safeguarding the Public Health: Newark, 1845–1918* (Westport, Conn.: Greenwood Press, 1975), p. 129.

52. Henry R. M. Landis, "Tuberculosis Campaign and Some of Its Accomplishments," in Phipps Institute, *Sixteenth Report*, art. 1, p. 2.

53. *Ibid.*, pp. 2–3.

54. *Ibid.*, p. 3.

55. *Ibid.*, pp. 4–5.

56. *Ibid.*, pp. 3, 4.

57. *Ibid.*

58. Knopf, *History of the National Tuberculosis Association*, p. 17; Henry R. M. Landis, "Non-Tuberculosis Complications of Tuberculosis," *Therapeutic Gazette*, Dec. 1922, p. 4, reprinted in Phipps Institute, *Sixteenth Report*, art. 6, pp. 1, 4.

Henry R. M. Landis, "The Tuberculosis Problem and the Negro," *Virginia Medical Monthly*, Jan. 1923, p. 5, reprinted in Phipps Institute, *Sixteenth Report*, art. 3. Landis's prior study was "Respiratory Symptoms Due to Latent Syphilis," in *Contributions to Medicine and Biological Research, Dedicated to Sir William Osler . . . by His Pupils and Co-Workers*, reprinted in the Henry Phipps Institute, *Fifteenth Report* (Philadelphia: The Institute, 1921), art. 6, pp. 625–631.

59. *Ibid.* Kemp was hired as a staff nurse at the Institute's main black clinic. In 1922, a year later, she was made supervisor of the Institute's northwest black clinic, a post she held for eight years. She was transferred back to Phipps in 1931, where she stayed until retiring in 1940 (Mary E. Carnegie, *The Path We Tread: Blacks in Nursing, 1854–1984* [Philadelphia: J. B. Lippincott, 1986], pp. 149–151).

60. "Report of the Director . . . to the Advisory Council," in Henry Phipps Institute, *Sixteenth Report* (Philadelphia: The Institute, 1923), pp. 1–4. S. A. Knopf, a prominent tuberculosis authority who was at one time president of the National Tuberculosis Association, wrote in 1922 that the sympathetic attitude of the Institute's staff toward its patients could not be matched at any other medical institution in America (Knopf, *A History of the National Tuberculosis Association*, p. 17).

61. Landis, "Clinic for Negroes," pp. 437–438 and quote on p. 432.

62. *Ibid.*, pp. 437–438.

Chapter III

1. John F. Bauman, "Black Slums/Black Projects: The New Deal and Negro Housing in Philadelphia," *Pennsylvania History* 41 (July 1974): 316; *Philadelphia Public Ledger*, May 4, 1923, May 29, 1923, and June 19, 1923, as well as issues for June 17, 1923, and June 30, 1923; "Antituberculosis Work Among Negroes of Philadelphia," *JNMA* 15 (1923): 195. On the tuberculosis crisis in New York City and Indianapolis during the early 1920s, see Gilbert Osofsky, *Harlem: The Making of a Ghetto* (New York: Harper & Row, 1971), pp. 152–154, and Emma Lou Thornbrough, "Segregation in Indiana During the Klan Era of the 1920s," in *The Making of Black America*, vol. 2: *The Black Community in Modern America*, ed. August Meier and Elliot Rudwick (New York: Atheneum, 1969), p. 191.

2. Vincent P. Franklin, "The Philadelphia Race Riot of 1918," *Pennsylvania Magazine of History and Biography* 99 (July 1975): 337–338, 348–350.

3. John T. Emlen to Bernard J. Newman, April 20, 1923, Papers of the Housing Association of Delaware Valley, 1909–1972, TUUA. Emlen was a head of the Armstrong Association and had authored the widely cited 1913 study, "The Movement for the Betterment of the Negro in Philadelphia."

4. Bernard J. Newman to Henry McKee Minton, Feb. 3, 1923; R. R. Wright to Bernard J. Newman, Feb. 2, 1923; Bernard J. Newman to Carl Murphy, editor of the *Baltimore Afro-American*, Feb. 14, 1923; all in Papers of the Housing Association, TUUA.

5. Philadelphia Housing Association, *Know Your City* (pamphlet; Philadelphia: The Association, 1923), TUUA; Bernard J. Newman, "Housing in Philadelphia, 1912," p. 19, in Papers of the Housing Association, TUUA.

6. Philadelphia Housing Association, *Know Your City*. On living conditions see "Housing in Philadelphia, 1923," pp. 18–19, in Papers of the Housing Association, TUUA. On subdividing see "Negro Migrants in Philadelphia in 1923," *Monthly Labor Review* 19 (Nov. 1924): 54–55. This report was based on *Philadelphia Housing Association Annual Report for 1923: Housing in Philadelphia* (Philadelphia: The Association, 1924). The housing report stated: "The worst aspect of the Philadelphia houses was the unsanitary conditions. On the 87 properties there were 374 violations of the housing and sanitation law." Among these violations were thirty-nine cases of overcrowding, nine windowless rooms, thirty-nine cases of defective plumbing, twenty-nine badly leaking roofs, fifty-four cases of inadequate fire protection, and "other conditions of filth and disrepair" (p. 54).

7. Philadelphia Migration Committee, "Report of the Committee on Negro Migration," July 11, 1923, report delivered at the meeting held in the offices of the Philadelphia Housing Association, p. 1, TUUA.

8. *Ibid.*, pp. 1–2.

9. Philadelphia Migration Committee, "Tentative Program of the Sub-Committee on Health," Aug. 1, 1923, p. 1, TUUA.

10. *Ibid.*; Louis J. Dublin, "Introductory Note," Aug. 1935, *Cumulative Index to the Statistical Bulletin of the Metropolitan Life Insurance Company* (15 vols.; n.p.: Metropolitan Life Insurance Co., c. 1935), pp. 1–2; Marquis James, *The Metropolitan Life: A Study in Business Growth* (New York: Viking Press, 1947), pp. 338–339, 393–398; "Census of Public Health Nursing in the United States," *Public Health Nurse* 18 (May 1926): 289. The nursing survey was taken on January 1, 1924.

11. Philadelphia Migration Committee, "Tentative Program of the Sub-Committee on Health," p. 2; Henry M. Minton, "Reduction in Negro Mortality," paper read before the All-Philadelphia Conference on Social Work, April 1924, reprinted in Henry Phipps Institute, *Eighteenth Report* (Philadelphia: The Institute, 1925), pp. 10–16, esp. p. 12–13.

12. "Negro Migrants in Philadelphia in 1923," p. 55. In New York City, by comparison, the Public Health Department appointed sixty additional sanitary inspectors during its 1869 smallpox epidemic. These inspectors joined the department's house-to-house check that contacted 150,000 families. Also, some 700,000 residents were vaccinated or offered vaccinations (John Duffy, *A History of Public*

Health in New York City, 1866–1966 [New York: Russell Sage Foundation, 1974], p. 149).

13. City of Philadelphia, Bureau of Health, *Annual Report of the Division of Medical Inspection, 1923* (Philadelphia: The City, 1923), p. 620. Writing in *Opportunity*, the National Urban League publication, Minton placed the number of smallpox cases during the period from December 13, 1922, to December 27, 1923, at seventy-nine (Minton, "Negro Physicians and Public Health Work," *Opportunity: Journal of Negro Life* 2 [1924]: 74).

14. Philadelphia Bureau of Health, *Annual Report of the Division of Medical Inspection, 1923*, p. 620. On smallpox epidemics in New York, Baltimore, and Milwaukee, see Duffy, *History of Public Health in New York City*, pp. 149–153; William T. Howard Jr., *Public Health Administration and the Natural History of Disease in Baltimore, Maryland, 1797–1920* (Washington, D.C.: Carnegie Institution of Washington, 1924), pp. 287–296; Judith W. Leavitt, *The Healthiest City: Milwaukee and the Politics of Health Reform* (Princeton, N.J.: Princeton University Press, 1982).

15. Minton, "Negro Physicians and Public Health Work," p. 74; Philadelphia Bureau of Health, *Annual Report of the Division of Medical Inspection of Public Schools, 1923* (Philadelphia: The City, 1923), p. 685.

16. Philadelphia Housing Association, *Know Your City*.

The municipal health agencies in Philadelphia were organized under the city's Department of Public Health. This department was divided into two large bureaus—the Bureau of Health and the Bureau of Hospitals. The Health Bureau was composed of several divisions, including a medical inspection of public schools division responsible for examinations and limited care of public school children, a housing and sanitation division responsible for inspection of housing, sanitation nuisances, and meat-milk-cattle-food products; and a child hygiene division responsible for public health clinics for children. The Hospital Bureau also was composed of subunits, namely, the city-run health facilities like the Philadelphia General Hospital and the Philadelphia Hospital for Contagious Diseases (Nathan Sinai and A. B. Mills for the Committee on the Costs of Medical Care, *A Survey of the Medical Facilities of the City of Philadelphia, 1929* [Chicago: University of Chicago Press, 1931], p. 108). At this time the Migration Committee's membership was as follows: John T. Emlen and A. L. Manly, Armstrong Association; J. Prentice Murphy, Children's Bureau; Elim A. E. Palmquist, Federation of Churches; Clarence R. White, Durham Public School; Mrs. Edmund Stirling, Inter-Racial Committee; Henry M. Minton, M.D., Mercy Hospital; Henry J. Barringer, Octavia Hill Association; Harvey Dee Brown, Philadelphia Health Council; Bernard J. Newman and Marie-Nelson Rowe, Philadelphia Housing Association; George R. Bedinger, Public Charities Association; Karl de Schweinitz, Society for Organizing Charity; Kenneth M. Coolbrough, State Employment Bureau; Albert G. Fraser,

Traveler's Aid Society; and Irwin J. Gorden, Welfare Federation (Philadelphia Migration Committee, "Report").

17. City of Philadelphia, *Reports of the Various Departments of the City of Philadelphia for the Year Ending December 31, 1923: Division of Housing and Sanitation* (Philadelphia: The City, 1924), p. 767. New personnel hirings are in the 1926 report (City of Philadelphia, Bureau of Health, *Annual Report of the Division of Housing and Sanitation, 1926* [Philadelphia: The City, 1926], p. 346). Neither the papers of the Migration Committee nor those of its head, Bernard J. Newman, mention any specific reasons why City Council would not provide appropriations to increase the Public Health Department's inspectors. Certainly the City Council's refusal to fund more inspectors seems unreasonable considering the small economic support the Migration Committee was seeking; in fact, the Committee pointed out during its meeting with Taylor that additional inspectors would cost virtually nothing since the applications for rental property licenses rendered by these inspectors would net the city more than the cost of their salaries (Bernard J. Newman to N. H. Taylor, July 12, 1923, Papers of the Housing Association, TUUA).

18. Bureau of Health, *Annual Report of the Division of Medical Inspection, 1923*, p. 607.

19. Minton, "Negro Physicians and Public Health Work," p. 73.

20. After 1923 and through the twenties, Bernard Newman continued to collect and publish data on the severe housing shortage that was affecting the city's blacks. However he did this under the auspices solely of the Philadelphia Housing Association and not of any citywide, interagency group like the Migration Committee (Philadelphia Housing Association, *Housing in Philadelphia, 1924* [Philadelphia: The Association, 1924], pp. 14–15, and Philadelphia Housing Association, *Housing in Philadelphia, 1925* [Philadelphia: The Association, 1925], pp. 24–27, both in Papers of the Housing Association, TUUA).

21. "The Philadelphia Health Council and Tuberculosis Committee," *Philadelphia—World's Medical Centre* (n.p.: n.pub., c. 1930), pp. 49–50, PCPS; Philadelphia Bureau of Health, *Annual Report of the Division of Tuberculosis, 1923*, p. 157. The upshot of political conservatism in the Pennsylvania legislature was that, beginning in the latter half of 1923, state appropriations for Department of Health programs were greatly reduced. The combined funds for such services as medical inspection of schools, child health care, and tuberculosis treatment dropped from $5.3 million to $4 million for the biennia of June 1, 1921–May 31, 1923 and June 1, 1923–May 31, 1925 (*Pennsylvania State Manual, 1923–1924* [Harrisburg: Pennsylvania Bureau of Publications, 1924], pp. 926, 944; *Pennsylvania State Manual, 1925–1926* [Harrisburg: Pennsylvania Bureau of Publications, 1926], p. 612).

22. Sylvester K. Stevens and Donald H. Kent, eds., *County Government and Archives in Pennsylvania* (Harrisburg: Pennsylvania Historical and Museum Commission, 1947), pp. 451–452. The Hamburg Sanatorium central office was located

in Philadelphia. Both Cresson and Hamburg treated a small number of black patients (see Table 12), but Cresson's black population was minute in 1924 and Hamburg's was declining. Furthermore, based on the statements of Tuberculosis Division officials, it is evident that the black patients received differential treatment, such as being given shorter stays or being placed in segregated wards (*Pennsylvania State Manual, 1925–1926*, pp. 358–359; Pennsylvania Department of Welfare, *Negro Survey of Pennsylvania* [Harrisburg, Pa.: The Department, 1928], p. 84).

23. *Philadelphia Public Ledger*, April 19, 1922; U.S. Public Health Service, *Municipal Health Department Practice for the Year 1923: Based Upon the 100 Largest Cities in the United States* (Public Health Bulletin No. 164; Washington, D.C.: GPO, 1926), pp. 28–29, chart between pp. 38 and 39, and p. 90.

24. Sadie T. Mossell, *A Study of the Negro Tuberculosis Problem in Philadelphia* (Philadelphia: Whittier Center and Henry Phipps Institute, 1923), pp. 18–19; Monroe N. Work, ed., *Negro Year Book: An Encyclopedia of the Negro, 1921–1922* (Tuskegee Institute, Ala.: Negro Year Book Publishing Co., 1922), p. 372.

25. Philadelphia Bureau of Health, *Annual Report of the Division of Tuberculosis, 1923*, pp. 158–160.

26. *Ibid.*, p. 160; "Philadelphia Health Council and Tuberculosis Committee," p. 50; Philadelphia Bureau of Health, *Annual Report of the Division of Tuberculosis, 1923*, p. 160; Millberry, "Medical and Dental Expansion After 1900," typescript in "The Negro in Philadelphia, 1938–1939, 1941," Records of the Works Progress Administration Pennsylvania History Survey, Ethnic Survey, 1938–1941, Record Group 41, PSA, p. 15.

27. Philadelphia Bureau of Health, *Annual Report of the Division of Tuberculosis, 1923*, p. 160.

28. Minton, "Negro Physicians and Public Health Work," p. 73; Millberry, "Medical and Dental Expansion," p. 15.

29. Whittier Center, *The Story of the Whittier Center* (Philadelphia: The Center, 1924), pp. 13–15, TUUA.

30. Minton, "Negro Physicians and Public Health Work," p. 73; Whittier Center, *Story of the Whittier Center*, p. 14.

31. The personnel of the three Negro Bureau clinics, as given by the Whittier Center, were as follows: Health Clinic No. 1 (Phipps Institute), Dr. Henry M. Minton, Dr. Griffin A. Saunders, Dr. Scott, Miss Johnson, Miss Turner, Mrs. Bradley, Miss Alexander; Health Clinic No. 2 (Jefferson Hospital), Dr. Thomas S. Burwell, Dr. Taylor, Dr. William H. Barnes, Dr. Moore, Dr. Lennon, Miss Sightler; Health Clinic No. 3 (20th St. and Ridge Ave.), Dr. Johnson, Dr. Scott, Dr. Chauncey Kemp, Mrs. Nancy Kemp, Miss Sasportas (Whittier Center, *Story of the Whittier Center*, p. 15).

32. Minton, "Negro Physicians and Public Health Work," p. 74. On cross-cultural dynamics, see Rachel E. Specter, *Cultural Diversity in Health and Illness*

(New York: Appleton-Century-Crofts, 1979), pp. 239–243; Wilbur H. Watson, "Folk Medicine and Older Blacks in the Southern United States," in *Black Folk Medicine: The Therapeutic Significance of Faith and Trust*, ed. Wilbur H. Watson (New Brunswick, N.J.: Transactions Books, 1984), pp. 53–66; and Kurt W. Deuschle, "Cross-Cultural Medicine: The Navajo Indians as Case Exemplar," *Daedalus* 115 (Spring 1986): 175–177. Generally, the area of cross-cultural dynamics was not broken open to the larger field of medical sociology until 1955, when Benjamin Paul's classic study appeared. See Benjamin Paul, ed., *Health, Culture, and Community* (New York: Russell Sage Foundation, 1955).

33. Minton, "Negro Physicians and Public Health Work," p. 74.

34. Millberry, "Medical and Dental Expansion," pp. 14–15. Tucker was a charter member of the National Association of Colored Graduate Nurses and this organization's president from 1910 to 1912 (Mabel K. Staupers, *No Time for Prejudice: A Study of the Integration of Negroes in Nursing in the United States* [New York: Macmillan, 1961], pp. 18, 186–187). The Freedmen's, Provident, and Lincoln nursing schools were among the nation's few institutions designed to train black nurses.

35. *Ibid.*, p. 15; Frank A. Craig, "A Study of the Housing and Social Conditions in Selected Districts of Philadelphia," in Henry Phipps Institute, *Eleventh Report* (Philadelphia: The Institute, 1915). The city's Board of Education during the 1920s and 1930s did not keep systematic data on the racial composition of the specific schools. In most cases they were notoriously segregated. The state's 1928 Department of Welfare survey on black social conditions included a section "Reviving Segregation in the Public Schools of Pennsylvania." It highlighted Philadelphia especially, stating that "in Philadelphia, there are 12 schools which have 100 percent Negro attendance. All the teachers are Negroes including the principal. Negro children living in school districts bordering on the districts of these 12 schools are sent out of their district to the school having all Negro pupils and teachers, and white children living in the district of the schools having all Negro pupils and teachers are sent out of their district to schools which have 100 percent white attendance" (Pennsylvania Department of Welfare, *Negro Survey*, p. 58). See also Kenton Jackson, "Education: Present-Day Education," in "The Negro in Philadelphia, 1938–1939, 1941," Records of the Works Progress Administration Pennsylvania History Survey, Ethnic Survey, 1938–1941, Record Group 41, PSA, p. 4.

36. Hospital and Library Service Bureau of the American Conference on Hospital Service, "Educational Facilities for Colored Nurses and Their Employment," *Public Health Nurse* 17 (April 1925): 203–204. One 1924 survey found that, of 1,688 accredited nursing schools throughout the country, only 54 admitted blacks. Half of the schools open to blacks were connected with black hospitals or health department units serving blacks. Another expert concluded that the possibility of

black women's receiving education at white nursing schools was out of the question. He explained that all future "opportunities" for blacks to acquire nursing education were to be found in the nation's black nursing schools (Franklin O. Nichols, "Opportunities and Problems of Public Health Nursing Among Negroes," *Public Health Nurse* 16 [March 1924]: 122). On the substantial number of Philadelphia black nurses working in the city's public health agencies and black hospitals, see Roberta West, *History of Nursing in Pennsylvania* (n.p.: Pennsylvania State Nurses Association, 1932?), p. 33; Millberry, "Medical and Dental Expansion," pp. 13–15.

37. "Census of Public Health Nursing," pp. 289, 311. This estimate was derived from the data in the National Public Health Nursing organization survey, "Census of Public Health Nursing" (pp. 289, 311), and the federal census figures for trained nurses in Philadelphia for 1920 and 1930. In 1920, there were 3,848 white nurses and 87 black nurses, and in 1930, 7,712 white nurses and 115 black nurses. For the ten years from 1920 to 1930, this computes to an average yearly increase of 386 white nurses and 7 black nurses. Thus, at the end of 1923 one can estimate that there were approximately 5,006 white nurses and 108 black nurses in the city.

38. Whittier Center, *The Work of the Whittier Center* (Philadelphia: The Center, c. 1927), p. 5, TUUA; H. R. M. Landis, "The Negro Nurse in Public Health Work," *Child Health Bulletin* 3 (Jan. 1927), reprinted in the Henry Phipps Institute, *Nineteenth Report* (Philadelphia: The Institute, 1927), pp. 18–19.

39. Landis, "Negro Nurse in Public Health Work," pp. 19–20.

40. *Ibid.*, p. 20. In 1928 the Pennsylvania Department of Welfare carried out an extensive statewide survey on living and work conditions of blacks throughout the state that reached conclusions similar to those of Dr. Landis. On the basis of these returns, the Department made recommendations in three areas: industrial conditions, housing, and health and sanitation. In the last area, the Department's key program suggestion was: "City health departments should be induced to engage the services of colored nurses, and . . . Negro physicians. . . . Our only reason for urging the employment of Negro nurses and physicians is that such persons can understand and sympathize with the people of their own race, and secure their confidence more readily than whites" (Pennsylvania Department of Welfare, *Negro Survey*, pp. 94–95).

41. Philadelphia Bureau of Health, *Annual Report of the Division of Tuberculosis, 1927* (Philadelphia: The City, 1927), p. 171.

42. Philadelphia Department of Public Health, *Annual Report of the Division of Communicable Disease, Tuberculosis Section, 1928* (Philadelphia: The City, 1928), pp. 258–260.

43. *Ibid.*, pp. 258–259.

44. *Ibid.*, p. 258.

45. *Ibid.*, pp. 259–260.

46. Hospital of the Woman's Medical College of Pennsylvania, *Twenty-Fourth Annual Report for the Year Ending May 31, 1928*, pp. 9, 27, AWMC; Hospital of the Woman's Medical College of Pennsylvania, *Twenty-Fifth Annual Report for the Year Ending May 31, 1929*, p. 8, AWMC.

The makeshift clinics that the Philadelphia Bureau of Health maintained were one of its major institutional deficiencies by 1929. A survey of the Bureau in that year reported that "nine of the ten child health centers are in rented quarters and all are inadequately equipped and too confined in space for efficient operation" (Sinai and Mills, *Survey of the Medical Facilities of the City of Philadelphia*, p. 109).

In 1923 the tuberculosis clinic and the "eye, ear, nose and throat" clinics were described by the hospital's medical director as "always crowded. . . . In clinic hours the waiting benches are always full. More clinic rooms are urgently needed." Similar conditions obtained in 1929, when the dispensary had a "severe handicap in the lack of space." Each year including 1928 the hospital far exceeded the number of "free service days" paid for by the state for in-patient treatment of the indigent (Hospital of the Woman's Medical College of Pennsylvania, *Nineteenth Annual Report for Year Ending May 31, 1923*, pp. 6–7, AWMC; Woman's Medical College, *Twenty-Fourth Annual Report*, p. 9; Alumnae Association of the Woman's Medical College of Pennsylvania, *Minutes of the Fifty-Fourth Annual Meeting*, June 13, 1929, p. 19, AWMC).

47. Philadelphia Department of Public Health, *Annual Report of the Division of Communicable Disease, Tuberculosis Section, 1928*, pp. 259–260.

48. W. Montague Cobb, *Progress and Portents for the Negro in Medicine* (New York: National Association for the Advancement of Colored People, 1948), p. 18; Committee on the Costs of Medical Care, *Medical Care for the American People* (Publication No. 28; Chicago: University of Chicago Press, 1932), pp. 5–12; Edwin R. Embree to Julius F. Rosenwald, May 10, 1928, JRFA-FU.

49. H. R. M. Landis, "Tuberculosis and the Negro," *Annals of The American Academy of Political and Social Science*, special issue: *The American Negro* 140 (Nov. 1928): 86–89, esp. p. 89; Henry L. Phillips to Edwin R. Embree, May 7, 1928, JRFA-FU.

50. Council on Medical Education and Hospitals of the American Medical Association, "Investigation of Negro Hospitals," *Journal of the American Medical Association* 92 (April 1929): 1376.

51. Campaign Committee, *For the Health of a Race* (Philadelphia: Holmes Press, 1928), p. 5. See also Francis F. Kane, "The Campaign of 1928," *The Modern Hospital*, Feb. 1929; Henry M. Minton, "Some of the Problems of Hospital Administration," reprint from *JNMA* 20 (1928) in JRFA-FU, p. 4; S. Lillian Clayton to Edwin R. Embree, May 24, 1928, JRFA-FU.

52. Campaign Committee, *For the Health of a Race*, p. 11; Mercy Hospital and School for Nurses, *Annual Report, 1923–1924* (Philadelphia: The Hospital, 1924),

p. 7; Mercy Hospital and School for Nurses, *Annual Report, 1924–1925* (Philadelphia: The Hospital, 1925), pp. 7–9. The campaign occurred in 1924 and intended to raise $40,000. It was, however, only a partial success. A valuable case study of ethnocentrism and fund-raising efforts for hospitals during the pre-World War II period is provided by Morris J. Vogel in *The Invention of the Modern Hospital: Boston, 1870–1930* (Chicago: University of Chicago Press, 1980).

53. *The Pennsylvania Manual, 1929* (Harrisburg: Pennsylvania Bureau of Publications, 1929), pp. 133, 229; statement by S. Lillian Clayton cited in Henry L. Phillips to Edwin R. Embree, May 7, 1928, JRFA-FU.

54. On Hill see Milton M. James, "Leslie Pickney Hill," *Negro History Bulletin* 24 (1961): 135–138. On Rhodes see "526 South 16th Street," *Brown American*, Jan. 1937, p. 9; Thomas Yenser, ed., *Who's Who in Colored America: A Biographical Dictionary of Notable Living Persons of African Descent, 1938–1940* (5th ed.; Brooklyn, N.Y.: Thomas Yenser, 1940), pp. 436. On Asbury and Henry see *Philadelphia Public Ledger*, Sept. 23, 1933, and Sept. 24, 1933; *Who's Who in Colored America, 1938–1940*, pp. 33, 248.

55. John H. Stanfield, *Philanthropy and Jim Crow in American Social Science* (Westport, Conn.: Greenwood Press, 1985), pp. 96–118; E. H. Beardsley, "Making Separate, Equal: Black Physicians and the Problems of Medical Segregation in the Pre-World War II South," *Bulletin of the History of Medicine* 57 (Fall 1983): 382–396.

The Rosenwald Fund was founded in 1917 by Julius Rosenwald, a business magnate and president of Sears and Roebuck Company. Until its closing in 1948 the Fund, along with other largely northern-based philanthropic foundations—like John D. Rockefeller's General Education Board (1902), the Anna T. Jeanes Fund (1905), and the Phelps-Stokes Fund (1910)—that emerged around the same time, had a major impact on the social and educational institutions of black America. The Rosenwald Fund subsidized black public schools and libraries, as well as higher education and health projects for blacks, in both the North and the South. For a detailed analysis of the Fund's involvement in the early twentieth-century black American community, see Stanfield, *Philanthropy and Jim Crow*, pp. 97–118; John H. Franklin, *From Slavery to Freedom* (New York: Alfred A. Knopf, 1974), pp. 278–280, 415; August Meier and Elliot Rudwick, *From Plantation to Ghetto* (New York: Hill & Wang, 1970), p. 202; Kenneth R. Manning, *Black Apollo of Science: The Life of Ernest Everett Just* (New York: Oxford University Press, 1983), pp. 122–123; and Gilbert A. Belles, "The College Faculty, the Negro Scholar, and the Julius Rosenwald Fund," *Journal of Negro Education* 54 (1969): 383–392.

56. Campaign Committee, *For the Health of a Race*, p. 27.

57. *Ibid.*, p. 3.

58. *Ibid.*, pp. 3, 8.

59. *Ibid.*, p. 9.

60. *Ibid.*, p. 8. Mercy student nurses were required to complete special two-month public health courses at both the Phipps Institute and the Visiting Nurses Association (Mercy Hospital and School for Nurses, *Annual Report of the Board of Directors, 1923–1924* [Philadelphia: The Hospital, 1924], p. 25).

61. Campaign Committee, *For the Health of a Race*, p. 9.

62. *Ibid.*, p. 10; Mercy Hospital and School for Nurses, *Biennial Report, 1928–1930* (Philadelphia: The Hospital, 1930), p. 12; Haven Emerson et al., *Philadelphia Hospital and Health Survey, 1929* (Philadelphia: Philadelphia Chamber of Commerce, 1929), pp. 709–710.

63. Mercy Hospital, *Biennial Report, 1928–1930*, p. 12; Henry M. Minton to Edwin R. Embree, Oct. 2, 1930, JRFA-FU.

64. Minton to Embree, Oct. 2, 1930.

65. Emerson, *Philadelphia Hospital and Health Survey, 1929*, pp. 695–696.

66. Cobb, *Progress and Portents*, pp. 24–25; E. R. Embree, *Julius Rosenwald Fund: A Review to June 30, 1928* (Chicago: The Fund, 1928), p. 14; C. A. Mills, "Distribution of American Research Funds," *Science* 107 (February 6, 1948), p. 127.

67. Charles S. Johnson, *The Economic Status of Negroes* (Nashville: Fisk University Press, 1933), p. 19; Margaret B. Tinkcom, "Depression and War—1929–1946," in *Philadelphia: A 300-Year History*, ed. Russell F. Weigley (New York: W. W. Norton, 1982), p. 609.

68. Philadelphia Bureau of Health, *Annual Report of the Division of Tuberculosis, 1930* (Philadelphia: The City, 1930), p. 406.

69. *Ibid.*, pp. 406–407.

70. A. Gordon, "Frederick Douglass Memorial Hospital and Training School," in *Philadelphia—World's Medical Centre*, p. 59. This publication was apparently composed by associates of the University of Pennsylvania medical institutions or the County Medical Society of Philadelphia. Gordon also stated that "the Douglass Hospital was among the first to direct a city-wide educational campaign during the need for early diagnosis of tuberculosis." The hospital's chest clinic was also now to be opened in the evening hours (p. 59).

71. Philadelphia Bureau of Health, *Annual Report of the Division of Tuberculosis, 1930*, p. 407.

72. *Philadelphia—World's Medical Centre*, p. 50.

73. Philadelphia Bureau of Health, *Annual Report of the Division of Tuberculosis, 1932* (Philadelphia: The City, 1932), p. 409; *ibid.*, p. 408. During 1932, the number of blacks who died from tuberculosis was 469 compared to 582 in 1930 (Philadelphia Bureau of Health, *Annual Report of the Division of Tuberculosis, 1930*, p. 406; Philadelphia Bureau of Health, *Annual Report of the Division of Tuberculosis, 1933* [Philadelphia: The City, 1933], p. 384).

244

74. Philadelphia Bureau of Health, *Annual Report of the Division of Tuberculosis, 1933*, p. 384.

75. Marion M. Torchia, "The Tuberculosis Movement and the Race Question, 1890–1950," *Bulletin of the History of Medicine* 49 (Summer 1975): 152–168.

76. *Philadelphia Tribune*, June 22, 1933; Frederick Douglass Memorial Hospital, *Thirty-Eighth Year, Annual Report, New Series, June 1st, 1933, to May 31st, 1934*, p. 2, PCPS; *Philadelphia Tribune*, June 22, 1933. In fact, in 1930 twenty-two nursing trainees at Douglass, the majority of its nursing school personnel, quit in the middle of the school year because the hospital could not guarantee restoration of state accreditation for its nursing program. Without such accreditation, the nursing candidates would not be able to find employment as graduate nurses at accredited hospitals and medical facilities in Pennsylvania. The hospital was able to locate only a handful of replacements for these lost nurses ("Frederick Douglass Memorial Hospital," Philadelphia Public Ledger Index, Jan. 1 and 2, 1930, Philadelphia Free Library, Newspaper Collections).

77. *Philadelphia Tribune*, June 22, 1933.

78. Douglass Memorial Hospital, *Thirty-Eighth Annual Report*, p. 2; Free Hospital for Poor Consumptives and White Haven Sanatorium Association, *Thirty-Seventh Annual Report, March 1, 1934–February 28, 1935* (Philadelphia: The Hospital, 1935), pp. 3–4; Russell F. Minton, "The History of Mercy-Douglass Hospital," *JNMA* 43 (May 1951): 154. From 1925 through 1929 the annual appropriation for Douglass Hospital was $17,000. However, in 1932, when the cut-off of state funds occurred, the hospital was receiving only $12,000 per year, and this was the sum allocated to Douglass once Mossell resigned (*Pennsylvania State Manual*, 1927 [Harrisburg: Pennsylvania Bureau of Publications, 1927], p. 653; *Pennsylvania State Manual, 1935–1936* [Harrisburg: Pennsylvania Bureau of Publications, 1936], p. 1076).

79. Douglass Memorial Hospital, *Thirty-Eighth Annual Report*, p. 2.

80. Philadelphia Bureau of Health, *Annual Report of the Division of Tuberculosis, 1936* (Philadelphia: The City, 1936), p. 526; Esmond R. Long, "Report of the Henry Phipps Institute of the University of Pennsylvania for the Period 1933–1937," in *Phipps Institute Twenty-Seventh Report* (Philadelphia: The Institute, 1937), pp. 6, 11, 14, 15, 18.

81. Millberry, "Medical and Dental Expansion," pp. 9, 14, 15.

82. *Ibid.*, pp. 13–15.

83. *Ibid.*, p. 11.

Chapter IV

1. On the distinction between medical problems deriving from accidental as opposed to epidemiological causes, see Edward A. Suchman, "Conceptual Analysis

of the Accident Phenomena," in *Medical Men and Their Work: A Sociological Reader*, ed. Elliot Freidson and Judith Lorbes (Chicago: Aldine-Atherton, 1972), pp. 377–380, 383–384.

2. H. Viscount Nelson, "Black Life in the Ghetto: Philadelphia's Thirtieth Ward, 1900–1940," paper presented at the Black History in Pennsylvania Conference, Lincoln University, April 20, 1978, p. 1; Andrew Billingsley and Jeanne M. Giovannoni, *Children of the Storm: Black Children and American Child Welfare* (New York: Harcourt Brace Jovanovich, 1970), pp. 115–125; John F. Bauman, "Black Slums/Black Projects: The New Deal and Negro Housing in Philadelphia," *Pennsylvania History* 41 (July 1974): 319.

3. The development of one essentially centralized black housing district in the cities of Chicago, Detroit, and New York City (i.e., Manhattan) has been documented in numerous studies. On Chicago see E. Franklin Frazier, "The Impact of Urban Civilization on Negro Life," in *E. Franklin Frazier on Race Relations: Selected Writings*, ed. G. Franklin Edwards (Chicago: University of Chicago Press, 1968), art. 10, pp. 167–168; Thomas L. Philpott, *The Slum and the Ghetto: Neighborhood Deterioration and Middle-Class Reform, Chicago, 1880–1930* (New York: Oxford University Press, 1978), esp. pp. 121–133; and Arnold R. Hirsch, *Making the Second Ghetto: Race and Housing in Chicago, 1940–1960* (New York: Cambridge University Press, 1983), esp. pp. 2–18. On Detroit, see David A. Levine, *Internal Combustion: The Races in Detroit, 1915–1926* (Bridgeport, Conn.: Greenwood Press, 1976), and August Meier and Elliot Rudwick, *Black Detroit and the Rise of the UAW* (New York: Oxford University Press, 1979). On Manhattan, see Roi Ottley and William J. Weatherby, eds., *The Negro in New York: An Informal Social History* (New York: New York Public Library, 1967), esp. pp. 182–186, 266; Gilbert Osofsky, *Harlem: The Making of a Ghetto* (New York: Harper & Row, 1971), esp. pp. 122–123, 137–140. Chester Rapkin and William G. Grigsby, *The Demand for Housing in Racially Mixed Areas: A Study of the Nature of Neighborhood Change* (Berkeley: University of California Press, 1960), p.6, distinguishes Harlem from Philadelphia's black community.

4. John F. Bauman, "Public Housing in the Depression: Slum Reform in Philadelphia Neighborhoods in the 1930s," in *The Divided Metropolis: Social and Spatial Dimensions of Philadelphia, 1800–1975*, ed. William W. Cutler III and Howard Gillette Jr. (Westport, Conn.: Greenwood Press, 1980), pp. 227–248, quote on p. 235; Margaret S. Marsh, "The Impact of the Market Street 'El' on Northern West Philadelphia: Environmental Change and Social Transformation, 1900–1930," in *Divided Metropolis*, ed. Cutler and Gillette, pp. 188–190; Rapkin and Grigsby, *Demand for Housing*, pp. 6–15; Theodore Hershberg, "A Tale of Three Cities: Blacks, Immigrants, and Opportunity in Philadelphia, 1850–1880, 1930, 1970," in *Philadelphia: Work, Space, Family, and Group Experience in the Nineteenth Century*, ed. Theodore Hershberg (New York: Oxford University Press,

1981), pp. 470, 476. The construction of public housing projects in the late 1930s through the 1940s to assuage Philadelphia's needy black residents and irate civic leaders is analyzed in Bauman, "Public Housing in the Depression," pp. 236–237, 242–243.

5. Joseph J. Boris, ed., *Who's Who in Colored America: A Biographical Dictionary of Notable Living Persons of Negro Descent in America, 1927* (1st ed.; New York: Who's Who in Colored America, 1927), and Thomas Yenser, ed., *Who's Who in Colored America: A Biographical Dictionary of Notable Living Persons of Negro Descent, 1938–1940* (5th ed.; Brooklyn, N.Y.: Thomas Yenser, 1940).

6. Carter G. Woodson, *The Negro Professional Man and the Community* (Washington, D.C.: Association for the Study of Negro Life and History, 1934), p. 81.

7. The relationship between black professionals and the black public in northern and border cities is addressed in *ibid.*, p. 332; Louis T. Wright, "The Negro Physician," *The Crisis* 36 (Sept. 1929): 305; Horace R. Cayton and George S. Mitchell, *Black Workers and the New Unions* (College Park, Md.: McGrath Publishing Co., 1939), p. 373; Eugene P. Foley, "The Negro Businessman: In Search of a Tradition," in *The Negro American*, ed. Talcot Parsons and Kenneth B. Clark (Boston: Beacon Press, 1966), pp. 567–568, 572. As World War II approached, a growing demand for physicians as opposed to clergypersons was evident in the black community as well as among Philadelphia's white upper class. In his social historical analysis of the city's upper class, E. Digby Baltzell made the distinction between the "high prestige technical elite" comprised of physicians and architects and the "intellectual elite" of clergymen, educators, artists, and authors (E. Digby Baltzell, *An American Business Aristocracy* [New York: Collier Books, 1962], pp. 59–63).

8. *American Medical Directory: A Register of Legally Qualified Physicians of the United States* (Chicago: American Medical Association), vols. for 1925, 1929, and 1938; Joseph J. Boris, ed., *Who's Who in Colored America: A Biographical Dictionary of Notable Living Persons of Negro Descent in America, 1928–1929* (2nd ed.; New York: Who's Who in Colored America, 1929); *Who's Who in Colored America*, vols. for 1927 and 1938–1940. *Who's Who in Colored America* is invaluable as a source for analyzing the character of leading blacks in various periods. See Preston Valien and Carrell Horton, "Some Demographic Characteristics of Outstanding Negro Women," *Journal of Negro Education* 23 (Fall 1954): 406–420. For a complete discussion of the Afro-American professional elite during the interwar years using quantitative analysis of *Who's Who in Colored America* volumes, see David McBride and Monroe H. Little, "The Afro-American Elite, 1930–1940: A Historical and Statistical Profile," *Phylon* 42 (Summer 1981): 105–119.

9. Herbert M. Morais, *The History of the Negro in Medicine* (New York: Publishers Co., 1968), p. 94; Numa P. G. Adams, "Sources of Supply of Negro Health Personnel, Section A: Physicians," *Journal of Negro Education* 6 (July 1937):

470; Max Seham, *Blacks and American Medical Care* (Minneapolis: University of Minnesota Press, 1973), p. 45.

10. John H. Lewis, "Number and Geographic Location of Negro Physicians in the United States," *Journal of the American Medical Association* 104 (1935): 1272–1273; Woodson, *Negro Professional Man*, p. 85; Adams, "Sources of Supply: Physicians," p. 470.

11. Moreover, this figure is likely to have been considerably higher, perhaps double—that is, two in five. The AMA *Medical Directory* tended to omit physicians with degrees from conditionally accredited institutions or many of the black medical schools.

12. Morais, *History of the Negro in Medicine*, pp. 89–90.

13. There were slightly more Medico-Chirurgical black graduates practicing in 1938 than in 1929 (that is, five as opposed to two). However, this probably was the result of black graduates from this school who moved out of Philadelphia during the pre-Depression years, only to return sometime before 1938.

14. Adams, "Sources of Supply: Physicians," pp. 470–471. Adams's findings indicated that during the 1927–1928 school year there were 233 students at Howard University's medical school. This decreased to 213 for the 1931–1932 year, and 133 for the 1935–1936 year. Similarly Meharry's enrollment fell from 211 to 183 between 1927–1928 and 1935–1936. The number of black medical students at white schools also dropped, from 73 to 53 between 1930–1931 and 1935–1936.

15. Adams, "Sources of Supply: Physicians," p. 471; Charles T. Stewart and Corazon M. Siddayao, *Increasing the Supply of Medical Personnel* (Washington, D.C.: American Enterprise Institute for Policy Research, 1973), pp. 16–17; Julius B. Richmond, *Currents in American Medicine: A Developmental View of Medical Care and Education* (Cambridge, Mass.: Harvard University Press, 1969), p. 6. According to Richmond, graduates of American medical schools increased from about 4,000 in 1925 to nearly 5,400 in 1938. Between 1931 and 1938 the number of physicians admitted to the United States as immigrants increased from 329 to 738 (U.S. Department of Commerce, Bureau of the Census, *Historical Statistics of the U.S.: Colonial Times to 1970* [Washington, D.C.: GPO, 1973], pt. 1, p. 76).

16. Adams found no record of a black having attended any tax-supported southern medical school, whether private or public, "even in those states in which the Negro population is approximately equal to or greater than the white population, although in these states the Negro pays taxes in proportion to what he owns as do all other free, adult citizens" (Adams, "Sources of Supply: Physicians,' p. 472).'

17. Morais, *History of the Negro in Medicine*, p. 97; Woodson, *Negro Professional Man*, pp. 81–82; Adams, "Sources of Supply: Physicians" p. 476. Woodson found that only 2.9 percent of the black physicians he surveyed were children of physicians (p. 82).

18. Adams, "Sources of Supply: Physicians," pp. 470–471. The Depression no doubt made these handicaps much more intense for prospective physicians, both black and white. See Richmond, *Currents in American Medicine*, p. 8.

19. Adams, "Sources of Supply: Physicians," p. 471.

20. Richmond, *Currents in American Medicine*, pp. 9–10, 23–24; Stewart and Siddayao, *Increasing the Supply of Medical Personnel*, p. 16; Morais, *History of the Negro in Medicine*, p. 97.

21. Lewis, "Number and Geographic Location of Negro Physicians," p. 1273. Other, somewhat later research verified the fact that the accessibility of Howard University's medical school and other professional schools enhanced the number of those professionals in the District of Columbia (G. Franklin Edwards, *The Negro Professional Class* [Glencoe, Ill.: Free Press, 1959], pp. 46–48).

22. A WPA field worker surveying the blacks of Pittsburgh wrote in 1941: "Not only do the Negro sick face discrimination, but even the Negro healers-of-the-sick face vicious barriers." The investigator pointed out that a black had not graduated from the University of Pittsburgh Medical School since 1914. There were only fifty black doctors in Allegheny County (that is, metropolitan Pittsburgh), only three of these physicians were permitted to practice in the hospitals, and two of them were limited to the out-patient or clinic department. Black interns were barred from the hospitals, and training of black nurses was disallowed until the advent of World War II, when a few entered Passavant Hospital ("The Negro in Pittsburgh: Field Notes, 1941," typescript in Records of the Works Progress Administration Pennsylvania History Survey, Ethnic Survey, 1938–1941, Record Group 41, PSA, p. 6).

23. Lewis, "Number and Geographic Location of Negro Physicians," p. 1273.

24. "The Education of the Intern," editorial in *Hospitals*, Nov. 1936, reprinted in *Pennsylvania Medical Journal* 40 (June 1937): 761–762.

25. After 1936, when Douglass Hospital lost its accreditation for training interns, the three to five internships it usually offered to black medical school deans were no longer available.

26. Seham, *Blacks and American Medical Care*, p. 72.

27. W. Montague Cobb suggested that such an attitude provided the underpinning of the segregated medical policies of the 1920s, 1930s, and 1940s (W. Montague Cobb, *Medical Care and the Plight of the Negro* [New York: National Association for the Advancement of Colored People, 1947], pp. 21–22, 35–37).

28. Howard K. Petry, ed., *A Century of Medicine: The History of the Medical Society of the State of Pennsylvania, 1848–1948* (Philadelphia[?]: Medical Society of the State of Pennsylvania, 1952), p. 288.

29. Dietrich C. Reitzes, *Negroes and Medicine* (Cambridge, Mass.: Harvard University Press, 1958), p. 51.

30. Morais, *History of the Negro in Medicine*, p. 99.

31. "Negro in Pittsburgh" suggests that a few blacks held part-time positions in one or two of the out-patient clinics of the predominantly white hospitals.

32. V. M. Alexander, and G. E. Simpson, "Negro Hospitalization," *Opportunity* 15 (Aug. 1937): 231–232, 248.

33. Millberry, "Medical and Dental Expansion," in "The Negro in Philadelphia, 1938–39, 1941," Records of the Works Progress Administration Pennsylvania History Survey, Ethnic Survey, 1938–1941, Record Group 41, PSA, pp. 10–11.

34. PSMDPA Membership List, 1936, typescript in possession of Douglass S. Dore, Philadelphia, a retired businessman active in the Philadelphia black community from the 1930s to the present. This list contains 195 names and is hereafter cited as "PSMDPA List."

35. Richmond, *Currents in American Medicine*, p. 10; *ibid.*; Rosemary Stevens, *American Medicine and the Public Interest* (New Haven, Conn.: Yale University Press, 1973), pp. 148–152; "Trends in Specialization," in President's Commission on the Health Needs of the Nation, *Building America's Health* (Raleigh, N.C.: Health Publications Institute, 1953), excerpt reprinted in Committee on Medical Teaching of the Association of Teachers of Preventive Medicine, *Readings in Medical Care* (Chapel Hill: University of North Carolina Press, 1958), p. 226.

36. Stevens, *American Medicine and the Public Interest*, p. 162; Cobb, *Medical Care and the Plight of the Negro*, pp. 17–18.

37. No distinctions between full-time or part-time specialist practitioners were made in the survey.

38. In 1931 about 17.1 percent of the nation's physicians were full-time specialists, and 23.5 percent in 1940 (Stevens, *American Medicine and the Public Interest*, p. 181).

39. Millberry, "Medical and Dental Expansion" pp. 7–8; Adams, "Sources of Supply: Physicians," pp. 474–475. Barnes was virtually a legend in the black community by 1938; he had worked with Dr. Chevalier L. Jackson at Temple University and is considered to have been the first black doctor to use the bronchoscope. Boston headed the surgery department at Mercy, and Scott supervised that hospital's surgical clinic. Stubbs was the medical director of Douglass Hospital (Millberry, "Medical and Dental Expansion," pp. 7–8).

40. Adams, "Sources of Supply: Physicians," pp. 474–475; Morais, *History of the Negro in Medicine*, pp. 95–95.

41. Stevens, *American Medicine and the Public Interest*, p. 198. On the psychological and educational theories extant in 1930 against the equal educability of black Americans, see Charles S. Johnson, *The Negro in American Civilization: A Study in Negro Life and Race Relations in the Light of Social-Research* (New York: Holt, Rinehart & Winston, 1930). Also see I. A. Newby, *Jim Crow's Defense: Anti-Negro Thought in America, 1900–1930* (Baton Rouge: Louisiana State Uni-

versity 1965), esp. pp. 191–199.

42. Stevens, *American Medicine and the Public Interest*, p. 200.

43. Mercy Hospital, *Biennial Report, 1933/1934* (Philadelphia: The Hospital, 1934), pp. 21–22.

44. *Ibid.*, p. 18.

45. Morais, *History of the Negro in Medicine*, p. 99; National Medical Fellowships, *Negroes in Medicine* (Chicago: n. pub., 1951[?]), p. 4; interview with Elizabeth P. McDougald, civil rights activist and daughter of John Q. McDougald, a prominent black gynecologist, Philadelphia, Feb. 14, 1977.

46. Millberry, "Medical and Dental Expansion," pp. 9–10.

47. Interview with Douglass S. Dore, Philadelphia, Oct. 10, 1978; *Philadelphia Tribune*, Feb. 13, 1954.

48. In 1784 the Prince Hall Freemasons was founded. This was the first and most prestigious black fraternal order. In 1843 the Grand United Order of Odd Fellows was established, followed by the Elks in 1898 (John H. Franklin, *From Slavery to Freedom* [New York: Alfred A. Knopf, 1974], pp. 154, 226; Benjamin Brawley, *A Social History of the American Negro* [London: Collier Books, 1921], p. 241; Charles H. Wesley, *History of the Improved Benevolent and Protective Order of Elks of the World, 1898–1954* [Washington, D.C.: Association for the Study of Negro Life and History, 1955]).

49. Woodson, *Negro Professional Man*, pp. 105–106. On the "unifying" historical and sociological function of black fraternal orders, see William A. Musaskin, *Middle-Class Blacks in a White Society: Prince Hall Freemasonry in America* (Berkeley: University of California Press, 1975).

50. Russell A. Dixon, "Sources of Supply of Negro Health Personnel, Section B: Dentists," *Journal of Negro Education* 6, yearbook no. 17 (July 1937): 477.

51. Millberry, "Medical and Dental Expansion," p. 17.

52. Dixon, "Sources of Supply: Dentists," p. 478.

53. *Ibid.*, p. 478.

54. *Ibid.*, p. 480.

55. A review of available yearbooks for the city's dental schools suggests that fewer blacks were attending these schools that had been doing so around World War I.

56. Dixon, "Sources of Supply: Dentists," p. 478.

57. Millberry, "Medical and Dental Expansion," p. 15; Mercy Hospital, *Biennial Report, 1933/1934*, p. 19.

58. Mercy Hospital, *Biennial Report, 1933/1934*, p. 19; Millberry, "Medical and Dental Expansion," pp. 16, 18; Kenneth E. Neiman, "A History of Dentistry in Montgomery County," *Bulletin of the Historical Society of Montgomery County* 17 (Fall 1970): 139–140.

59. Millberry, "Medical and Dental Expansion," p. 18; PSMDPA List. Three

city dentists were among the selections for *Who's Who in Colored America* in 1938.

60. Donald A. Yett, *An Economic Analysis of the Nurse Shortage* (Lexington, Mass.: Lexington Books, 1975), p. 4; Estelle M. Riddle, "Sources of Supply of Negro Health Personnel, Section C: Nurses," *Journal of Negro Education* 6 (July 1937): 483, 490.

61. Calculations based on data in Table 2 and U.S. Department of Commerce, Bureau of the Census, *Fifteenth Census of the United States, 1930* (Washington, D.C.: GPO, 1933), *Population*, vol. 4: *Occupations by States*, pp. 1414–1415.

62. Yett, *Economic Analysis of the Nurse Shortage*, p. 9.

63. Riddle, "Sources of Supply: Nurses," p. 490.

64. Millberry, "Medical and Dental Expansion," p. 16.

65. Mercy Hospital Training School for Nurses, *White Caps 1933/1934*, p. 15, Schomburg Center for Research in Black Culture, New York.

66. Millberry, "Medical and Dental Expansion," p. 16.

67. Norman K. Denzin, "Incomplete Professionalization: The Case of Pharmacy," in *Medical Men and Their Work*, ed. Freidson and Lorbes, pp. 55–64.

68. This was especially true in before World War II, when third-party payment medical coverage was not widely institutionalized (Stewart and Siddayao, *Increasing the Supply of Medical Personnel*, pp. 11–14).

69. Millberry, "Medical and Dental Expansion," pp. 1–6; Bureau of the Census, *1930 Census, Distribution*, vol. 1: *Retail Distribution*, pt. 3, p. 789; F. Marion Fletcher, *The Negro in the Drug Manufacturing Industry: The Racial Policies of American Industry* (Philadelphia Industrial Research Unit, Wharton School of Finance and Commerce, University of Pennsylvania, Report No. 21; Philadelphia: University of Pennsylvania Press, 1970), p. 20. Black women were among those managing these newer stores. Among them were Susie Hampton, Margaret Logan, and Dr. Anna H. Brown (Millberry, "Medical and Dental Expansion," pp. 3–6).

70. Fletcher, *Negro in the Drug Manufacturing Industry*, pp. 8, 25.

71. Millberry, "Medical and Dental Expansion," p. 5; PSMDPA List. James C. Alexander, key organizer of the Druggists Association, worked in drugstores in Pittsburgh and Atlantic City before starting his own in Philadelphia in 1918. At the time of his death on February 20, 1939, he had been in the drug business for a longer continuous period than any other black druggist in Philadelphia (Millberry, "Medical and Dental Expansion," p. 5).

72. Fletcher, *Negro in the Drug Manufacturing Industry*, p. 20; Millberry, "Medical and Dental Expansion," p. 5.

73. Cobb, *Progress and Portents*, p. 41; Millberry, "Medical and Dental Expansion," p. 7.

74. Millberry, "Medical and Dental Expansion," p. 8.

75. August Meier and Eliot Rudwick, *From Plantation to Ghetto* (New York: Hill and Wang, 1970), p. 238. For additional description of the intensifying political

restiveness among black professionals and working-class folk during the New Deal era—a politics that stessed physical and economic well-being over integrationist idealism—see Paula Giddings, *When and Where I Enter: The Impact of Black Women of Race and Sex in America* (New York: Bantam Books, 1984), pp. 210–211, and Nancy J. Weiss, *Farewell to the Party of Lincoln: Black Politics in the Age of FDR* (Princeton, N.J.: Princeton University Press, 1983), pp. 209–235.

76. Raymond P. Alexander, *The Doctor Virginia M. Alexander Scholarship Foundation* (pamphlet; Philadelphia: Alexander Scholarship Foundation, 1961), pp. 4–5.

77. "Can a Colored Woman Be a Physician?" *The Crisis* 40 (Feb. 1933): 33.

78. *Ibid.*, pp. 5, 7.

79. Dorothy B. Porter, "Introduction: Fifty Years of Collection," in *Black Access: A Bibliography of Afro-American Bibliographies*, ed. Richard Newman (Westport, Conn.: Greenwood Press, 1984), p. xxii; Sylvia G. L. Dannett, "Dr. Helen Dickens," in *Profiles of Negro Womanhood*, vol.2: *Twentieth Century*, ed. Sylvia G. L. Dannett (Yonkers, N.Y.: Educational Heritage Series, 1966), p. 92; Alexander, *Dr. Alexander Scholarship Foundation*, p. 6; Paul E. Baker, *Negro-White Adjustment: An Investigation and Analysis of Methods in the Interracial Movement in the United States* (New York: Associate Press, 1934).

80. V. M. Alexander and G. E. Simpson, "Negro Hospitalization," *Opportunity* 15 (Aug. 1937): 248.

81. *Ibid.*, pp. 231–232.

82. *Ibid.*, p. 232.

83. *Ibid.*, p. 248; "The Henry Phipps Institute," in Henry Phipps Institute, *Twenty-Ninth Report, 1940/1941* (Philadelphia: The Institute, 1941), pp. 6–7; Edgar S. Everhart, chief, Venereal Disease Division, Department of Health, "Exhibit No. 7," in Pennsylvania General Assembly, *Final Report of the Temporary Commission on the Conditions of the Urban Colored Population Appendix to the Legislative Journal, Session of 1943* 5 (1943): 4892; Frederick D. Stubbs, "Community Health," remarks delivered at the 31st Annual Conference of the NAACP, Tindley Temple, Philadelphia, June 20, 1940, in *Papers of the National Association for the Advancement of Colored People*, ed. August Meier and Elliot Rudwick, Annual Conference Proceedings, 1910–1950, group II, ser. A, box 28, p. 6, frame 0894.

84. In New York City, as early as 1917, the local NAACP became involved in the political struggle to integrate fully the professional staff and training programs at Harlem Hospital, a struggle that was finally victorious in 1930 (Michael L. Goldstein, "Black Power and the Rise of Bureaucratic Autonomy in New York City Politics: The Case of Harlem Hospital, 1917–1931," *Phylon* 41 [1980]: 191, 198). In Cleveland, in the late 1920s, the NAACP branch became embroiled in a bitter dispute to integrate Cleveland's municipal hospital, Cleveland City Hospital, that resulted in appointment of black physicians to its regular staff as well as black

applicants to internships and nurses' training programs (William Giffin, "The Mercy Hospital Controversy Among Cleveland's Afro-American Civic Leaders, 1927," *Journal of Negro History* 61 [Oct. 1976]: 333; Kenneth L. Kusmer, *A Ghetto Takes Shape: Black Cleveland, 1870–1930* [Urbana: University of Illinois Press, 1976], pp. 268–269). The divergent timing of the entry of these two NAACP branches into local hospital issues and the substantially later involvement of the Philadelphia NAACP in its local black community's hospital integration battles illustrate the observation that local NAACP branches usually "in practice acted autonomously in setting their own specific programs" (August Meier and Elliot Rudwick, "Integration vs. Separatism: The NAACP and CORE Face Challenge from Within," in *Along the Color Line: Explorations in the Black Experience*, ed. August Meier and Elliot Rudwick [Urbana: University of Illinois Press, 1976], p. 245).

85. "Frederick Douglass Stubbs, M.D., 1906–1947," *JNMA* 50 (March 1958): 222; interview with Dr. Wilbur H. Strickland Jr., former staff member at Douglass and Mercy-Douglass hospitals, Philadelphia, June 16, 1986; Stubbs, "Community Health," p. 7. Strickland was a life-long colleague of Stubbs's.

86. Stubbs, "Community Health," pp. 7–9.

87. *Negroes in Medicine*, p. 4.

Chapter V

1. G. Gordon Brown, *Law Administration and Negro-White Relations in Philadelphia: A Study in Race Relations* (Philadelphia: Bureau of Municipal Research, 1947), pp. 29–30. The urban background of many, if not most, southern black migrants to Philadelphia during the 1930s, 1940s, and 1950s is significant because it runs counter to the notion that these newcomers lacked "urban norms" and hence brought many of the public health and social ills upon themselves after arriving in Philadelphia (Juanita P. Morisey, "Differences Between Migrant and Non-Migrant Negro Children in a Philadelphia School," M.A. thesis, University of Pennsylvania, 1960).

2. On the impact of World War II in diversifying black employment nationally, see William H. Harris, *The Harder We Run: Black Workers Since the Civil War* (New York: Oxford University Press, 1982), pp. 112–122, and Mary F. Berry and John W. Blassingame, *Long Memory: The Black Experience in America* (New York: Oxford University Press, 1982), pp. 199–200.

3. John Hope Franklin, *From Slavery to Freedom* (New York: Alfred A. Knopf, 1974), pp. 573–607; Harold Cruse, *The Crisis of the Negro Intellectual* (New York: Morrow & Co., 1967), p. 324; Richard M. Dalfiume, "The 'Forgotten Years' of Negro Revolution," *Journal of American History* 4 (June 1968): 90–106. Liberal

activists also shaped measures to eliminate anti-Semitism from medical education and professional practice (Frank Kingdom, "Discrimination in Medical Colleges," *American Mercury* 61 [Oct. 1945]: 395; Lawrence Bloomgarden, "Medical School Quotas and National Health," *Commentary* 15 [Jan. 1935]: p. 31).

4. Russell F. Minton, "The History of Mercy-Douglass Hospital," *JMNA* 43 (May 1951): 155. The New York City health care establishment was considered especially discriminatory because there were no black-controlled health facilities in the city and because Harlem Hospital had for years segregated black physicians into lower-level or "adjunct" staff positions.

5. *Philadelphia Tribune*, Oct. 12, June 1, October 3, and April 13, 1939.

6. The surveys of the Negro in Philadelphia and Pittsburgh heretofore cited in Millberry, "Medical and Dental Expansion After 1900," typescript in "The Negro in Philadelphia, 1938–39, 1941," Records of the Works Progress Administration Pennsylvania History Survey, Ethnic Survey, 1938–1941, Record Group 41, PSA, and "The Negro in Pittsburgh: Field Notes," typescript in Records of the Works Progress Administration Pennsylvania History Survey, Ethnic Survey, 1938–1941, Record Group 41, PSA.

7. Commonwealth of Pennsylvania, *Final Report of the Pennsylvania State Temporary Commission on the Conditions of the Urban Colored Population to the General Assembly of the State of Pennsylvania* (Harrisburg: The Commonwealth, 1943), p. i; *Philadelphia Tribune*, Oct. 10, 1940.

8. Haven Emerson et al., *Philadelphia Hospital and Health Survey, 1929* (Philadelphia: Philadelphia Chamber of Commerce, 1929), p. 545.

9. Pennsylvania General Assembly, "Preliminary Report on the Conditions of the Urban Colored Population to the General Assembly of the State of Pennsylvania," May 1941, typescript, Fisher Government Documents Collection, Free Library of Philadelphia, pp. 51–53; Commonwealth of Pennsylvania, *Final Report of the Temporary Commission on the Conditions of the Urban Colored Population: Appendix to the Legislative Journal, Session of 1943* 5 (1943): 4788–4789, 4793, 4796, 4800 (hereafter referred to as *Legislative Journal—Final Report on the Urban Colored Population*).

10. Evidence that inadequate health care and unsanitary housing were at the root of the health problems of Philadelphia's black poor was presented repeatedly in Commonwealth of Pennsylvania, "Preliminary Report on the Conditions of the Urban Colored Population" and *Legislative Journal—Final Report on the Urban Colored Population*. See also Frederick D. Stubbs, "Community Health," remarks delivered at the 31st Annual Conference of the NAACP, Philadelphia, June 20, 1940, in *Papers of the National Association for the Advancement of Colored People*, ed. August Meier and Elliot Rudwick, Annual Conference Proceedings, 1910–1950, group II, ser. A, box 28, p. 7, frame 0894.

11. Pennsylvania Department of Welfare, Faculty Committee of the University

of Pennsylvania, *A Survey and a Statement of Principles on Tax-Supported Medical Care for the Needy and Medically Needy of Pennsylvania* (Philadelphia: The Commonwealth, Jan. 1957), pp. 132–133.

12. General Assembly, "Preliminary Report on the Urban Colored Population," pp. 53–54; Elizabeth H. Pitney, research secretary, Philadelphia Tuberculosis and Health Association, "Exhibit No. 5," *Legislative Journal—Final Report on the Urban Colored Population*, p. 4891. On the resourcefulness of teaching hospitals in taking on large numbers of patient referrals in general, see Robert H. Ebert, "Medical Education in the United States," in *Doing Better and Feeling Worse*, ed. John H. Knowles (New York: W. W. Norton, 1979), p. 178.

13. Emerson et al., *Philadelphia Hospital and Health Survey, 1929*, p. 597.

14. *Legislative Journal—Final Report on the Urban Colored Population*, p. 4788.

15. Pitney, "Exhibit No. 5," pp. 4791, 4891. This document reported that in 1941 the tuberculosis death rate for blacks (199 deaths per 100,000 black population) was still over five times higher than that of whites (38 per 100,000) (p. 4891).

16. Charles T. Stewart and Corazon M. Siddayao, *Increasing the Supply of Medical Personnel* (Washington, D.C.: American Enterprise Institute for Policy Research, 1973), pp. 11–14; Richard Harris, *A Sacred Trust* (Baltimore: Penguin Books, 1969), p. 76.

17. James A. Hamilton, *Patterns of Hospital Ownership and Control* (Minneapolis: University of Minnesota Press, 1961), pp. 7–8. The number of admissions to American hospitals increased more in the 1940–1950 decade than in any previous decade. The total admitted to all hospitals (that is, general, mental, tuberculosis, and other types) was 10,088,000 in 1940 and 17,024,000 in 1950. The number of hospitals and beds throughout the nation also grew during this decade from 6,291 to 6,430 hospitals and 1,226,245 to 1,456,912 beds (U.S. Department of Commerce, Bureau of the Census, *Historical Statistics of the United States: Colonial Times to 1957* [Washington, D.C.: GPO, 1960], pp. 35, 37).

18. The so-called "full employment" wartime conditions eventually caused a marked drop in the state's overall black and white unemployment. Yet this drop was actually a gradual process. In fact, during the first two years of World War II, hiring by industry was sluggish and the acute unemployment problems that had emerged during the Depression persisted in many key industries (Sylvester K. Stevens, "The Impact of the War on the Pennsylvania Economy," *Pennsylvania History* 11 [April 1944]: 118, 120; Sylvester K. Stevens, *Pennsylvania: Titan of Industry* [3 vols.; New York: Lewis Historical Publishers Co., 1948], vol. 1, pp. 342–345).

19. Throughout the nation in 1940, blacks still were double the proportion of whites in the unskilled, low-wage job categories. Nationally blacks doubled whites in their proportion in non-skilled labor from 1940 to 1960: 38.6 percent to 33.5

percent. Blacks increased their numbers in all job categories between 1940 and 1944, but declined subsequently (Ray Marshall, *The Negro in Organized Labor* [New York: John Wiley and Sons,1964], pp. 167–168.

20. On the severe staff shortage that was compounded by mobilization for World War II at Philadelphia General Hospital, the city's largest hospital complex, see Stephanie A. Stachniewicz and Jean K. Axelrod, *The Double Frill: The History of the Philadelphia General Hospital School of Nursing* (Philadelphia: Alumni Association of the School of Nursing, Philadelphia General Hospital, and G. F. Stickley Co., 1978), pp. 103–106.

21. Earlier in the 1930s, the final report of the Committee on the Costs of Medical Care, a panel of experts in medicine and the social sciences who wrote some of the most comprehensive studies on the organization of American medical practice ever to appear, proposed turning hospitals into comprehensive centers for all medical activities. Stanley J. Reisner, in *Medicine in the Reign of Technology* (London: Cambridge University Press, 1978), p. 152, comments: "Physicians in the twentieth century have gradually accepted the idea that the interrelationship among doctor, patient, and technology requires some mechanism to integrate the provision of medical services. . . . This centralization has in many ways improved the quality of medical care available to the average patient. At the same time, it has created many pockets in which few or no local medical services are available to patients."

22. Kenneth Boulding, quoted in Harry I. Greenfield, *Allied Health Manpower: Trends and Prospects* (New York: Columbia University Press, 1969), p. 10.

23. Paul Starr, *The Social Transformation of American Medicine* (New York: Basic Books, 1982), chap. 3; Eli Ginzberg with Miriam Ostow, *Men, Money, and Medicine* (New York: Columbia University Press, 1969), pp. 47–59; Hamilton, *Patterns of Hospital Ownership and Control*, p. 9; Edwin L. Crosby, "The Hospital as a Community Health Center," *Public Health Reports* 73 (Sept. 1958): 769; Greenfield, *Allied Health Manpower*, p. 10.

24. Joseph W. Mountin et al., *Hospital Facilities in the United States*, pt. 2: *Trends in Hospital Development, 1928–1936* (Public Health Bulletin No. 243; Washington, D.C.: U.S. Public Health Service, National Institute of Health, 1938), pp. 31–53.

25. John D. Stoeckle and Lucy M. Candib, "The Neighborhood Health Center: Reform Ideas of Yesterday and Today," in *Neighborhood Health Centers*, ed. Robert M. Hollister et al. (Lexington, Mass.: Lexington Books, 1974), p. 36; Pennsylvania Department of Welfare, *Survey and Statement of Principles*, p. 49.

26. For example, Dr. W. Harry Barnes became a municipal police surgeon, while Minton concentrated on directing Mercy Hospital.

27. Greenfield, *Allied Health Manpower*, p. 3; George J. Stigler, *Trends in Employment in the Service Industries: A Study of the National Bureau of Economic*

Research (Princeton, N.J.: Princeton University Press, 1956), pp. 92–100.

28. *Ibid.*; Christopher Jencks and David Riesman, *The Academic Revolution* (Garden City, N.Y.: Anchor Books, 1969), p. 218. "Many urban hospitals became vast institutions, able to accommodate both private and clinic patients. Maternity care in general hospitals and in maternity hospitals was always divided along the two-class system. By the 1940's hospitals in urban centers were organized to operate efficiently. Tasks were divided according to skills, and the number of hospital workers and the numbers of tasks were continually multiplying" (Richard W. Wertz and Dorothy C. Wertz, *Lying-In: A History of Childbirth in America* [New York: Free Press, 1977], p. 167).

29. According to labor experts, by 1940 black female domestics were shifting away from household work to service work in institutional settings, such as hotels, restaurants, and rest homes since wages were usually higher there and hours were more consistent (Jean C. Brown, *The Negro Women Workers* [Bulletin of the U.S. Women's Bureau No. 165; Washington, D.C.: GPO, 1935], p. 2). Female labor tended to form the bulk of surplus labor for the modernizing hospitals (Ginzberg, *Men, Money, and Medicine*, pp. 151–162).

30. Elizabeth Kelly, *Opportunities for Negro Women in the Medical and Other Health Services* (U.S. Women's Bureau Bulletin; Washington, D.C.: GPO, Oct. 1947), p. 6.

31. Interview with Mrs. E. S., retired member, National Union of Hospital and Health Care Employees, Local 1199C, Philadelphia, June 10, 1977.

32. *Philadelphia Tribune*, Sept. 12, 1960. It was impossible to gain access to personnel records of Philadelphia hospitals because of these institutions' administrative policies. Based on my other sources, including interviews with former hospital employees, I suspect that Philadelphia General, the Hospital of the University of Pennsylvania, and Mt. Sinai had significant numbers of blacks in the lowest employment levels in 1940.

33. Quoted in Dietrich C. Reitzes, *Negroes and Medicine* (Cambridge, Mass.: Harvard University Press, 1958), p. 63.

34. *Final Report on the Urban Colored Population*, p. 178. After observing the twenty-eight city hospitals that treated the largest number of black patients, the Pennsylvania Urban Commission confirmed the popular charge that blacks were being used as guinea pigs in some hospitals. The Commission concluded that, in Philadelphia and elsewhere in the state, "a higher percentage of Negroes are used for experimental demonstration and teaching purposes than whites." The Commission's research was based on a variety of sources: the testimony of public health officials, field visits, interviews of neighborhood residents, physicians and nurses, and other experts (black and white), and previous social scientific studies (*ibid.*, pp. 172–174).

35. *Ibid.*, pp. 180–181, 183.

36. *Ibid.*, pp. 178, 179.

37. *Ibid.*, pp. 189–191, 196, 198–208.

38. *Ibid.*, pp. 212–213.

39. *Ibid.*

40. *Ibid.*

41. *Ibid.*

42. *Ibid.*, pp. 214–215.

43. *Ibid.*, pp. 215–216.

44. In nearby Coatesville, the five-bed Clement Atkinson Memorial Hospital, founded by a local black physician, Whittier C. Atkinson, also served to relieve the black medical needs ("Atkinson General Practitioner of the Year of Pennsylvania's Medical Society," *JNMA* 53 [Jan. 1961]: 85–86; *Legislative Journal—Final Report on the Urban Colored Population*, p. 4799).

45. "Doctor Recalls Pioneering Training of Negro Aides," *Philadelphia Sunday Bulletin*, April 18, 1970.

46. *Final Report on the Urban Colored Population*, pp. 218–219.

47. *Ibid.*, p. 219. Construction of a nurses' home, which had been started at Douglass in the 1920s and had remained unfinished due to recurrent funding cutoffs, was finally completed in 1943 (*Philadelphia Tribune*, July 3, 1943).

48. Minton, "A List of Some of the Projects Completed by Me During My Superintendency at Mercy Hospital" (ca. 1939), JRFA-FU, p. 1.

49. Edgar S. Everhart, chief, Venereal Disease Division, Department of Health, "Exhibit No. 7," *Legislative Journal—Final Report on the Urban Colored Population*, p. 4892; Frederick D. Stubbs, "Summary of Status of Douglass Memorial Hospital," *Legislative Journal—Final Report on the Urban Colored Population*, pp. 4799–4800; Pitney, "Exhibit No. 5," p. 4891.

50. *Philadelphia Tribune*, Nov. 11, 1944; "Professional News," *JNMA* 37 (May 1945): 104.

51. This estimate is based on the AMA *Medical Directory* for 1938 (pp. 1450–1451). The beds of the Philadelphia Hospital for Mental Diseases at Byberry (5,500 beds) and the Naval Hospital (650 beds) were not included in this estimate. If they are included, this would mean black hospitals provided only about 1 percent of the city's total hospital beds.

52. *Final Report of the Commission on the Urban Colored Population*, pp. 221–221. X-ray technicians did not appear among the employee breakdowns, and radiologists themselves evidently performed the x-rays at these two black hospitals. Such technicians had to be certified. As of 1946 six Mercy staff had been trained and certified as x-ray technicians at Mercy by the chief of radiology, Russell F. Minton ("Doctor Recalls Pioneering Training").

53. *Final Report of the Commission on the Urban Colored Population*, pp. 220–222.

54. *Ibid.*, p. 220.

55. *Ibid.*, p. 221.

56. *Ibid.*, p. 222.

57. *Ibid.*, pp. 56–66.

58. The Commission's last allocation of $15,000 came by a legislative act passed on June 1, 1943 (*Laws of the General Assembly of the Commonwealth*, 1943 sess. [Harrisburg, Pa.: The Commonwealth, 1943], no. 345, p. 817).

59. Committee of Teachers of the Philadelphia Public Schools, *Negro Employment: A Study of the Negro Employment Situation in Philadelphia and Its Relation to the School Program* (Philadelphia: The Committee?, 1943/1944?), pp. 10, 11.

60. *Ibid.*, p. 16. At the same time, two black women technicians were operating a successful clinical laboratory, processing pre-marital blood tests for the state. They, however, appear to have worked in extreme isolation.

61. *Philadelphia Tribune*, June 4, 1943.

Chapter VI

1. "Professional News," *JNMA* 37 (Sept. 1945): 171; Midian O. Bousfield, "An Account of Physicians of Color in the United States," *Bulletin of the History of Medicine* 17 (Jan. 1945): 83; interview with Wilbur H. Strickland, Philadelphia, June 16, 1986.

2. Paul B. Cornely, "Distribution of Negro Physicians in the U.S. in 1942," *Journal of the American Medical Association* 124 (March 25, 1944): 826. Nationally there were fewer black doctors in 1948 (3,753) than in 1942 (3,810) (W. Montague Cobb, "Medical Care for Minority Groups," *Annals of the Academy of Political and Social Sciences* 273 [Jan. 1951]: 171; Joseph L. Johnson, "The Supply of Negro Health—Physicians," *Journal of Negro Education* 18 [1949]: 348, 351, 353).

3. Paul B. Cornely, "Distribution of Negro Dentists in the United States," *National Negro Health News* 16 (Jan.-March 1948): 14–15. There were only ten black students in Philadelphia's five medical schools and that of the University of Pittsburgh in the 1947–1948 academic year (Johnson, "Supply of Negro Health—Physicians," p. 15).

4. Patricia J. Sullivan, "Patterns of Negro Segregation in the Hospitals of Philadelphia," unpublished study, Department of Sociology, University of Pennsylvania, 1946, excerpts reprinted in G. Gordon Brown, *Law Administration and Negro-White Relations in Philadelphia: A Study in Race Relations* (Philadelphia: Bureau of Municipal Research, 1947), app. B, pp. 171, 176–177.

5. Commonwealth of Pennsylvania, *Final Report of the Pennsylvania State Temporary Commission on the Conditions of the Urban Colored Population to the General Assembly of the State of Pennsylvania* (Harrisburg: The Commonwealth, 1943), p. 220.

6. Interview with Dr. Russell F. Minton, former medical director of Mercy-Douglass Hospital, Philadelphia, Nov. 20, 1978.

7. Sullivan, "Patterns of Negro Segregation," pp. 176–177.

8. Brown, *Law Administration and Negro-White Relations*.

9. *Ibid.*, p. 56.

10. *Ibid.*, pp. 56–57.

11. *Ibid.*, p. 57.

12. In fact, unlike some institutions in Illinois and New York, there were no black faculty in any discipline in any of the colleges or universities in Philadelphia (*ibid.*; "Negro Profs at White Colleges," *Ebony* 2 [Oct. 1947]: 15–16).

13. Following the war, among the many programs that the NAACP's National Health Committee advocated were the national health insurance bill (1946) and the elimination of segregated admission policies of medical schools (1948 and 1949). Drs. W. Montague Cobb and Louis T. Wright were the national leaders in this movement (W. Montague Cobb, "The National Health Program of the NAACP," *JNMA* 45 [Sept. 1953]: 333–339).

14. Papers of the Health Committee, NAACP, Philadelphia Branch, Executive Secretary Files, 1943–1967, TUUA.

15. Minutes of the Health Committee, Philadelphia NAACP, March 5, 1946, TUUA; M. Lorenzo Walker, "DeHaven Hinkson, M.D., 1891– ," *JNMA* 66 (July 1974): 342.

16. *Ibid.*

17. *Ibid.*

18. Minton interview, Nov. 20, 1978.

19. Walker, "DeHaven Hinkson," p. 342.

20. Minton interview, Nov. 20, 1978.

21. Walker, "DeHaven Hinkson,' p. 342.

22. Minutes of the Health Committee, Philadelphia NAACP, March 5, 1946.

23. "Northeastern Regional Conference of the NACGN, May 16, 17, 18, 1946—Sponsored by the Local Association of Colored Graduate Nurses of Philadelphia and Vicinity and National Nursing Council," in Papers of the NACGN, Conference Programs, 1916–1951, Schomberg Center for Research in Black Culture, New York, pp. 2, 4. Local officers at this time were Louise I. Brashears, Doylestown; Marie F. Carter, Philadelphia; Ella J. King, Philadelphia; Elizabeth F. Meredith, Philadelphia; Fleta M. Brodhead, Philadelphia; and Eleanor Selah, Chester. John T. Graver, the director of Mercy, and Wilbur H. Strickland, the director of Douglass, also gave addresses (pp. 1, 2).

24. Russell F. Minton, "The History of Mercy-Douglass Hospital," *JNMA* 43 (May 1951): 154–155.

25. Elliot M. Rudwick, "A Brief History of Mercy-Douglass Hospital in Philadelphia," *Journal of Negro Education* 20 (Winter 1951): 54–57.

26. Records of the Department of State, Records of the Administrative Bureau, Solicitation Registration File, 1926–1961 (RG-26), Physio-Therapy Society File, PSA (hereafter abbreviated PTS File).

27. Adolphus W. Anderson Sr. to Secretary of Commonwealth of Pennsylvania, Philadelphia, Oct. 20, 1947, PTS File; "Articles of Agreement, Physio-Therapy Society and Adolphus W. Anderson, Sr.," Oct. 8, 1978, PTS File.

28. Minutes of the Physio-Therapy Society, June 8, 1947.

29. James Summerville, *Educating Black Doctors: A History of Meharry Medical College* (University: University of Alabama Press, 1983), p. 123; Minutes of the Physio-Therapy Society, April 6, 1947, PTS File.

30. Josephine B. Keene, *Directory of Negro Business and Professional Women of Philadelphia and Vicinity* (Philadelphia: n. pub., 1939), [p. 16].

31. Minutes of the Physio-Therapy Society, July 6, 1947.

32. *Ibid.*, Aug. 3, 1947.

33. *Ibid.*, Nov. 30, 1947.

34. *Laws of Pennsylvania, 1925*, no. 347, pp. 644–646.

35. Physio-Therapy Society, "Application for Certificate of Registration Under Solicitation Law," Nov. 12, 1947, PTS File.

36. Henrietta Woffenden, investigator, Bureau of Community Work, to Esther Forstrand, Philadelphia Health and Welfare Council, Philadelphia, Jan. 23, 1948, PTS File.

37. Henrietta Woffenden to Esther Forstrand, Jan. 23, 1948; Katherine E. Matchett, Health and Welfare Council, to Woffenden, Harrisburg, January 27, 1948; Woffenden to Hugh Smith, Better Business Bureau, Philadelphia, Jan. 23, 1948; Smith to Woffenden, Harrisburg, Jan. 26, 1948, Woffenden to Wayne L. Hopkins, Armstrong Association, Philadelphia, Jan. 28, 1948; Hopkins to Woffenden, Harrisburg, Jan. 30, 1948, all in PTS File.

38. Hopkins to Woffenden, January 30, 1949.

39. Henrietta Woffenden to Dr. C. Rufus Rorem, Hospital Council of Philadelphia, Philadelphia, Jan. 23, 1948, and Rorem to Woffenden, Harrisburg, Feb. 9, 1948, PTS File.

40. Henrietta Woffenden to Charles S. Paxson, Philadelphia Hospital Association, Philadelphia, Jan. 23, 1948, and Paxson to Woffenden, Harrisburg, Jan. 30, 1948, PTS File.

41. Henrietta Woffenden to PCMS, Philadelphia, Feb. 11, 1948, and William F. Irwin, PCMS, to Woffenden, Harrisburg, Feb. 18, 1948, PTS File.

42. Henrietta Woffenden to College of Physicians, Philadelphia, Feb. 11, 1948; Woffenden to College of Physicians, March 24, 1948; Dr. F. William Sunderman to Woffenden, Philadelphia, March 24, 1948, all in PTS File.

43. Dr. George M. Piersol to Dr. Hubley R. Owen, Division of Medical Services, School District of Philadelphia, April 5, 1948, PTS File.

44. Dr. Hubley R. Owen to Henrietta Woffenden, Harrisburg, April 7, 1948, PTS File.

45. Dr. Egbert T. Scott to Henrietta Woffenden, Harrisburg, March 25, 1948, PTS File.

46. Henrietta Woffenden to John W. Harris, Philadelphia, May 11, 1948, and Woffenden to Hon. Herbert E. Millen, Philadelphia, May 28, 1948, PTS File.

47. Ira J. Mills, Bureau of Community Work, to Dr. Wilbur H. Strickland, Philadelphia, Aug. 13, 1948, PTS File.

48. Besides Philadelphia's Mercy and Douglass hospitals, black medical facilities in Chicago, New York, Cleveland, and Chattanooga were also under pressure by hospital authorities and political forces to either "modernize" or shut down.

49. W. Montague Cobb, *Medical Care and the Plight of the Negro* (New York: National Association for the Advancement of Colored People, 1947), pp. 20–26; Minton interview, Nov. 20, 1978.

50. Rudwick, "Brief History of Mercy-Douglass Hospital," p. 58. Among the Advisory Council's members were Drs. Joseph Stokes, Children's Hospital; William Belke, Episcopal Hospital; Burgess Gordon and Paul Swenson, Jefferson; Charles R. Drew and Joseph L. Johnson, Howard; R. Buerki and I. S. Ravdin, Pennsylvania; P. F. Lucchesi, Philadelphia General; Lloyd B. Greene, Pennsylvania Hospital; W. Edward Chamberlain, Temple; and William G. Leaman, Woman's Medical College (Minton, "History of Mercy-Douglass Hospital," p. 156).

51. Minton, "History of Mercy-Douglass Hospital," p. 156. As a pre-med student, Minton had helped install the first electrical circuits throughout the building.

52. *Ibid.*

53. Herbert M. Morais, *The History of the Negro in Medicine* (New York: Publishers Co., 1968), p. 152; Richard Harris, *A Sacred Trust* (Baltimore: Penguin Books, 1969), p. 75.

54. Minton, "History of Mercy-Douglass Hospital," pp. 153–154.

55. Jack Greenberg, *Race Relations and American Law* (New York: Columbia University Press, 1959), pp. 89–90; Michael Meltsner, "Equality and Health," *University of Pennsylvania Law Review* 115 (Nov. 1966): 26–28.

Chapter VII

1. Leonard U. Blumberg, *Migration as a Program for Urban Social Work: A Pilot Study of Recent Negro Migrants into Philadelphia* (Philadelphia: Urban League of Philadelphia, 1958), p. 2.

2. *Ibid.*; Milton M. Gordon, "The Girard College Case: Desegregation and A Municipal Trusts," *Annals of the American Academy of Political and Social Science*

304 (March 1956): 53–61. On the dramatic decline in deaths attributed to tuberculosis in American cities during the post-World War II period, see Leona Baumgartner, "Urban Reservoirs of Tuberculosis," *American Review of Tuberculosis and Pulminary Diseases* 79 (May 1959): 688–689.

3. John Hope Franklin, *From Slavery to Freedom* (New York: Alfred A. Knopf, 1974), pp. 556–557; Louis E. Lomax, *The Negro Revolt* (New York: Harper & Brothers, 1962), pp. 73–74; Anthony Lewis and the *New York Times, Portrait of a Decade: The Second American Revolution* (New York: Bantam Books, 1965), pp. 3–9.

4. Several letters, legal memoranda, and internal reports from Judge Millen regarding this matter are in the James H. Duff Papers, Governor's General Correspondence, 1943–1951 (MG 190), PSA. See specifically Herbert E. Millen to James H. Duff, April 12, 28, 1949; May 4, 9, 1949; June 13, 1949; Oct. 10, 1949; Jan. 27, 1950; and May 4, 1950; also, Duff to Millen, April 13, 1949; May 2, 1949; and June 3, 1949.

5. John W. Harris Jr., secretary, Mercy-Douglass Hospital Campaign Fund, "Proposed Plan for Re-Building Mercy-Douglass Hospital," April 28, 1949, mimeo., Duff Papers, PSA, p. 1.

6. *Ibid.*

7. Wilbur H. Strickland and K. J. Hall, "Mercy-Douglass Hospital: Proposals in Reference to New Hospital Building Referred to Governor James H. Duff in His Letter of May 2nd, 1949," mimeo., Duff Papers, PSA.

8. Millen to Duff, May 4, 1950.

9. Dietrich C. Reitzes, *Negroes and Medicine* (Cambridge, Mass.: Harvard University Press, 1958), p. 62.

10. Russell F. Minton, "The History of Mercy-Douglass Hospital," *JNMA* 43 (May 1951): 157.

11. Strickland and Hall, "Mercy-Douglass Hospital," attached document.

12. James Summerville, *Educating Black Doctors: A History of Meharry Medical College* (University: University of Alabama Press, 1983), pp. 91–92.

13. *Philadelphia Tribune*, June 20, 1950.

14. *Philadelphia Tribune*, June 27, 1950.

15. Minton, "History of Mercy-Douglass Hospital," p. 156.

16. E. Washington Rhode, "Under the Microscope," *Philadelphia Tribune*, Jan. 20, 1953. See also the article "Mercy-Douglass Staff Integrated" in the same issue.

17. Minton, "History of Mercy-Douglass Hospital," p. 155.

18. *Philadelphia Tribune*, June 17, 1950.

19. *Ibid.*, Oct. 28, 1950. On October 26, 1950, Foster delivered a paper on blood disorders, "The Detection of Protein-Bound Iodine in Blood," as the opening address at the American Association of Clinical Chemists, which was convening at Hahnemann (*ibid.*).

20. Michael Meltsner, "Equality and Health," *University of Pennsylvania Law Review* 115 (Nov. 1966): 26.

21. In New Jersey during 1950 the Division Against Discrimination of the state's Department of Education, in cooperation with the New Jersey Hospital Association, surveyed the racial policies of eighty-five non-profit hospitals in twenty-one counties. They found that virtually all these institutions admitted black patients, but that semi-private and private room admission policies were often adjusted according to the race of patients. Twenty-five hospitals would "not mix Negro and white patients under any circumstances." Black physicians were obtaining courtesy privileges at the hospitals, and black medical professionals were increasingly admitted to previously all-white nursing schools, although dormitory arrangements for these black students sometimes posed problems (*New York Times*, Jan. 2, 1950).

22.. Alphonso A. Woods to Charles A. Shorter, Philadelphia, October[?], 1952, Papers of the NAACP, Philadelphia Branch, Executive Secretary Files, 1948–1963, Discrimination—Hospitals (1952), TUUA.

23. Ralph White to Alphonso W. Shockley, Philadelphia, Oct. 27, 1952, and Charles A. Shorter to Carleton C. Richards, Philadelphia, Nov. 12, 1952, both in Papers of the NAACP, Philadelphia Branch.

24. Alphonso W. Shockley to Charles A. Shorter, Philadelphia, Nov. 7, 1952, Papers of the NAACP, Philadelphia Branch. Dickerson was referring to the poor treatment of black patients. That same year a black girl who had been severely burned in a fire was refused aid at a local hospital and subsequently died from her injuries (*Philadelphia Tribune*, Jan. 3, 1953).

25. Charles A. Shorter to Carleton C. Richards, Nov. 12, 1952, Papers of the NAACP, Philadelphia Branch.

26. *Dorland's Medical Directory: Philadelphia and Metropolitan Area*, Oct. 1954 (n.p.: John P. Dorland, 1954), p. 421; *American Medical Directory: A Register of Legally Qualified Physicians of the United States, 1950* (Chicago: American Medical Association, 1950).

27. W. Montague Cobb, "The National Health Program of the NAACP," *JNMA* 45 (Sept. 1953): 336.

28. Carleton C. Richards to Branch Health Committee Members, April 10, 1953, Papers of the NAACP, Philadelphia Branch.

29. W. Montague Cobb to Carleton C. Richards, Washington, D.C., May 21, 1953, Papers of the NAACP, Philadelphia Branch.

30. William J. McKenna, "The Negro Vote in Philadelphia Elections," *Pennsylvania History* 32 (Oct. 1965): 409, 414; *New York Times*, Sept. 9, 1951.

31. Dean's Committee, "Official Proposal of the Philadelphia Dean's Committee for the Establishment of a System of Affiliations Between the Philadelphia General Hospital and the Medical Schools of Philadelphia," March 23, 1953, Papers of the

NAACP, Philadelphia Branch; Stephanie A. Stachniewicz and Jean K. Axelrod, *The Double Frill: The History of the Philadelphia General Hospital School of Nursing* (Philadelphia: Alumni Association of the School of Nursing, Philadelphia General Hospital and G. F. Stickley Co., 1978), p. 153.

32. Dean's Committee, "Official Proposal."

33. *Ibid.*

34. John H. Strange, "Blacks and Philadelphia Politics, 1963–1968," in *Black Politics in Philadelphia*, ed. Miriam Ershkowitz and Joseph Zikmund (New York: Basic Books, 1973), pp. 125, 127. Under the conditions of the new City Charter of 1951, Philadelphia's FEPC was replaced by the City Commission on Human Relations. It also was expanded from five appointees to nine.

35. City Commission on Human Relations, communique, April [?], 1953, Papers of the NAACP, Philadelphia Branch.

36. *Philadelphia Tribune*, May 19, 1953.

37. Strange, "Blacks and Philadelphia Politics," p. 123; McKenna, "Negro Vote in Philadelphia Elections," p. 414.

38. *Philadelphia Tribune*, Feb. 27, 1954, and March 27, 1954.

39. Reitzes, *Negroes and Medicine*, p. 334.

40. *Philadelphia Tribune*, Feb. 27, 1954.

41. Minutes of the ACLU, Philadelphia Chapter, Committee on Equality, Feb. 23, 1954, and April 27, 1954, Philadelphia. Members included Francis Bosworth (chairman), Sadie T. M. Alexander, John Briner, Walter A. Gay, W. Glenn George, Julian E. Goldberg, Jerome Kaplan, George O'Neal, William A. Rabill, and Arthur Seidel.

42. ACLU, Philadelphia Chapter, Committee on Equality, "Inventory of Racial Discrimination and Integration in 44 Philadelphia Hospitals as of June, 1954," June 1954, p. 1. The "Analysis" section, conducted by Robert B. Johnson, was completed in March 1956.

43. *Ibid.*, pp. 1–3.

44. *Ibid.*, p. 2.

45. Armstrong Association of Philadelphia, Annual Report, 1953, p. 8, TUUA.

46. ACLU, "Inventory of Racial Discrimination," pp. 6–7.

47. Ruth M. Raup and Elizabeth A. Williams, "Negro Students in Medical Schools in the United States," *Journal of Medical Education* 39 (May 1964): 447.

48. Numericaly, between the 1949–1950 and 1955–1956 academic years, black enrollment in predominantly white schools increased from 138 to 216 (*ibid.*, p. 448).

49. ACLU, "Inventory of Racial Discrimination," p. 3. This pattern of enrollment of black nursing students also appeared at the nation's Catholic nursing schools. A greater number of Catholic nursing schools enrolled black students in

1954 and 1955 than in any other previous or subsequent years through 1960. Seven Catholic nursing schools in Pennsylvania had black matriculants as of 1952. Some of these schools were no doubt in the Philadelphia area, since the Church's northern urban schools tended to integrate well ahead of those in other regions. Blacks attending these Pennsylvania schools could not always participate fully in certain school-related training programs or social affairs, however, because of racial opposition on the part of elements in the nursing school, affiliated hospitals, or nearby white communities (Margaret A. Foley, "Negro Students: A Comparative Study of Enrollments in Catholic Schools of Nursing," *Hospital Progress* 34 [Oct. 1954]: 66–68; Thomas J. Shanahan, "Negroes in Nursing Education: A Report on Catholic Schools," *Hospital Progress* 42 [July 1961]: 100–102).

50. Interview with Dr. Russell F. Minton, a former medical director of Mercy-Douglass, Philadelphia, Nov. 20, 1978; interview with Elizabeth P. McDougald, Philadelphia, Feb. 14, 1977; Robert M. Cunningham Jr., "Discrimination and the Doctor," *Medical Economics* 29 (Jan. 1952): 119–124, reprinted in Committee on Medical Care Teaching of the Association of Teachers of Preventive Medicine, *Readings in Medical Care* (Chapel Hill: University of North Carolina Press, 1958), p. 182.

51. *American Medical Directory, 1956* and *1950*; census data for Philadelphia.

52. Paul B. Cornely, "Segregation and Discrimination in Medical Care in the United States," *American Journal of Public Health* 46 (Sept. 1958): 1074–1081.

53. The 1950 estimate is based on the census returns on Philadelphia for that year and on Reitzes, *Negroes and Medicine*, p. 393.

54. Reitzes, *Negroes and Medicine*, pp. 393–394.

55. *Ibid.*, p. 400.

56. *Ibid.*, pp. 345, 388, 395.

57. *Ibid.*, p. 397.

58. *Ibid.*, p. 370.

59. Raup and Williams, "Negro Students in Medical Schools," p. 447; Andrew A. Sorensen, "Black Americans and the Medical Profession, 1930–1970," *Journal of Negro Education* 41 (Fall 1972): 339.

60. Woman's Medical College, "Black Graduates," mimeo., c. 1972, Medical College of Pennsylvania Collection, AWMC, p. 2.

61. Raup and Williams, "Negro Students in Medical Schools," pp. 448–449.

62. Author's survey of black medical school graduates in Philadelphia listed in the *American Medical Directory, 1950*.

63. Reitzes, *Negroes and Medicine*, p. 391.

64. Cornely, "Segregation and Discrimination," p. 1079.

65. Reitzes, *Negroes and Medicine*, p. 341.

66. Temple Burling, Edith M. Lentz, and Robert N. Wilson, *The Give and*

Take in Hospitals: A Study of Human Relations in Hospitals (New York: Putnam's Sons, 1966), p. 8.

67. U.S. Department of Commerce, Bureau of the Census, *Historical Statistics of the United States: Colonial Times to 1957* (Washington, D.C.: GPO, 1960), pp. 37, 80.

68. At Philadelphia General, the need for greater numbers of employees to administer medications and therapeutic exercises, as well as prepare trays, laundry, and food, is detailed in Stachniewicz and Axelrod, *Double Frill*, pp. 153–179.

69. Virginia H. Walker, *Nursing and Ritualistic Practice* (New York: Macmillan, 1967), p. 59.

70. Edwin L. Crosby, "The Hospital as a Community Health Center," *Public Health Reports* 73 (Sept. 1958): 766, 769. The net disbursements to a sample of major hospitals in the city for 1951 and 1957 had to be increased as follows: Hahnemann Hospital, $252,000 to $341,150; Jefferson Hospital, $363,000 to $570,000; Pennsylvania Hospital, $255,500 to $381,000; Temple University Hospital, $206,250 to $585,000; Univ. of Pennsylvania Hospital, $374,500 to $454,659; and Children's Hospital, $82,500 to $105,959 (Commonwealth of Pennsylvania, Office of the Auditor General, *Biennial Report, 1949–1951* [Harrisburg, Pa.: The Commonwealth, 1951], pp. 160, 162, 167, and *1957–1959* [Harrisburg, Pa.: The Commonwealth, 1959], pp. 130, 132, 136, 137).

71. Blumberg, *Migration as a Program for Urban Social Work*, p. 9–10.

72. Philadelphia Community Policy Committee on Health and Hospital Services, *First Report: Financial Situation of Voluntary Hospitals* (Philadelphia: The City, April 1959), p. 5. By the close of 1959 requests by hospitals in Philadelphia and other parts of the state for federal monies (Hill-Burton grants) were three times greater than what was available (Governor's Office, news release, Dec. 9, 1959, mimeo., David L. Lawrence Papers, Governor's General File, 1958–1962, MG 191, PSA).

73. Interview with Mrs. V. T., Philadelphia, June 10, 1978; Charles A. Shorter to Carleton C. Richards, Philadelphia, Oct. 17, 1954, Papers of the NAACP, Philadelphia Branch.

74. Philadelphia Commission on Human Relations, *Annual Report, 1955*, pp. 30, 32; *1956*, pp. 58, 60; *1957*, pp. 65, 67; *1958*, pp. 61, 63; *1959*, pp. 59, 65.

75. Walker, *Nursing and Ritualistic Practice*, p. 166; Eli Ginzberg with Miriam Ostow, *Men, Money, and Medicine* (New York: Columbia University Press, 1969), pp. 91–92; Harry I. Greenfield, *Allied Health Manpower: Trends and Prospects* (New York: Columbia University Press, 1969), pp. 140–141.

76. William J. Curran and E. Donald Shapiro, *Law, Medicine, and Forensic Science* (Boston: Little, Brown, 1970), p.609.

77. Philadelphia Commission on Human Relations, "Hospital Employment Study, Finding and Conclusions Summarized," mimeo., July 14, 1966, Commis-

sion on Human Relations Records, CP-BMRA, pp. 1–2.

78. Robert McCleary, *One Life, One Physician* (Washington, D.C.: Public Affairs Press, 1971), pp. iii–iv, 1; Ivan Illich, *Medical Nemesis: The Expropriation of Health* (New York: Pantheon Books, 1975), p. 23.

79. The Commission kept data for this category only for the years 1955 and 1956. In this period, the Commission pursued seven hospital-related complaints. This was about one-sixth of all the cases it reviewed in this category during those two years (Commission on Human Relations, *Annual Report, 1955*, p. 34, and *1956*, p. 62).

80. Commission on Human Relations, *Annual Report, 1961*, pp. 17–18.

81. Interview with Mrs. E. E., Philadelphia, June 10, 1978.

82. Mrs. V. T. interview, June 10, 1978.

83. U.S. Commission on Civil Rights, *The National Conference and the Reports of the State Advisory Committees to the U.S. Commission on Civil Rights, 1959* (Washington, D.C.: GPO, 1960), p. 343. A public controversy occurred when Dr. Cornelius G. Wooding, the only black pathologist at the City Medical Examiner's Office in Philadelphia, was fired because he would not engage in what he believed was graft and corruption ("Philly Doctor Charges Bias in Firing," *Jet* 11 [Jan. 31, 1957]: 10).

84. Two such groups were the Philadelphia Fellowship Commission and the Philadelphia Jewish Community Relations Council (Philadelphia Fellowship Commission, *A Five-Year Study of the Selection of Medical Students* [pamphlet; Philadelphia: The Commission, 1957]). Important academic studies on this issue in other American cities also surfaced around this time; see Stanley Lieberson, "Ethnic Groups and the Practice of Medicine," *American Sociological Review* 23 (Oct. 1958): 542–549; David M. Solomon, "Ethnic and Class Differences Among Hospitals as Contingencies in Medical Careers," *American Journal of Sociology* 66 (1961): 463–471.

85. Philadelphia Fellowship Commission, *Five-Year Study*, pp. 30–34.

86. Philadelphia Commission on Human Relations, *Hospital Employment Study, Final Report*, June 30, 1966, pp. 29–32.

87. *Philadelphia Tribune*, May 26, 1959.

88. *Ibid.*, March 20, 1954; Reitzes, *Negroes and Medicine*, p. 52.

CHAPTER VIII

1. Kelly, Harbison, and Belz have pointed out: "In the early 1960's, the rapid spread of sit-ins and freedom marches, [and] the rise to prominence of new civil rights leaders such as James Farmer and Martin Luther King . . . all testified to the growing sense of outrage in the Negro community. The civil rights revolution was moving into a new stage, characterized by civil disobedience, direct action,

and even the resort to violence. In the lower South, also, there was an ominous rise in white violence, as reactionaries countered sit-downs and freedom marches with mass arrests, intimidations, and, on occasion, even with bombings and the murder of civil rights workers. These developments convinced the Kennedy administration and the liberal bloc in Congress that further federal legislation was imperative" (Alfred H. Kelly, Winfred A. Harbison, and Herman Belz, *The American Constitution: Its Origins and Development* [New York: W. W. Norton, 1983], p. 620). Also see Mary F. Berry and John W. Blassingame, *Long Memory: The Black Experience in America* (New York: Oxford University Press, 1982), pp. 181–185; Charles C. Alexander, *Holding the Line: The Eisenhower Era, 1952–1961* (Bloomington: Indiana University Press, 1975), pp. 194–201; Randall W. Bland, *Private Pressure on Public Law: The Legal Career of Justice Thurgood Marshall* (Port Washington, N.Y.: Kennikat Press, 1973), pp. 114–116; Derrick A. Bell Jr., *Race, Racism, and American Law* (Boston: Little, Brown, 1973); Harold C. Fleming, "The Federal Executive and Civil Rights, 1961–1965," in *The Negro American*, ed. Talcott Parsons and Kenneth B. Clark (Boston: Beacon Press, 1966), pp. 374–375.

2. Michael Meltsner, "Equality and Health," *University of Pennsylvania Law Review* 115 (Nov. 1966): 22–38; Bell, *Race, Racism, and American Law*, pp. 253–257; James L. Curtis, *Blacks, Medical Schools, and Society* (Ann Arbor: University of Michigan Press, 1971), pp. 24–27, 59–61; Jack Greenberg, *Race Relations and American Law* (New York: Columbia University Press, 1959), pp. 89–90; U.S. Commission on Civil Rights, *Equal Opportunity in Hospitals and Health Facilities* (Special Publication No. 2; Washington, D.C.: GPO, March 1965), pp. 6–10.

3. Russell F. Minton, "Proceedings: Imhotep National Conference on Hospital Integration," *JNMA* 50 (March 1958): 142.

4. [Daniel B. Taylor], "Recent Developments at Mercy-Douglass Hospital in Philadelphia, Pennsylvania," *JNMA* 47 (Sept. 1955): 356.

5. *Ibid.*

6. "Mercy-Douglass Hospital—Editional," *JNMA* 53 (Jan. 1961): 79. The national recognition accorded Philadelphia General's internship and residency programs during this period is described in Stephanie A. Stachniewicz and Jean K. Axelrod, *The Double Frill: The History of the Philadelphia General Hospital School of Nursing* (Philadelphia: Alumni Association of the School of Nursing, Philadelphia General Hospital, and G. F. Stickley Co., 1978), pp. 151, 169. On the nationwide shortage of interns and residents, which intensified between 1940 and 1960, see Rosemary Stevens, *American Medicine and the Public Interest* (New Haven, Conn.: Yale University Press, 1973), pp. 300–301, 380–381.

7. "Howard University College of Medicine," *JNMA* 50 (July 1958): 308; "Meharry Medical College," *JNMA* 50 (July 1958): 308; *Philadelphia Tribune*, Jan. 1, 1963.

8. The Imhotep Conferences took place annually from 1957 through 1966 and were coordinated by the NMA and Dr. W. Montague Cobb, medical professor at Howard University and editor of the *JNMA*. At the first conference, at which Russell Minton and John Procope from Mercy-Douglass spoke, black medical and social welfare leaders from twenty-one states attended, including delegates from sixteen constituent societies of the NMA, twenty-six branches of the NAACP, and four branches of the National Urban League. Also in attendance were representatives from major medical interest groups including the AMA, the American Hospital Association, American Nursing Health Council, and the AFL-CIO (W. Montague Cobb, "The Black Physician in America," *New Physician* 19 [Nov. 1970]: 915–916).

9. "Proceedings: Imhotep Conference," pp. 142–143.

10. *Ibid.*, p. 143.

11. The community donations amounting to approximately 1 percent of Mercy-Douglass revenues was in line with the shrinking national norm. Between 1962 and 1966 philanthropy averaged just 2.4 percent of total hospital revenues nationwide (Henry B. Hansmann, "The Role of Nonprofit Enterprise," *Yale Law Journal* 89 [April 1980]: 860 n. 89).

12. The use of expensive personnel and equipment to provide the highest quality of care for too large a number of patients was one of the chief financial pitfalls faced by hospitals throughout America during the early 1960s. See Millard F. Long, "Efficient Use of Hospitals," in *The Economics of Health and Medical Care*, ed. S. J. Axelrod (Ann Arbor: University of Michigan Press, 1964), p. 212.

13. *Philadelphia Tribune*, March 19, 1963, April 27, 1963; *Philadelphia Tribune* Office Library, Clipping File, Sept. 11, 1973, and July 24, 1973.

14. A review of the officers of the NMA for the mid-1950s reveals few Philadelphia physicians. As of 1955, for instance, no doctor from the city was serving as a member of the NMA's board of trustees or house of delegates, nor as a general officer or administrative secretary. Of the Association's thirteen scientific sections, which reviewed policies and research in the various medical specialties, only the radiological section had a Philadelphia doctor (James L. Martin); the other fifty-eight members were from other parts of the country ("Officers of the NMA for 1955," *JNMA* 46 [Nov. 1954]: 442). Also, in 1956, when some urban areas were designated separate "zones" within the NMA's nationwide regional organization by virtue of the size and cohesion of these local areas' membership, Philadelphia was not one ("Area, Regional, and Zone Directors and State Vice-Presidents," *JNMA* 48 [March 1956]: 145). Lastly, Pennsylvania statewide membership in the NMA had declined from 8.2 percent of the national membership body in 1951 to 4.3 percent in 1955 ("NMA Activities," *JNMA* 48 [Jan. 1956]: 76).

15. *Philadelphia Tribune*, Jan. 1, 1963.

16. The closing occurred despite a bequest by Dr. Eugene Hinson left to the

hospital in 1960 for the purpose of supporting the nursing program (*Philadelphia Tribune*, June 11, 1960, and Aug. 9, 1960).

17. In 1960, after sixty years of operation, Meharry's nursing school closed *Philadelphia Tribune*, Aug. 9, 1960; Summerville, *Educating Black Doctors: A History of Meharry Medical College* (University: University of Alabama Press, 1983), p. 114.

18. Rhoda L. Goldstein, "Negro Nurses in Hospitals," *American Journal of Nursing* 60 (Feb. 1960): 215. By 1961 a state law had been enacted requiring nursing schools throughout Pennsylvania to open their programs to blacks (M. Elizabeth Carnegie, "Are Negro Schools of Nursing Needed Today?" *Nursing Outlook* 12 [Feb. 1964]: 54).

19. Carnegie, "Are Negro Schools of Nursing Needed?" p. 56.

20. U.S. Department of Commerce, Bureau of the Census, *Seventeenth Census of the United States, 1950* (Washington, D.C.: GPO, 1952), vol. 2: *Characteristics of the Population*, pt. 38: *Pennsylvania; Eighteenth Census of the United States, 1960* (Washington, D.C.: GPO, 1962), *Pennsylvania*, pts. 4 and 5, pp. 749, 751. In 1950, the Bureau of the Census began using the Standard Metropolitan Area (SMA), based on counties, for enumerating data on urban population, employment, race, and so on. Thus, the figures for 1950, 1960, and 1970 for blacks in the medical occupations in Philadelphia were combined with those of surrounding cities and counties, which no doubt included a sprinkling of black physicians and dentists. Camden, New Jersey, and Chester, Pennsylvania, in particular, had large black populations and some black medical professionals. Since the census data provide no exact figures for these cities, a sharper estimate of the number of black medical professionals in Philadelphia proper was not possible.

21. A national study of the number and distribution of black physicians also indicated that a decline in the supply of these professionals occurred following the integration of American medical schools. See A. A. Sorenson, "Black Americans and the Medical Profession," *Journal of Negro Education* 41 (1972): 337–342.

22. Donna McGough, "Physicians' Field of Practice and Hospital Affiliation: A Comparison of Negro Physicians and Sample of Non-Negro Physicians Practicing in Philadelphia" [1965], in Philadelphia Commission on Human Relations, "Hospital Employment Study," April 1966, mimeo., pp. 3, 6, CP-BMRP.

23. *Ibid.*, pp. 3–4.

24. *Ibid.*

25. See note 20.

26. Bureau of the Census, *1960 Census: Pennsylvania*, pt. 4; U.S. Department of Commerce, Bureau of the Census, *Nineteenth Census of the United States, 1970* (Washington, D.C.: GPO, 1973), *Pennsylvania, General Social and Economic Characteristics*. These estimated figures for 1965 were based on the differences in the number of non-whites in these health occupations in 1970 as opposed to 1960.

These differences were then divided by two to yield a mid-decade (or 1965) estimate. On the national trend in the early 1960s toward including greater numbers of black technical and paraprofessional medical workers, see Marli S. Melton, "Health Manpower and Negro Health: The Negro Physician," *Journal of Medical Education* 43 (July 1968): 800–802.

27. Philadelphia Commission on Human Relations, *Annual Report, 1961*, p. 57; *1962*, p. 57; *1963*, p. 30.

28. "Alice G. McClaughlin versus Temple University Hospital," Case #8-4-2231, 1963, Commission on Human Relations Closed Case Files, CP-BMRA.

29. "Kathryn R. Hendrix versus Philadelphia Department of Public Health," Case #1-5-2171, 1963, Commission on Human Relations Closed Case Files.

30. "Lane versus University of Pennsylvania Hospital," Case #5-3-2341, 1964, Commission on Human Relations Closed Case Files.

31. "Mattie Williams versus Woman's Hospital," Case #9-15-2257, *1964*, Commission on Human Relations Closed Case Files.

32. "Evan Dickson versus Graduate Hospital," Case #4-2-2406, 1965, Commission on Human Relations Closed Case Files.

33. *Philadelphia Tribune*, April 22, 1961. None of the five cases resulted in any civil or punitive legal action by the Commission on behalf of the complainants.

34. Commission on Human Relations, "Hospital Employment Study," p. 58, *Philadelphia Tribune*, April 22, 1961. On the similar symbolic importance of a like agency in New York City from the late 1950s through the mid-1960s, see Gerald Benjamin, *Race Relations and the New York City Commission on Human Rights* (Ithaca, N.Y.: Cornell University Press, 1974), esp. pp. 239–259.

35. Lester A. Sobel, ed., *Civil Rights, 1960–66* (New York: Facts on File, 1967), pp. 259–260; "Other Philadelphia," *Newsweek* 64 (Sept. 7, 1964): 30; " 'Doing No Good,' All Negro Riot," *Time* 84 (Sept. 4, 1964): 32. On the tensions that led up to this riot, see *New York Times*, June 9, 1963.

36. Jack Elinson and Conrad E. A. Herr, "A Sociomedical View of Neighborhood Health Centers," in *Neighborhood Health Centers*, ed. Robert M. Hollister et al. (Lexington, Mass.: Lexington Books, 1974), pp. 126–127.

37. *Philadelphia Tribune*, June 27, 1964; miscellaneous correspondence of officials of the Commission on Human Relations and Temple University Hospital and factual materials collected by the EEOC during its investigation of Temple University Hospital for alleged discrimination in Commission on Human Relations Cases and Non-Cases File, Pa-Z, 1959–65, CP-BMRA.

38. "Negro in Philadelphia," *Philadelphia Sunday Bulletin*, Jan. 24, 1965, clipping in Negro History File, PSA. On Moore's activism during this period in general, see Paul Lermack, "Cecil Moore and the Philadelphia Branch NAACP: The Politics of Negro Pressure Group Organization," in *Black Politics in Philadelphia*, ed. Miriam Ershkowitz and Joseph Zikmund (New York: Basic Books, 1973), pp.

145–160.

39. U.S. Civil Rights Commission, *Equal Opportunity in Hospitals and Health Facilities* (Special Publication No. 2; Washington, D.C.: GPO, March 1965), pp. 6–9.

40. Kessing's Research Report, *Race Relations in the U.S.A., 1954–68* (New York: Charles Scribner's Sons, 1970), pp. 137–139.

41. Sobel, ed., *Civil Rights, 1960–66*, pp. 259–262; Commission on Human Relations, "Hospital Employment Study," p. 1.

42. *Philadelphia Tribune*, May 5, 1962.

43. "Statement of Mrs. Sadie T. M. Alexander on Survey of Hospital Employment Policies and Practices to Be Conducted by Philadelphia Commission on Human Relations, Presented December 21, 1965, Philadelphia," Commission on Human Relations Files.

44. "Statement of Congressman Robert N. C. Nix, Sr., on Survey of Hospital Employment Policies and Practices to Be Conducted by Philadelphia Commission on Human Relations, Presented December 21, 1965," Commission on Human Relations Files; "Statement of Mrs. Sadie T. M. Alexander."

45. "Statement of Congressman Robert N. C. Nix"; "Statement of Mrs. Sadie T. M. Alexander."

46. McGough, "Physicians' Field of Practice and Hospital Affiliation," pp. 7–8. Given the many decades of separation between black medical practitioners and the larger Philadelphia medical community, it is not surprising that the EEOC investigation involved not only unraveling the internal administrative bureaucracy of a hospital suspected of perpetuating discriminatory acts against black personnel but evaluating hospital economics as well as racial preferences of white patients. As one investigator stated: "Since the pattern is for Negro physicians to have largely non-white patients many of whom are low-income, it may be considered not economical for a hospital to have them on their staff in comparison to a white physician whose patients have higher incomes . . . Whereas it may not reflect racial discrimination directly, it does reflect economic discrimination which falls hardest on low-income families, a large portion of whom are Negro, and physicians who serve them" (*ibid.*, p. 7). The researcher emphasized that even though economic and racial factors were intertwined in a way that yielded racially discriminatory effects, the latter factor was found to be the most important. The surveyors emphasized that this conclusion had not been reached by means of general impressions, but by advanced statistical techniques (*ibid.*).

47. Commission on Human Relations, "Hospital Employment Study," pp. 57, 84–85.

48. Indeed, after 1965, the disproportionate concentration of blacks in the lowest-paying hospital jobs was for the first time critically recognized by labor exports studying hospital systems in other parts of the country. See Harry I.

Greenfield, *Allied Health Manpower: Trends and Prospects* (New York: Columbia University Press, 1969), pp. 97–98; Eleanor G. Gilpatrick and Paul K. Corliss, *The Occupational Structure of New York City Municipal Hospitals* (New York: Praeger, 1970), pp. 64–67.

Appendix A

1. *American Medical Directory: A Register of Legally Qualified Physicians of the United States* (Chicago: American Medical Association), vols. for 1925, 1929, and 1938.

Index

Lewis, Julian H., 90; surveys distribution of black physicians (1935), 98
Love, Ida T., 153, 155
Luchessi, P. F., 167
Lyman, David R., 49

Masons, 109
McArthur, Camilla, 69
McKnight, Etheridge, criticizes discrimination in health care during 1940s, 141
Medical professionals, black. *See* Black medical professionals
Medical schools, black enrollment nationally, 16, 94. *See also names of specific medical schools*
Medico-Chirurgical College, 14–16
Meharry Medical College, 16, 92, 94, 98, 121, 167
Meharry School of Dentistry, 111
Mercy Hospital (Philadelphia), 5, 9, 40, 66, 69, 128, 148, 149; and black physicians of West Philadelphia, 102; clinics at, 55, 56; considers merger with Douglass, 152; Convalescent Hospital for Colored Women, 142; dental clinic at, 112; during the Depression, 77; early funding of, 10; idea of, 156, 159; national campaign for nursing school, 72–77; neighboring community of, 86; new physician-activists at, 126; and North Philadelphia health problems, 119; nursing students contribute to, 114; personnel make-up (1942), 142–143; problem of lay support, 157; public health services during early 1940s, 142; purchases new site, 26; smallpox vaccination clinic at, 62, 67; specialty training at (before World War II), 106; training school for nurses, 70; work of its graduate nurses in 1930s, 83. *See also* Mercy-Douglass Hospital; Physio-Therapy Society
Mercy-Douglass Hospital (Philadelphia), 187; association with Pennsylvania Medical School, 188–190; closes

temporarily, 172–173; construction funds approved, 166–167; financial crisis intensifies, 191; idea of, 156, 159; most black physicians affiliated with, 193; movement to improve expands, 164–166; nursing school closes, 191; residents at Children's Hospital, 168; seeks academic affiliation, 185–186; site of, 157–158. *See also* Mercy Hospital
Methodist Church Board of Lay Activities, 170
Methodist Episcopal Hospital, 25
Metropolitan Life Insurance Company, 59–60
Migration Committee: distinct from city health department, 66; established, 57–58; on smallpox epidemic among blacks, 60–63; studies health conditions of black migrants, 58–60
Millen, Herbert E., 127, 158, 165–166, 185
Minton, Henry M., 142, 198; background, 46–47; on campaign for Mercy Hospital's nursing school, 76; with Migration Committee, 58, 59, 60; on NAACP Health Committee, 150; on public health work of black doctors and nurses, 47–48, 49; supervises black clinics, 47
Minton, Russell F., 127, 186; completes graduate training, 107; heads Mercy-Douglass, 189–190; on NAACP Health Committee, 150; seeks resurgence for Mercy-Douglass, 189–190; tours black hospitals nationwide, 126
Mont Alto Sanatorium, and black patients, 64–65, 129
Moody, Charles, 14
Moore, J. Hampton, 49
Moore, Lillian Atkins, 24
Mortality rates. *See* Black community of Philadelphia
Mossell, Nathan Francis, 3, 4, 5, 13, 14, 118, 165, 186, 198, 220n; with Migration Committee, 58; resignation incident at Douglass, 81–82; response against his activism, 77